Introduction to National Rural Employment Guarantee Act (NREGA)

The National Rural Employment Guarantee Act (NREGA)

V.D. Rohtagi

Sumit Enterprises
NEW DELHI - 110002

First Published 2009

ISBN 978-81-8420-148-2

Published by:
SUMIT ENTERPRISES
4649B/21, Ansari Road, Darya Ganj
New Delhi-110 002
E-mail: sumit_enterprises2007@yahoo.com
Phones: 011-23279353
Mob: 9810217567

PRINTED IN INDIA

Published by Sri Lokesh Gupta for Sumit Enterprises, New Delhi-110 002, Typeset by Pooja Computer, Dehi, Printed at Sachin Printers, Delhi.

PREFACE

The National Rural Employment Guarantee Act 2005 is a law whereby any adult who is willing to do unskilled manual labor at the minimum wage is entitled to being employed on public works within fifteen days. This Primer is a simple introduction to the Act. Through a question-answer format, the Primer discussed the basis features of the Act, and suggests a few ideas about what concerned citizens can do to intensify the campaign for a full-fledged Employment Guarantee Act.

Though the Indian economy has achieved a substantial growth rate of 9 percent, the problem of unemployment and poverty in the rural areas of the country continues to be a cause of serious concern. During the last three decades, the rich have become richer and the poor miserably poorer. Even the marginal farmers have become landless labourers. Due to ineffective delivery system and mismanagement of several employment programmes initiated by the Central Government, the poor have not been benefited from them.

To provide means of livelihood and reduce the quantum of poverty especially in rural areas, the ruling United progressive Alliance (UPA) Government at the Centre enacted a law to enable the poor people in the rural areas to get 100 days employment with legal guarantee. This pro-active measure became a law when the National Rural Employment Guarantee Bill was unanimously passed by the Parliament on August 23, 2005 and notified in September, 2005.

The book presents the findings of a pilot study on implementation of the National Rural Employment Guarantee Scheme (NREGS), conducted in four districts --Sitapur, Raebareli, Unnao, and Barabanki -eight blocks, sixteen villages, interviewing 400 beneficiaries (25 per village) on the worksite. Major findings reveal that the beneficiaries, while expressing satisfaction on the new initiatives taken by the Government, demanded increase in wage rates, work site facilities as enshrined in the Act and increase in the number of working days in a financial year. The study also reveals that there is wide appreciation of the NREGA in the rural areas with significant representation of beneficiaries from scheduled castes and Other Backward Classes. There is need for vigorous identification of job opportunity well in advance and strict monitoring of the implementation process. Creating greater awareness about the scheme through various local media facilities available in the rural areas vigorous efforts to involve women workers in warranted.

Though the sample size of the study is small, it reveals interesting findings. It would be necessary to explore all the aspects of implementation process and plug various loopholes.

—Author

CONTENTS

1

INTRODUCTION

The National Rural Employment Guarantee Act (NREGA, also known as National Rural Employment Guarantee Scheme, NREGS) is Indian legislation enacted on August 25, 2005. The NREGA provides a legal guarantee for one hundred days of employment in every financial year to adult members of any rural household willing to do public work-related unskilled manual work at the statutory minimum wage.

This act was introduced with an aim of improving the purchasing power of the rural people, primarily semi or un-skilled work to people living below poverty line in rural India. It attempts to bridge the gap between the rich and poor in the country. Roughly one-third of the stipulated work force must be women.

POLITICAL BACKGROUND

The act was brought about by the UPA coalition government headed by Dr. Manmohan Singh. The promise of this project was one of the major factors that gained UPA victory in the Indian general election, 2004.

Dr. Jean Drèze, a Belgian born economist, at the Delhi School of Economics, has been a major influence on this project.

THE PLAN

Central Government shall meet the cost towards the payment of wage, 3/4 of material cost and certain percentage of administrative cost. State Government shall meet the cost towards unemployed allowance, 1/4 of material cost and administrative cost of State council.

Adult members of rural households submit their name, age and address with photo to the Gram Panchayat. The Gram panchayat registers households after making enquiry and issues a job card. The job card contains the details of adult member enrolled and his /her photo. Registered person can submit an application for work in writing (for at least fourteen days of continuous work) either to panchayat or to Programme Officer.

The pànchayat/programme officer will accept the valid application and issue dated receipt of application, letter providing work will be sent to the applicant and also displayed at panchayat office. The employment will be provided within a radius of 5 km: if it is above 5 km extra wage will be paid.

If employment under the scheme is not provided within fifteen days of receipt of the application daily unemployment allowance will be paid to the applicant.

The scheme starting from February 2, 2006 in 200 districts (out of a total of 593 in the country) will cover all districts in five years. The government announced the addition of another 130 districts in the financial year 2007-8.

2006-2007

For financial year 2006-2007 budgetary support for NREGA is Rs 11300 crores. The Congress-led UPA government decided to further extend this scheme across the country at the beginning of the financial year 2008-09, the year the government faces a new general elections. Though the government has already planned to extend the scheme, country's supreme audit institution, the Comptroller and Auditor General (CAG) of India, in its performance audit of the implementation of NREGA found out "significant deficiencies" and had even advised the government to plug these shortcomings before extending the scheme further.

2008

In April 2008 NREGA expanded to cover the entire India.

IT Implementation

NREGA is the first programme having been implemented with full IT support. TATA Consultancy Services, India's largest

IT/ITES sector company has designed the software solution for the state of Andhra Pradesh. NIC, a government of India undertaking, developed solution has been implemented in other areas.

NATIONAL RURAL EMPLOYMENT GUARANTEE ACT, 2005

An Act to provide for the enhancement of livelihood security of the households in rural areas of the country by providing at least one hundred days of guaranteed wage employment in every financial year to every household whose adult members volunteer to do. Unskilled annual work and for matters connected therewith or incidental thereto. BE it enacted by Parliament m the Fifty-sixth Year of the Republic of India as follows:

PRELIMINARY

(1) This Act may be called the National Rural Employment Guarantee Act, 2005.

(2) It extends to the whole of India except the State of Jammu and Kashmir.

(3) It shall come into force on such date as the Central Government may, by notification in the Official Gazette, appoint; and different dates maybe appointed for different States or for different areas in a State and any reference in any such provision to the Short title, extent and commencement.

Commencement of this Act shall be construed as a reference to the coming into force of that provision in such State or, as the case may be, in such area: Provided that this Act shall be applicable to the whole of the territory to which it extends within a period of five years from the date of enactment of this Act.

2. In this Act, urness the context otherwise requires:

(a) "adult" means a person who has completed his eighteenth years of age;

(b) "applicant" means the head of a household or any of its other adult members who has applied for employment under the Scheme;

(c) "Block" means a community development area within a district comprising a group of Gram Panchayats;

(d) "Central Council" means the Central Employment Guarantee Council constituted under sub-section (1) of section 10;

(e) "District Programme Coordinator" means an officer of the State Government designated as such under sub-section (1) of section 14 for implementation of the Scheme in a district;

(f) "household" means the members of a family related to each other by blood, marriage or adoption and normally residing together and sharing meals or holding a common ration card;

(g) "implementing agency" includes anydepartrnent of the Central Government or a State Government, a Zila Parishad, Panchayat at intermediate level, Gram Panchayat or any local authority or Government undertaking or non-governmental organisation authorised by the Central Government or the State Government to undertake the implementation of any work taken up under a Scheme;

(h) "minimum wage", in relation to any area, means the minimum wage fixed by the State Government under section 3 of the Minimum Wages Act, 1948 for agricultural labourers as applicable in that area;

(i) "National Fund" means the National Employment Guarantee Fund established under sub-section (1) of section 20;

(j) "notification" means a notification published in the Official Gazette;

(k) "preferred work" means any work which is taken up for implementation on a priority basis under a Scheme;

(l) "prescribed" means prescribed by rules made under this Act;

(m) "Programme Officer" means an officer appointed under sub-section (1) of section 15 for implementing the Scheme;

(n) "project" means any work taken up under a Scheme for the purpose of providing employment to the applicants;

(o) "rural area" means any area in a State except those areas covered by any urban local body or a Cantonment Board established or constituted under any law for the time being in force;

(p) "Scheme" means a Scheme notified by the State Government under subsection (1) of section 4;

(q) "State Council" means the State Employment Guarantee Council constituted under sub-section (1) of section 12;

(r) "unskilled manual work" means any physical work which any adult person is capable of doing without any skill or special training;

(s) "wage rate" means the wage rate referred to in section 6.

GUARANTEE OF EMPANELMENT RURAL AREAS

(1) Save as otherwise provided, the State Government shall, in such rural area in Guarantee of the State as may be notified by the Central Government, provide to every household whose rural adult members volunteer to do unskilled manual work not less than one hundred days of employment.

(2) Every person who has done the work given to him under the Scheme shall be entitled to receive wages at the wage rate for each day of work.

(3) Save as otherwise provided in this Act, the disbursement of daily wages shall be made on a weekly basis or in any case not later than a fortnight after the date on which such work was done.

(4) The Central Government or the State Government may, within .the limits of its economic capacity and development, make provisions for securing work to every adult member of a household under a Scheme for any period beyond the period guaranteed under sub-section (1), as may be expedient. Provided that different rates of wages may be specified for different areas: Provided further that the wage rate specified from time to time under any such notification shall not be at a rate less than sixty rupees per day. (2) Until such time as a wage rate is fixed by the Central Government in respect of any area in a State, the minimum wage fixed by the State Government under section 3 of the Minimum Wages Act, I948 for agricultural labourers, shall be considered as the wage rate applicable to that area. 11 of 1948. Payment of 7.

(1) If an applicant for employment under the Scheme is not provided such unemployment employment within fifteen days of receipt of his application seeking employment or from allowance.

The date on which the employment has been sought in the case of an advance application, whichever is later, he shall be entitled to a daily unemployment allowance in accordance with this section.

(2) Subject to such terms and conditions of eligibility as may be prescribed by the State Government and subject 10 the provisions of this Act and the Schemes and the economic capacity of the State Government, the unemployment allowance payable under sub-section (1) shall be paid to the applicants of a household subject to the entitlement of the household at such rate as may be specified by the State Government, by notification, in consultation with the State Council: Provided that no such rate shall be less than one-fourth of the wage rate for the first thirty days during the financial year and not less than one-half of the wage rate for the remaining period of the financial year.

(3) The liability of the State Government to pay unemployment allowance to a household during any financial year shall cease as soon as:

- The applicant is directed by the Gram Panchayat or the Programme Officer to report for work either by himself or depute at least one adult member of his household; or
- The period for which employment is sought comes to an end and no member of the household of the applicant had turned up for employment; or
- The adult members of the household of the applicant have received in total at least one hundred days of work within the financial year; or
- The household of the applicant has earned as much from the wages and unemployment allowance taken together which is equal to the wages for one hundred days of work during the financial year.

(4) The unemployment allowance payable to, the household of an applicant jointly shall be sanctioned and disbursed by the Programme Officer or such local authority (including the Panchayats at the district, intermediate or village level) as the State Government may, by notification, authorise in this behalf.

(5) Every payment of unemployment allowance under sub-section (1) shall be made or offered not later than fifteen days from the date on which it became due for payment.

(6) The State Government may prescribe the procedure for payment unemployment allowance under this Act.

Non-8. (1) If the Programme Officer is not in a position to disburse the unemployment disbursement allowance in time or at all for any reason beyond his control, he shall report the matter to of the District Programme Coordinator and announce such reasons in a notice to be displayed on his notice board and the notice board of the Gram Panchayat and such other certain conspicuous places as he may deem necessary. (2) Every case of non-payment or delayed payment of unemployment allowance shall be reported in the annual report submitted by the District Programme Coordinator to the State Government along with the reasons for such non-payment or delayed payment. (3) The State Government shall take all measures to make the payment of unemployment allowance reported under sub-section (1) to the concerned household as expeditiously as possible.

If it does not report for work within fifteen days of being notified by the Programme officer or the implementing agency to report for the work; or (c) continuously remains absent from work, without obtaining a permission from the concerned implementing agency for a period of more than one week or remains absent for a total period of more than one week in any month, shall not be eligible to claim the unemployment allowance payable under this Act for a period of three months but shall be eligible to seek employment under the Scheme at any time.

IMPLEMENTING AND MONITORING AUTHORITIES

(1) With effect from such date as the Central Government may, by notification specify, there shall be constituted a Council to be called the Central Employment Guarantee Council to discharge the functions, and perform the duties, assigned to it by or under this Act.

(2) The headquarters of the Central Council shall be at Delhi.

(3) The Central Council shall consist of the following members to be appointed by the Central Government, namely:-

(a) a Chairperson;

(b) not more than such number of representatives of the Central Ministries including the Planning Commission not below the rank of Joint Secretary to the Government of India as may be determined by the Central Government;

(c) not more than such number of representatives of the State Governments as may be determined by the Central Government;

(d) not more than fifteen non-official members representing Panchayati Raj Institutions, organisations of workers and disadvantaged groups: Provided that such non-official members shall include two chairpersons of District Panchayats nominated by the Central Government by rotation for a period of one year at a time: Provided further that not less than one-third of the non-official members nominated under this clause shall be women: Provided also that not less than one-third of the non-official members shall be belonging to the Scheduled Castes, the Scheduled Tribes, the Other Backward Classes and Minorities;

(e) such number of representatives of the States as the Central Government may, by rules, determine in this behalf;

(f) a Member-Secretary not below the rank of Joint Secretary to the Government of India.

(4) The tends and conditions subject to which .the Chairperson and other members of the Central Council may be appointed and the time, place and procedure of the meetings (including the quorum at such meetings) of the Central Council shall be such as may be prescribed by the Central Government.

(1) The Central Council shall perform and discharge the following functions and duties, namely:

(a) establish a central evaluation and monitoring system;

(b) advise the Central Government on all matters concerning the implementation of this Act;

(c) review the monitoring and redressal mechanism from time to time and recommend improvements required;

(d) promote the widest possible dissemination of information about the Schemes made under this Act;

(e) monitoring the implementation of this Act;

(f) preparation of annual reports to be laid before Parliament by the Central Government on the implementation of this Act;

(g) any other duty or function as may be assigned to it by the Central Government.

(2) The Central Council shall have the power to undertake evaluation of the various Schemes made under this Act and for that purpose collect or cause to be collected statistics pertaining to the rural economy and the implementation of the Schemes.

(1) For the purposes of regular monitoring and reviewing the implementation of this Act at the State level, every State Government shall constitute a State Council to be known as the (name of the State) State Employment Guarantee Council with a Chairperson and such number of official members as may be determined by the State Government and not more than fifteen non-official members nominated by the State Government from Panchayati Raj institutions, organisations of workers and disadvantaged groups: Provided that not less than one-third of the non-official members nominated under this clause shall be women: Provided further that not less than one third of the non-official members shall be belonging to the Scheduled Castes, the Scheduled Tribes, the Other Backward Classes and Minorities.

(2) The terms and conditions subject to which the Chairperson and members of the State Council may be appointed and the time, place and procedure of the meetings (including the quorum at such meetings) of the State Council shall be such as may be prescribed by the State Government.

(3) The duties and functions of the State Council shall include-

(a) advising the State Government on all matters concerning the Scheme and its implementation in the State;

(b) determining the preferred works;

(c) reviewing the monitoring and redressal mechanism from time to time and recommending improvements;

(d) promoting the widest possible dissemination of information about this Act and the Schemes under it;

(e) monitoring the implementation of this Act and the Schemes in the State and coordinating such implementation with the Central Council;

(f) preparing the annual report to be laid before the State Legislature by the State Government;

(g) any other duty or function as may be assigned to it by the Central Council or the State Government.

(3) The State Council shall have the power to undertake an evaluation of the Schemes operating in the State and for that purpose to collect or cause to be collected statistics pertaining to the rural economy and the implementation of the Schemes and Programmes in the State.

PRINCIPAL AUTHORITIES FOR PLANNING AND IMPLEMENTATION OF SCHEMES

District Programme Coordinator

(1) The Panchayats at district, intermediate and village levels shall be the principal authorities for planning and implementation of the Schemes made under this Act.

(2) The functions of the Panchayats at the district level shall be:

- To finalise and approve blockwise shelf of projects to be taken up under a programme under the Scheme;
- To supervise and monitor the projects taken up at the Block level and district level; and
- To carry out such other functions as may be assigned to it by the State Council, from time to time.

(3) The functions of the Panchayat at intermediate level shall be:

- To approve the Block level Plan for forwarding it to the district Panchayat at the district level for final approval;
- To supervise and monitor the projects taken up at the Gram Panchayat and Block level; and
- To carry out such other functions as may be assigned to it by the State Council, from time to time.

(4) The District Programme Coordinator shall assist the Panchayat at the district level in discharging its functions under this Act and any Scheme made thereunder.

(1) The Chief Executive Officer of the District Panchayat or the Collector of the district or any other district level officer of appropriate rank as the State Government may decide shall be designated as the District Programme Coordinator for the implementation of the Scheme in the district.

(2) The District Programme Coordinator shall be responsible for the implementation of the Scheme in the district in accordance with the provisions of this Act and the rules made thereunder.

(3) The functions of the District Programme Coordinator shall be:

- To assist the district panchayat in discharging its functions under this Act and any scheme made thereunder;
- To consolidate the plans prepared by the Blocks and project proposals received from other implementing agencies for inclusion in the shelf of projects to be approved by the Panchayat at district level;
- To accord necessary sanction and administrative clearance wherever necessary;
- To coordinate with the Programme Officers functioning within his jurisdiction and the implementing agencies to ensure that the applicants are provided employment as per their entitlements under this Act;
- To review, monitor and supervise the performance of the Programme Officers;
- To conduct periodic inspection of the works in progress; and
- To redress the grievances of the applicants.

(4) The State Government shall delegate such administrative and financial powers to the District Programme Coordinator as may be required to enable him to carry out his functions under this Act.

(5) The Programme Officer appointed under sub-section (1) of section 15 and all other officers of the State Government and local authorities and bodies functioning within the district shall be responsible to assist the District Programme Coordinator in carrying out his functions under this Act and the Schemes made thereunder.

(6) The District Programme Coordinator shall prepare in the month of December every year a labour budget for the next financial year containing the details of anticipated demand for unskilled manual work in the district and the plan for engagement of labourers in the works covered under the Scheme and submit it to the district panchayat.

Programme 15.

(1) At every Panchayat at intermediate level, the State Government shall appoint Officer a person who is not below the rank of Block Development Officer with such qualifications and experience as may be determined by the State Government as Programme Officer at the Panchayat at intermediate level.

(2) The Programme Officer shall assist the Panchayat at intermediate level in discharging its functions under this Act and any Scheme made thereunder. The Programme Officer shall be responsible for matching the demand for employment with the employment opportunities arising from projects in the area under his jurisdiction. The Programme Officer shall prepare a plan for the Block under his jurisdiction by consolidating the project proposals prepared by the Gram Panchayats and the proposals received from intermediate panchayats.

(3) The functions of the Programme Officer shall include:

- monitoring of projects taken up by the Gram Panchayats and other
- implementing agencies-within the Block;
- sanctioning and ensuring payment of-unemployment allowance to the eligible households;
- ensuring prompt and fair payment of wages to all labourers employed under a programme of the Scheme within the Block;
- ensuring that regular social audits of all works within the jurisdiction of the Gram Panchayat are carried out by the Gram Sabha and that prompt action is taken on the objections raised in the social audit;
- dealing promptly with all complaints that may arise in connection with the implementation of the Scheme within the Block; and
- any other work as may be assigned to him by the District Programme Coordinator or the State Government.

(4) The Programme Officers shall function under the direction, control and superintendence of the District Programme Coordinator.

(5) The State Government may, by order, direct that all or any of the functions of a Programme Officer shall be discharged by the Gram Panchayat or a local authority.

Responsibilities 16.

(1) The Gram Panchayat shall be responsible for identification of the of the Gram projects in the Gram Panchayat area to be taken up under a Scheme as per the Panchayats recommendations of the Gram Sabha and the Ward Sabhas and for executing and supervising such works.

(2) A Gram Panchayat may take up any project under a Scheme within the area of the Gram Panchayat as may be sanctioned by the Programme Officer.

(3) Every Gram Panchayat shall, after considering the recommendations of the Gram Sabha and the Ward Sabhas, prepare a development plan and maintain a shelf of possible works to be taken up under the Scheme as and when demand for work arises.

(4) The Gram Panchayat shall forward its proposals for the development projects including the order of priority between different works to the Programme Officer for scrutiny and preliminary approval prior to the commencement of the year in which it is proposed to be executed.

(5) The Programme Officer shall allot at least fifty per cent of the works in terms of its cost under a Scheme to be implemented through the. Gram Panchayats.

(6) The Programme Officer shall supply each Gram Panchayat with:

- the muster rolls for the works sanctioned to be executed by it; and
- a list of employment opportunities available elsewhere to the residents of the Gram Panchayat.

(7) The Gram Panchayat shall allocate employment opportunities among the applicants and ask them to report for work.

(8) The works taken up by a Gram Panchayat under a Scheme shall meet the required technical standards and measurements.'

(1) The Gram Sabha shall monitor the execution of works within the Gram Social audit of Panchayat work by Gram

(2) The Gram Sabha shall conduct regular social about of all the projects under the Scheme taken up within the Gram Panchayat.

(3) The Gram Panchayat shall make available all relevant documents including the muster rolls, bills, vouchers, measurement books, copies of sanction orders and other connected books of account and papers to the Gram Sabha for the purpose of conducting the social audit.

The State Government shall make available to the District Programme Coordinator Responsibilities and the Programme Officers necessary staff and technical support as may be necessary of State for the effective implementation of the Scheme.

Movement in Implementing Scheme

The State Government shall, by rules, determine appropriate grievance redressal Grievance mechanisms at the Block level and the district level for dealing with any complaint by any redressal person in respect of implementation of the Scheme and lay down the procedure for disposal mechanism of such complaints.

ESTABLISHMENT OF NATIONAL AND STATE EMPLOYMENT GUARANTEE FUNDS AND AUDIT

(1) The Central Government shall, by notification, establish a fund to be called National the National Employment Guarantee Fund for the purposes of this Act.

(2) The Central Government may after due appropriation Parliament by law in this behalf, credit by way of grants or loans such sums of money/as the Central Government may consider necessary to the National Fund.

(3) The amount standing to the credit of the National Fund shall be utilised in such manner and subject of such conditions and limitations as may be prescribed by the Central Government.

(1) The State Government may by notification establish a fund to be called the State Employment Guarantee Fund for the purposes of implementation of the Scheme.

(2) The amount standing to the credit of the State Fund shall be expended in such manner and subject to such conditions and limitations as may be prescribed by the State Government for the purposes of implementation of this Act and the Schemes made thereunder and for meeting the administrative expenses in connection with the implementation of this Act.

(3) The State Fund shall be held and administered on behalf of the State Government in such manner and by such authority as may be prescribed by the State Government.

(1) Subject to the rules as may be made by the Central Government in this behalf, Funding the Central Government shall meet the cost of the following, namely

Transparency and Accountability

Audit of Accounts

(a) The amount required for payment of wages for unskilled manual work under the Scheme;

(b) Up to three-fourths of the material cost of the Scheme including payment of wages to skilled and semi-skilled workers subject to the provisions of Schedule II;

(c) Such percentage of the total cost of the Scheme as may be determined by the Central Government towards the administrative expenses, which may include the salary and allowances of the Programme Officers and his supporting staff, the administrative expenses of the Central Council, facilities to be provided under Schedule II and such other item as may be decided by the Central Government.

(2) The State Government shall meet the cost of the following, namely:

(a) the cost of unemployment allowance payable under the Scheme;

(b) one-fourth of the material cost of the Scheme including payment of wages to skilled and semi-skilled workers subject to the provisions of Schedule II;

(c) the administrative expenses of the State Council.

(1) The District Programme Coordinator and all implementing agencies in the District shall be responsible for the proper utilisation and management of the funds placed at their disposal for the purpose of implementing a Scheme.

(2) The State Government may prescribe the manner of maintaining proper books and accounts of employment of labourers and the expenditure incurred in connection with the implementation of the provisions of this Act and the Schemes made thereunder.

(3) The State Government may, by rules, determine the arrangements to be made for the proper execution of Scheme and programmes under the Schemes and to ensure transparency and accountability at all levels in the implementation of the Schemes.

(4) All payments of wages in cash and unemployment allowances shall be made directly to ,the person concerned and in the presence of independent persons of the community on pre-announced dates.

(5) If any dispute or complaint arises concerning the implementation of a Scheme by the Gram Panchayat, the matter shall be referred to the Programme Officer.

(6) The Programme Officer shall enter every complaint in a complaint register maintained by him and shall dispose of the disputes and complaints within seven days of its receipt and in case it relates to a matter to be resolved by any other authority it shall be forwarded to such authority under intimation to the complainant.

(1) The Central Government may, in consultation with the Comptroller and Auditor General of India, prescribe appropriate arrangements for audits of the accounts of the Schemes at all levels.

(2) The accounts of the Scheme shall be maintained in such form and in such manner as may be prescribed by the State Government.

Whoever contravenes the provisions of this Act shall on conviction be liable to a fine which may extend to one thousand rupees.

PENALTY FOR NON COMPLIANCE.

Power to Delegate.

(1) The Central Government may, by notification, direct that the powers exercisable by it (excluding the power to make rules) may, in such circumstances and subject to such conditions and limitations, be exercisable also by the State Government or such officer subordinate to the Central Government or the State Government as it may specify in such notification.

(2) The State Government may, by notification, direct that the powers exercisable by it (excluding the power to make rules and Schemes) may, in such circumstances and subject to such conditions and limitations, be exercisable also, by such officer subordinate to it as it may specify in such notification.

(1) The Central Government may give such directions as it may consider necessary to the State Government for the effective implementation of the provisions of this Act.

(2) Without prejudice to the provisions of sub-section (1), the Central Government may, on receipt of any complaint regarding the issue or improper utilisation of funds granted under this Act in respect of any Scheme if prima facie satisfied that there is a case, cause an investigation into the complaint made by any agency designated by it and if necessary, order stoppage of release offends to the Scheme and institute appropriate remedial measures for its proper implementation within a reasonable period of time.

The provisions of this Act or the Schemes made thereunder shall have effect notwithstanding anything inconsistent therewith contained in any other law for the time being in force or in any instrument having effect by virtue of such law: Provided that where a State enactment exists or is enacted to provide employment guarantee for unskilled manual work to rural households consistent with the provisions of this Act under which the entitlement of the households is not less than and the conditions of employment are not inferior to what is guaranteed under this Act, the State Government shall have the option of implementing its own enactment: Provided further that in such cases the financial assistance shall be paid to the concerned State Government in such manner as shall be determined by the Central Government, which shall not exceed what the State would have been entitled to receive under this Act had a Scheme made under this Act had to be implemented.

(1) If the Central Government is satisfied that it is necessary or expedient so to do, it may, by notification, amend Schedule I or Schedule II and thereupon Schedule I or Schedule II, as the case may be, shall be deemed to have been amended accordingly. (2) A copy of every notification made under sub-section (1) shall be laid before each House of Parliament as soon as may be after it is made.

No suit, prosecution or other legal proceedings shall lie against the District Programme Coordinator, Programme Officer or any other person who is, or who is deemed to be, a public servant within the meaning of section 21 of the Indian Penal Code in respect of anything which is in good faith done or intended to be done under this Act or the rules or Schemes made thereunder.

(1) The Central Government may, by notification, and subject to the condition of previous publication, make rules to carry out the provisions of this Act.

(2) In particular, and without the prejudice of the foregoing power, such rules may provide for all or any of the following matters, namely:

(a) the number of representatives of the State Governments under clause (e) of sub-section (3) of section 10;

(b) the terms and conditions subject to which the Chairman and other members of the Central Council may be appointed, and the time, place and procedure of the meetings (including the quorum at such meetings) of the Central Council, under sub-section (4) of section 10;

(c) the manner in which and the conditions and limitations subject to which the National Fund shall be utilised under sub-section (3) of section 20;

(d) the rules relating to funding pattern to meet the cost of certain items under sub-section (1) of section 22;

(e) any other matter which is to be, or may be, prescribed or in respect of which provision is to be made by the Central Government by rules.

(1) The State Government may, by notification, and subject to the condition of previous publication, and consistent with this Act and the rules made by the Central Government, make rules to carry out the provisions of this Act.

Power of State Government to Make Rules.

Laying of rules and Schemes

(2) In particular, and without prejudice to the generality of the foregoing power, such rules may provide for all or any of the following matters, namely:

(a) the terms and conditions upon which eligibility for unemployment allowance may be determined under sub-section (2) of section 7;

(b) the procedure for payment of unemployment allowance under sub-section (6) of section 7;

(c) the terms and conditions subject to which the Chairperson and members of the State Council may be appointed, and the time, place and procedure of the meetings (including the quorum at such meetings) of their appointment to the State Council, under sub-section (2) of section 12;

(d) the grievance redressal mechanism at the Block level and the District level and the procedure to be followed in such matter under section 19;

(e) the manner in which and the conditions and limitations subject to which the State Fund shall be utilised under sub-section (2) of section 21;

(f) the authority who may administer and the manner in which he may hold the State Fund under sub-section (3) of section 21;

(g) the manner of maintaining books of account of employment of labourers and the expenditure under sub-section (2) of section 23;

(h) the arrangements required for proper execution of Schemes under subsection (3) of section 23;

(i) the form and manner in which the accounts of the Scheme shall be maintained under sub-section (2) of section 24;

(j) any other matter which is to be, or may be, prescribed or in respect of which provision is to be made by the State Government by rules.

(1) Every rule made by the Central Government under this Act shall be laid, as soon as may be after it is made, before each House of Parliament, while it is in session, for a total period of thirty days which may be comprised in one session or in two or more successive sessions, and if, before the expiry of the session immediately following the session or the successive sessions aforesaid, both Houses agree in making any modification in the rule or both the Houses agree that the rule should not be made, the rule shall have thereafter have effect only in such modified form or be of no effect, as the case may be; so, however, that any such modification or annulment shall be without prejudice to the validity of anything previously done under that rule.

(2) Every rule or Scheme made by the State Government under this Act shall, as soon as may be after it is made, be laid before each House of the State Legislature where there are two Houses, and where there is one House of the State Legislature, before that House.

Power to remove difficulties.

(1) If any difficulty arises in giving effect to the provisions of this Act, the Central Government may, by order published in the Official Gazette, make such provisions, not inconsistent with the provisions of this Act, as appear to it to be necessary or expedient for removing the difficulty: Provided that no order shall be made under this section after the expiry of three years from the commencement of this Act.

(2) Every order made under this section shall be laid, as soon as may be after it is made, before each House of Parliament.

MINIMUM FEATURES OF A RURAL EMPLOYMENT GUARANTEE SCHEME

1. The focus of the Scheme shall be on the following works in their order ofpriority:

(i) water conservation and water harvesting;

(ii) drought proofing (including afforestation and tree plantation);

(iii) irrigation canals including micro and minor irrigation works;

(iv) provision of irrigation facility to land owned by households belonging to the Scheduled Castes and Scheduled Tribes or to land of beneficiaries of land reforms or that of the beneficiaries under the Indira Awas Yojana of the Government of India;

(v) renovation of traditional water bodies including desilting of tanks;

(vi) land development;

(vii) flood control and protection works including drainage in water logged areas;

(viii) rural connectivity to provide all-weather access; and

(ix) any other work which may be notified by the Central Government in consultation with the State Government.

2. Creation of durable assets and strengthening the livelihood resource base of the rural poor shall be an important objective of the Scheme.

3. The works taken up under the scheme shall be in rural areas.

4. The State Council shall prepare a list of preferred works for different areas based on their ability to create durable assets.

5. The Scheme shall be subject to appropriate arrangements as may be laid down by the State Government under the rules issued by it for proper maintenance of the public assets created under the Scheme.

6. Under no circumstances shall the labourers be paid less than the wage rate.

7. When wages are directly linked with the quantity of work, the wages shall be paid according to the schedule of rates fixed by the State Government for different types of work every year, in consultation with the State Council.

8. The schedule of rates of wages for unskilled labourers shall be so fixed that a person working for seven hours would normally earn a wage equal to the wage rate.

9. The cost of material component of projects including the wages of the skilled and semi-skilled workers taken up under the Scheme shall not exceed forty per cent of the total project costs.

10. It shall be open to the Programme Officer and Gram Panchayat to direct any person who applied for employment under the Scheme to do work of any type punishable under it.

11. The Scheme shall not punnet engaging any contractor for implementation of the projects under it.

12. As far as practicable, a task funded under the Scheme shall be performed by using manual labour and not machines.

13. Every Scheme shall contain adequate provisions for ensuring transparency and accountability at all level of implementation.

14. Provisions for regular inspection and supervision of works taken up under the Scheme shall be made to ensure proper quality of work as well as to ensure that the total wages paid for the completion of the work is commensurate with the quality and quantity of work done.

15. The District Programme Coordinator, the Programme Officer and the Gram Panchayat implementing the Scheme shall prepare annually a report containing the facts and figures and achievements relating to the implementation of the Scheme within his or its jurisdiction and a copy of the same shall be made available to the public on demand and on payment of such fee as may be specified in the Scheme.

16. All accounts and records relating to the Scheme shall be made available for public scrutiny and any person desirous of obtaining a copy or relevant extracts therefrom may be provided such copies or extracts on demand and after paying such fee as may be specified in the Scheme.

17. A copy of the muster rolls of each Scheme or project under a Scheme shall be made available in the offices of the Gram Panchayat and the Programme Officer for inspection by any person interested after paying such fee as may be specified in the Scheme.

CONDITIONS FOR GUARANTEED RURAL EMPLOYMENT UNDER A SCHEME AND MINIMUM ENTITLEMENTSO F LABOURERS

1. The adult members of every household who:

(i) reside in any rural areas; and

(ii) are willing to do unskilled manual work, may submit their names, age and the address of the household to the Gram Panchayat at the village level (hereafter in this Schedule referred to as the Gram Panchayat) in the jurisdiction of which they reside for registration of their household for issuance of a job card.

2. It shall be the duty of the Gram Panchayat to register the household, after making such enquiry as it deems fit and issue a job card containing such details of adult members of the household affixing their photographs, as may be specified by the State Government in the Scheme.

3. The registration made under paragraph 2 shall be for such period as may be laid in the Scheme, but in any case not less than five years, and may be renewed from time to time.

4. Every adult member of a registered household whose name appears in the job card shall be entitled to apply for unskilled manual work under the Scheme.

5. All registered persons belonging to a household shall be entitled to employment in accordance with the Scheme made under the provisions of this Act, for as many days as each applicant may request, subject to a maximum of one hundred days per household in a given financial year.

6. The Programme Officer shall ensure that every applicant referred to in paragraph 5 shall be provided unskilled manual work in accordance with the provisions of the Scheme within fifteen days of receipt of an application or from the date he seeks work in case of advance application, whichever is later: Provided that priority shall be given to women in such a way that at least one-third of the beneficiaries shall be women who have registered and requested for work under this Act.

7. Applications for work must be for at least fourteen days of continuous work.

8. There shall be no limit on the number of days of employment for which a person may apply, or on the number of days of employment actually provided to him subject to the aggregate entitlement of the household.

9. Applications for work may be submitted in writing either to the Gram Panchayat or to the Programme Officer, as may be specified in the Scheme.

10. The Gram Panchayat and Programme Officer, as the case may be, shall be bound to accept valid applications and to issue a dated receipt to the applicant. Group applications may also be submitted.

11. Applicants who are provided with work shall be so intimated in writing, by meals of a letter sent to him at the address given in the job card and by a public notice displayed at the office of the Panchayats at the district, intermediate or village level.

12. As far as possible, employment shall be provided within a radius office kilometres of the village where the applicant resides at the time of applying.

13. A new work under the Scheme shall be commenced only if:

(a) at least fifty labourers become available for such work; and

(b) the labourers cannot be absorbed in the ongoing works: the State Government in this works, as determined by.

14. In cases the employment is provided outside such radius, it must be provided within the Block, and the labourers shall be paid ten per cent of the wage rate as extra wages to meet additional transportation and living expenses.

15. A period of employment shall ordinarily be at least fourteen days continuously with not more than six days in a week.

16. In all cases where unemployment allowance is paid, or due to be paid, the Programme Officer shall inform the District Programme Coordinator in writing the reasons why it was not possible for him to provide employment or cause to provide employment to the applicants.

17. The District Programme Coordinator shall, in his Annual Report to the State Council, explain as to why employment could not be provided in cases where payment of unemployment allowance is involved.

18. Provision shall be made in the Scheme for advance applications, that is, applications which may be submitted in advance of the date from which employment is sought.

19. Provision shall be made in the Scheme for submission of multiple applications by the same person provided that the corresponding periods for which employment is sought do not overlap.

20. The Gram panchayat shall prepare and maintain or cause to be prepared and maintained such registers, vouchers and other documents in such form and in such manner as may be specified in the Scheme containing particulars of job cards and passbooks issued, name, age and address of the head of the household and the adult members of the household registered with the Gram Panchayat.

21. The Gram Panchayat shall send such list or lists of the names and addresses of households and their adult members registered with it and supply such other information to the concerned Programme Officer at such periods and in such form as may be specified in the Scheme.

22. A list of persons who are provided with the work shall be displayed on the notice board of the Gram Panchayat and at the office of the Programme Officer and at such other p laces as the Programme Officer may deem necessary and the list shall be open for inspection by the State Government and any person interested.

23. If the Gram panchayat is satisfied at any time that a person has registered with it by furnishing false information, it may direct the Programme Officer to direct his name to be struck off from the register and direct the applicant to return the job card: Provided that no such action under this paragraph shall be directed unless the applicant has been given an opportunity of being heard in the presence of two independent persons.

24. If any personal injury is caused to any person employed under the Scheme by accident arising out of and in the course of

his employment, he shall be entitled to, free of charge, such medical treatment as is admissible under the Scheme.

25. Where hospitalisation of the injured worker is necessary, the State Government shall arrange for such hospitalisation including accommodation, treatment, medicines and payment of daily allowance not less than half of the wage rate required to be paid had the injured been engaged in the work.

26. If a person employed under a Scheme dies or becomes permanently disabled by accident arising out of and in the course of employment, he shall be paid by the implementing agency an ex gratia payment at the rate of twenty-five thousand rupees or such amount as may be notified by the Central Government, and the amount shall be paid to the legal heirs of the deceased or the disabled, as the case may be.

27. The facilities of safe drinking water, shade for children and periods of rest, first-aid box with adequate material for emergency treatment for minor injuries and other health hazards connected with the work being performed shall be provided at the work site.

28. In case the number of children below the age of six years accompanying the women working at any site are five or more, provisions shall be made to depute one of such women worker to look after such children.

29. The person deputed under paragraph 28 shall be paid wage rate.

30. In case the payment of wages is not made within the period specified under the Scheme, the labourers shall be entitled to receive payment of compensation as per the provisions of the Payment of Wages Act, 1936 (4 of 1936).

31. The wages under a Scheme may be paid either wholly in cash or in cash and kind provided that at least one-fourth of the wages shall be paid in cash only.

32. The State Government may prescribe that a portion of the wages in cash may be paid to the labourers on a daily basis during the period of employment.

33. If any personal injury is caused by accident to a child accompanying any person who is employed under a Scheme, such person shall be entitled to, free of charge, such medical treatment for the child as may be specified in the Scheme and in case of death or disablement, through an ex gratia payment as may be determined by the State Government.

34. In case of every employment under the Scheme, there shall be no discrimination solely on the ground of gender and the provisions of the Equal Remuneration Act, 1976 (25 of 1976), shall be complied.

2

IMPLEMENTATION OF NREGA

The National Rural Employment Guarantee Act, 2005 (NREGA) guarantees 100 days of employment in a financial year to any rural household whose adult members are willing to do unskilled manual work. The Act initially came into force in 200 districts with effect from 2 February 2006.

The basic objective of the Act is to enhance livelihood security in rural areas by providing at least 100 days of guaranteed wage employment on demand. This work guarantee can also serve other objectives: generating productive assets, protecting the environment, empowering rural women, reducing rural-urban migration and fostering social equity, among others. The Act requires every State to formulate a State Rural Employment Guarantee Scheme (REGS), which should conform to the minimum features specified under the Act. According to the Act, rural households have a right to register themselves with the local Gram Panchayats (GPs), and seek employment. Work is to be provided within 15 days from the date of demand, failing which the State Government will have to pay unemployment allowance at the stipulated rates.

The State Rural Employment Guarantee Schemes are implemented as Centrally Sponsored Schemes on a cost sharing basis between the Centre and the States. The Central Government will bear all costs, other than the following:

- 25 per cent of the cost of material and wages for semi-skilled/ skilled workers;
- Unemployment allowance; and

- Administrative expenses of the State Employment Guarantee Council.

Detailed Operational Guidelines have been issued by the Ministry of Rural Development (Ministry), Government of India. Together with the provisions of the Act, they prescribe:

- the types of works that can be covered under NREGA (subject to additions in respect of different States);
- the minimum entitlements of labour;

MINISTRY OF POWERRURAL DEVELOPMENT

- the roles and responsibilities of different functionaries right from the State Government to the District, Block and Panchayat level functionaries, including those of the Panchayati Raj Institutions (PRIs) at various levels;
- the detailed procedures for planning, financial management, registration and employment allotment, execution of works, and payment of wages and unemployment allowance;
- the detailed records to be maintained at different levels; and
- the mechanisms for social audit, as well as monitoring and evaluation of outcomes.

ORGANISATIONAL STRUCTURE AND FUNDING PATTERN

The organizational structure for implementation of NREGA is as follows:

ORGANISATIONAL STRUCTURE OF NREGA

MINISTRY OF RURAL DEVELOPMENT (MORD)

- Nodal Ministry for NREGA implementation
- Resource support to States
- Review, monitoring and evaluation of processes and outcomes
- Establish MIS

STATE EMPLOYMENT GUARANTEE COUNCIL (SEGC)

- Advise State Government on implementation

- Monitoring and Evaluation
- Decide on 'preferred works' under REGS
- Prepare Annual Reports

STATE GOVERNMENT

- Formulate Rural Employment Guarantee Scheme (REGS) and Rules
- Designate State Rural Employment Guarantee Commissioner
- Ensure timely release of State Share
- Ensure wide dissemination of information
- Ensure administrative, financial and technical support to implementing agencies

DISTRICT PANCHAYAT

- Finalise District Plans
- Monitor and supervise REGS in the District
- Execute works (other than Gram Panchayats works)

DISTRICT PROGRAMME COORDINATOR (DPC)

- Responsible for overall co-ordination and implementation of scheme in District

Intermediate Panchayat

- Planning at Block level
- Monitoring and supervision
- Executing works (other than G P works)

Programme Officer

- Coordinate the works undertaken by Gram Panchayat and implementing agencies at Block level

Other Implementing Agencies

- Line Departments, NGOs, Central and State Government Undertakings, and Self-Help Groups (SHGs)

Gram Sabha

- Recommend works to be taken up
- Monitor and supervise works

- Conduct social audits of implementation
- Forum for sharing information
- Ensure transparency and accountability

CENTRAL EMPLOYMENT GUARANTEE COUNCIL (CEGC)

- Advise GoI on NREGArelated matters
- Monitoring and Evaluation
- Prepare Annual Reports

Gram Panchayat

- Planning of works, registering households, issuing job cards, allocating employment
- Executing 50 *per cent* of the works, and monitoring implementation of the Scheme at the village level

The Government of India (GoI) has established a fund called the National Employment Guarantee Fund, from which grants are released directly to Districts2. Revolving funds are to be set up under REGS at the District, Block and Gram Panchayat levels, with separate bank accounts being opened for such funds at each level.

Request for Audit

In August 2006, the Ministry requested a performance audit of the implementation of NREGA, in view of the importance of the Act and the programme and to provide assurance that the processes under the Act were put in place and were being adopted effectively by the State Governments. This request was accepted, and a performance audit of implementation of NREGA, covering the initial 200 districts, was initiated during 2007-08.

Audit Objectives

The main audit objectives for the Performance Audit were to ascertain whether:

- Effective preparatory steps for planning, implementation and monitoring/evaluation of outcomes were taken by the Central and State Governments;
- The procedures for preparing perspective and annual plan at different levels for estimating the likely demand for

work, and preparing a shelf of projects were adequate and effective;

- There was an effective process for registration of households, allotment of job cards, and allocation of employment in compliance with the guidelines;
- NREGA works were properly planned, and economically, efficiently and effectively executed in a timely manner, and in compliance with the Act and the guidelines, and durable assets were created and properly accounted for;
- Wages and unemployment allowance were paid in accordance with the Act and the guidelines, and the intended objective of providing 100 days of annual employment at the specified wage rates was effectively achieved;
- Funds released for NREGA were accounted for, and utilized in compliance with the guidelines;
- There was an adequate and effective mechanism at different levels for monitoring and evaluation of NREGA outcomes; and
- There was an adequate and effective mechanism for social audit and grievance redressal.

Audit Criteria

The main sources of audit criteria for the performance audit were the following:

- The National Rural Employment Guarantee Act, 2005 (NREGA), and notifications issued thereunder;
- NREGA Operational Guidelines (2006); and
- Circulars and letters issued by the Ministry.

AUDIT SCOPE, SAMPLING AND METHODOLOGY

Audit Scope

The scope of audit was restricted to the initial 200 districts identified for implementation of NREGA. The period of audit coverage was from February 2006 to March 2007. Field audit of the relevant records of the Ministry, State Governments and District, Block and Panchayat level offices was conducted at the

Ministry and 263 States between May and September 2007. Subsequently, in order to assess the improvement in maintenance of records as a result of the performance audit, a limited scrutiny of record maintenance for one month (November 2007) was conducted between February and March 2008, covering 24 GPs in 6 States from within the original audit sample.

Audit Sampling

In each State, 25 per cent of the NREGA districts (subject to a minimum of two) were selected. In each district, two blocks were chosen, in each block four Gram Panchayats (GPs) were chosen, and in each selected GP, four works (preferably three completed and one ongoing) were selected for detailed examination.

Thus, records relating to 68 districts, 141 blocks within the selected sampled districts, and 558 GPs in the selected sampled blocks were selected for detailed examination. The limited scrutiny, which was conducted in February- March 2008, covered 6 states, 12 districts, 12 blocks and 24 GPs, which were selected from the original audit sample.

Audit Methodology

The performance audit commenced with an entry conference with the Ministry in April 2007, wherein the audit methodology, scope, objectives and criteria were explained. During the meeting, the Ministry also made a presentation on the status of NREGA.

After the conclusion of field audit, an exit conference was held with the team of the Ministry headed by Joint Secretary of the Ministry in December 2007, where the draft audit findings and recommendations were discussed at length. In addition, exit conferences were also held between August 2007 and January 2008 with the State Governments, where the Statespecific findings were discussed.

The draft performance audit report was issued to the Ministry in December 2007. The Ministry sent its response on the draft report, and also forwarded the comments of 21 State Governments on the report in February 2008. Further, the Secretary, Ministry of Rural Development along with her team also made a presentation highlighting their concerns relating to the issues covered in the draft report in February 2008. The concerns espoused by the Ministry during the presentation and their responses on the draft report have been suitably addressed/incorporated in the Report.

Subsequent to the original audit, some of the sampled districts were revisited to check the improvement in maintenance of records in February-March 2008, covering 24 GPs in 12 blocks in 12 districts in 6 States from within the original audit sample. The results of the scrutiny have been incorporated in the Report.

Audit gratefully acknowledges the cooperation and assistance extended by the Ministry, the State Governments, and their officials at various stages of conduct of the Performance Audit.

Responses of the Ministry and States

The Ministry had forwarded the responses of 21 State Governments, asking audit to examine the responses and make appropriate revision to the draft report. In response to audit's request for the Ministry's final response on the report and not merely the individual responses of the States, the Ministry stated (February 2008) that the audit findings related to:

- Either specific instances of irregularities/ deviations committed by the implementing agencies of the State Governments; or
- The general principles enunciated in the Act, scheme, guidelines and instructions of the GoI.

As regards specific instances of irregularities/ deviations, the Ministry stated that it could not be expected to comment on the findings of the audit team, as neither was the relevant evidence (which would presumably have been made available by the implementing agencies for examination by the audit teams) available with the Ministry, nor was it reasonably practical to have such evidence examined by the Ministry, which were admittedly numerous and spread over the country.

Further, the Ministry stated that the State Governments were not subordinate organs of the Government of India, but were coordinate authorities within the framework of both NREGA as well as the Constitution and, therefore, requested audit to proceed to finalise the observations pertaining to the States.

In this regard, audit holds the view that Audit does not agree with the Ministry's that it confines itself to the general principles of the Act and associated instructions, and has no role to play in reviewing the specific instances of irregularities/ deviations pointed out by audit. Tthe National Rural Employment Guarantee Act (NREGA) is a Central legislation, and the Ministry, as the nodal agency for NREGA, bears ultimate overall responsibility for co-ordinating and monitoring the implementation administration of NREGA and ensuring that the funds provided by GoI are economically, efficiently and effectively utilized by the implementing agencies. However, the responses of the State Governments have been suitably incorporated in this report, even though the Ministry has not examined these responses and givenoffered its comments thereon.

In its presentation in February 2008, the Ministry also sought to distinguish between the force of the Act and the State Schemes on the one hand, and the guidelines and advisories issued by the Ministry on the other. According to the Ministry, while the Act and the State schemes were binding, the guidelines and advisories were merely suggestive, with scope for flexibility. The Ministry, therefore, felt that there was a need to recognize the varying authority of processes, and nuance the findings according to the appropriate classification of the process. Further, in its response of February 2008, the Ministry stated that its advisories and guidelines were advisory and not mandatory or prescriptive.

While audit notes the distinction between processes specified under the Act, State Schemes and, guidelines, auditit holds the view and that advisoriesthough , the guidelines and advisories were suggestive, these needed to be followed in spirit as these wereall these processes are intended to facilitate the effective and efficient implementation of NREGA and achievement of its intended objectives. Instances of deviations from, or non-compliance with the specified processes would adversely affect the Act's implementation, and such instances noticed during field audit have been suitably highlighted in this report. In specific instances where the State Governments have consciously decided to deviate from the specified processes for compelling reasons, it is the Ministry's responsibility to ensure that adequate and effective alternative controls have been put in place for the same purpose.

PHYSICAL AND FINANCIAL PERFORMANCE

Physical Performance

According to the Ministry's reports, during the year 2006-07:

- 3.81 crore rural households had registered under the scheme;
- 2.12 crore households had demanded employment under the scheme, of which 2.10 crore households received employment.
- 0.22 crore households received the full 100 days of legally guaranteed employment. Statewise details of physical performance reported by Ministry.

Financial Performance

The total financial assistance provided by the GoI to all the State Governments up to 31 March 2007 was Rs. 12073.56 crore (including Opening Balance of Rs. 2052.92 crore, Central Share of Rs. 8958.02 crore, State Share of Rs. 813.42 crore and Miscellaneous Receipts of Rs. 249.20 crore). Of this, the State Governments could utilize Rs. 8823.36 crore (73 per cent).

AUDIT FINDINGS

Framing of Rules and Rural Employment Guarantee Scheme (REGS)Preparatory Steps

Rural Employment Guarantee Scheme (REGS) Requirement

- The Act provided that the State Governments could make rules for carrying out the provisions of the Act. The Rules, inter alia, were to, inter alia, determine the grievance redressal mechanism at the block level and the district level and procedure to be followed in such matter, lay down the terms and conditions to determine the eligibility for unemployment allowance, and provide for the manner of maintaining books of account of employment of labourer and the expenditure.

- According to the NREGA Operational Guidelines, the State Government should prescribe the time frame for each level i.e. GP, block and district levels for proposing, scrutinizing, and approving REGS works.

AUDIT FINDINGS

- The Governments of Arunachal Pradesh, Chhattisgarh, Gujarat, Haryana, Himachal Pradesh, Jammu & Kashmir, Jharkhand, Kerala, Maharashtra, Manipur, Punjab, Rajasthan and Tamil Nadu (13 States) did not formulate rules for carrying out the provisions of the Act as of March 2007.
- The Governments of Arunachal Pradesh, Andhra Pradesh, Assam, Chhattisgarh, Gujarat, Jharkhand, Karnataka, Kerala, Madhya Pradesh, Manipur, Nagaland, Orissa, Punjab, Sikkim, Uttarakhand and West Bengal (16 States) did not prescribe the time frame for each level i.e. GP, Block and District levels for proposing, scrutinising and approving REGS works.

NREG Act envisaged providing rural employment as a matter of right. It is therefore important to have appropriate grievance redressal mechanisms in place. NREG Act enjoined upon the state governments to determine, by rules, appropriate grievance redressal mechanisms at the block level and at the district level. As mentioned earlier 13 states had not framed rules.

The Act provided that any dispute or complaint was to be referred to the programme officer/ district programme coordinator, but in the absence of detailed grievance redressal mechanisms, it was not clear as to what action could programme officer/district programme co-ordinator take against a GP/programme officer or otherwise provide relief to the aggrieved labourers. As a result, the rural employment seekers were deprived of effective grievance redressal mechanisms. As stated later in this report, instances of nonissue of dated receipts of applications for work, delay in payment of wages and non-payment of unemployment allowance were noticed resulting in not only dilution of the purpose of the Act of providing 100 days' employment as a matter of right but also in violation of the Act.

The Act provides that whoesoever contravenes the provisions of this Act shall on conviction be liable to a fine which may extend to one thousand rupees'. But it is not clear as to whose power and responsibility is to convict those who contravene the provisions of this Act.

- A great deal of responsibility has been cast on the Gram Panchayat for implementation of the NREGA. The sarpanch is particularly responsible for attending to tasks like distribution of job cards, receipt of work application, selection of works, allotment of works, implementation and supervision of work etc. This implies that Sarpanch has to actively devote his time, attention and energy to the programme. But, unlike other functionaries, he is not paid any remuneration for these tasks. In the absence of legitimate incentive for the Sarpanch coupled with lack of effective grievance redressal mechanism, it is not clear how the Sarpanch's accountability in regard to NREGS could be ensured.

Ministry's Response

- Formulation of rules by the State Governments was only an option under Section 32(1) of the Act, and was not mandatory.
- The Act did not prescribe any time limit (for different levels). While the guidelines suggested that the States should consider fixing some time limits, this was advisory.

Responses of States

- Governments of Chhattisgarh, Gujarat, Punjab, Tamil Nadu, and Maharashtra stated that action had now been initiated to frame rules in respect of NREGS.
- The Governments of Andhra Pradesh, Chhattisgarh, Orissa, Sikkim and Uttar Pradesh have indicated that action for stipulating detailed timeframes would be taken now.

Implication

- While Section 32(1) of the Act requires is an "enabling" provision for the State Governments to make rules to carry out the provisions of the Act and Section 32(2) indicates some critical details of matters including determination of grievance redressal mechanism, which may be provided in the rules., including such important aspects as the manner of maintaining books of accounts, arrangements for proper execution of schemes etc. Formulation of such rules iswas thus essential therefore, for specifyicrucial ng detailed procedures, processes, formats etc., taking into consideration State-specific requirements, for the effective implementation of NREG Act.

- In the absence of defined time frames at GP, Block and District levels for proposing, scrutinizing and approving REGS works, there would might be difficulty in ensuring a shelf of projects in advance, which could adversely impact provision of employment on demand.

Recommendations

- Ministry may ensure that allThe State Governments should formulate detailed rules for the implementation of the Act, and also specify timeframes at different levels for proposing, scrutinizing and approving REGS works.
- All states should be persuaded to put in place effective grievance redressal mechanisms so as to ensure that the purpose of NREG Act to provide 100 days employment as a matter of right is not diluted. The situation of lack of legitimate incentive (except goodwill of villagers) for the Sarpanchas of the GPs also needs to be addressed.

State Employment Guarantee Councils (SEGCs) and Employment Guarantee Commissioners (EGCs)

Requirement

- The Act stipulates that every State Government should set up a State Employment Guarantee Council (SEGC), which is responsible for advising the State Government on the implementation, evaluation and monitoring of the Scheme, deciding on the "preferred works" to be implemented under REGS, recommending the proposals of works to be submitted to the GoI by the State Government, and preparing an Annual Report on REGS, to be presented to the State Legislature.

- The NREGA Operational Guidelines require each State Government to designate an officer, not below the rank of a Commissioner, as the State Rural Employment Guarantee Commissioner responsible for ensuring that all activities related to the objectives of the Act were carried out as intended.

Audit Findings

While 22 State Governments had constituted SEGCs, the Governments of Gujarat, Haryana, Sikkim and Uttarakhand (4 States) had not done so as of March 2007.Further, SEGCs in Meghalaya, Jammu & Kashmir and Arunachal Pradesh had not prepared the list of preferred works to be implemented under the Scheme, and the SEGCs in Meghalaya, Jammu & Kashmir, Arunachal Pradesh and Rajasthan had not prepared Annual Reports for submission to the State Legislature. Further,

- The SEGC in Uttar Pradesh was constituted only with nonofficial members.
- In Punjab and Arunachal Pradesh the SEGC had neither reviewed the monitoring and redressal mechanism of NREGA nor monitored the implementation of NREGA.
- In Tamil Nadu, though the SEGC was constituted, no periodicity of meeting was fixed and the Council met only once during 2006-07.
- While 16 18 State Governments had designated an officer as State Rural Employment Guarantee Commissioner, the State Governments of Arunachal Pradesh, Himachal Pradesh, Karnataka, Nagaland, Sikkim, Tripura, Uttar Pradesh and Uttarakhand West Bengal (9 7 States) had not done so as of March 2007.

Ministry's Response

- The Act did not stipulate a timeframe for setting up the SEGCs; hence, it could not be said that there was a delay in setting up the councils.

Responses of States

- The Government of Sikkim had now designated Commissioner and member Secretary of SEGC.

- The Governments of Haryana and, Gujarat and Punjab stated that the proposal to setup the SEGC was under consideration. while Uttra Pradesh had initiated the process for nomination of members of SEGC.
- The Government of Uttarakhand stated that an independent cell for SREGS was being formed at the state level. The Government of West Bengal stated that though a separate post of EGC had not been created the Special secretary of the Department of Panchayat and Rural Development looked after implementation of NREGA.

Implications

- The response of the Ministry is not acceptable. Section 12(1) of NREGA stipulates that for the purposes of regular monitoring and reviewing implementation at the State level, every State "shall" constitute a State council, and also stipulates the duties and functions of the council. If after two years of implementation of NREGA, some States have not set up the State councils, it is not known how the relevant functions were of regular monitoring and evaluation are being discharged.
- In the absence of a State Rural Employment Guarantee Commissioner, there is no single identified official responsible for ensuring that all activities required for fulfilling the objectives of the Act are carried out.

Recommendations

The Ministry may take steps to seeensure that SEGCs are constituted in all States. The Ministry may also ensure that all State Governments designate State Rural Employment Guarantee Commissioners., and these councils discharge their stipulated functions.The Ministry may also ensure that all State Governments appoint State Rural Employment Guarantee Commissioners.

Resource Support

Requirements NREGA, its Operational Guidelines and other circulars issued by the Ministry Ministry inter alia envisaged the following:

- As per the provisions of the NREGA, eEvery State Government was required to appoint a full-time dedicated Programme Officer (PO), not below the rank of Block Development Officer (BDO), in each Block, with necessary supporting staff for facilitating implementation of the Scheme at Block level.
- The operational guidelines also provided that iIt would be advisable to appoint an "Employment Guarantee Assistant" (EGAs) or "Gram Rozgar Sevak" (GRSs) in each GP, in view of the pivotal role of the GP in the implementation of REGS.
- The suggested model for administrative expenses included a technical assistant for every 10 Gram Panchayats.
- The State Government could also constitute panels of accredited engineers at the District and Block levels for the purpose of assisting with the estimation and measurement of works.
- The State Government could consider appointing Technical Resource Support Groups at the State and District levels to assist in the planning, designing, monitoring, evaluation and quality audit of various initiatives and also assist in training and handholding, with a view to improving the quality and cost effectiveness of the scheme.

Audit Findings

- The Governments of Arunachal Pradesh, Assam, Bihar, Haryana, Himachal Pradesh, Jammu & Kashmir, Jharkhand, Karnataka, Madhya Pradesh, Maharashtra, Meghalaya, Nagaland, Orissa, Punjab, Sikkim, Tamil Nadu, Tripura, Uttar Pradesh, Uttarakhand and West Bengal (20 States) did not appoint full-time dedicated Programme Officers (POs) in 102 test checked blocks. The existing Block Development Offices (BDOs) were appointed as POs and given the additional charge of the Scheme.
- While 17 State Governments had appointed Technical Assistants in 78 blocks, tThe Governments of Bihar, Himachal Pradesh, Jammu & Kashmir, Jharkhand, Karnataka, Madhya Pradesh, Maharashtra, Manipur,

Punjab, Rajasthan and West Bengal (11 States) did not appoint Technical Assistants in 57 test checked blocks.

- The Governments of Assam, Bihar, Chhattisgarh, Gujarat, Haryana, Himachal Pradesh, Jammu & Kashmir, Jharkhand, Karnataka, Madhya Pradesh, Manipur, Nagaland, Orissa, Sikkim, Tamil Nadu, Uttar Pradesh, Uttarakhand and West Bengal (18 States) did not appoint dedicated Gram Rozgar Sevaks in 303 test checked GPs.
- The Governments of Arunachal Pradesh, Assam, Bihar, Chhattisgarh, Gujarat, Haryana, Himachal Pradesh, Jharkhand, Karnataka, Maharashtra, Manipur, Nagaland, Orissa, Punjab, Rajasthan, Sikkim, Tamil Nadu and West Bengal (18 States) did not constitute panels of Accredited Engineers for the purpose of assisting with the estimation and measurement of work.
- The Governments of Arunachal Pradesh, Assam, Chhattisgarh, Gujarat, Haryana, Himachal Pradesh, Jammu & Kashmir, Jharkhand, Karnataka, Kerala, Maharashtra, Manipur, Meghalaya, Nagaland, Orissa, Punjab, Sikkim, Tamil Nadu, Tripura, Uttar Pradesh, Uttarakhand and West Bengal (22 States) did not set up a Technical Resource Support Group at State/ District level.

Good Practices

In Andhra Pradesh, two computer operators cum assistants per block, three technical assistants per block and one dedicated technical assistant for 6-7 GPs had been appointed.

At the district level, orders for appointing a panel of 10 engineers as District Resource Persons (DRPs) had been issued. At the State level, an EGS units and a technical support unit had been established.

Ministry's Response

- The Ministry's advisories to the State Governments to enable them to deploy adequate staff for NREGA at all levels were broad suggestive frameworks, and States had the option to determine their administrative arrangements, based on their own needs requirements.

Responses of States

- The process of appointment of dedicated POs, Gram Rozgar Sevaks/Administrative Assistant, Technical Assistant/JEs, AEs, Computer Assistants had been initiated by the Governments of Chhattisgarh, Gujarat, Jharkhand, Punjab, Tripura, Maharashtra, Uttar Pradesh and West Bengal.
- A panel of Accredited Engineers was now being prepared in Assam, Jharkhand and Maharashtra.
- The Governments of Chhattisgarh and Assam had initiated the process of constituting Technical Resource Support Groups.
- The Government of Uttarakhand had has now appointed Dy. Programme Officers at the block level on contract basis.
- The Government of Orissa was now contemplating appointment of Additional Programme Officers on contract basis for every block, and a GRS had now (2007-08) been appointed for each GP.

Implication

While the Act stipulated appointment of POs at the Block level and also mandated provision of necessary staff and technical support by the State Governments to the District Programme Coordinators (DPCs) and POs, the Ministry's guidelines and advisories provided further advice on staffing at various levels. Where the Ministry's guidelines and advisories for staffing have not been adhered to, alternative staffing arrangements should be made to ensure the effective implementation of the scheme. However, audit scrutiny revealed that the lack of adequate administrative and technical resource support at the District, Block and GP levels adversely affected the smooth and effective implementation of NREGA, as detailed below:

- Considering the fact the average block in the 200 districts in NREGA Phase-I has 20 GPs and 56 villages, nonappointment of a full-time dedicated Programme Officers (PO), who is pivotal to the successful implementation of NREGA, and giving the additional charge of PO to BDOs, who were responsible for other developmental schemes at the Block level, strikes at the root of effective implementation of NREGA. In the absence of dedicated technical resources, the administrative and technical scrutiny and approval of REGS works was, thus, routed through the normal departmental channels burdened with existing responsibilities. This was further compounded by the failure to specify time frames for processing and approval of proposals at different levels. This was reflected in the poor progress in taking up works proposed in the Annual Plans, and thus affecting the implementation of NREGA.

- The absence of Gram Rozgar Sewaks severely affected the maintenance of basic records at the GP level, without which it would be impossible to verify employment demand and allocation for each household. Also, the potential REGS beneficiaries would not have any one at the GP level to contact about their demand for employment.

Recommendations

- State Governments should assess the staffing requirement for A full-time dedicated administrative and technical organizational setup is required for the successful implementation of NREGA, especially in the 200 districts notified in Phase-I.and accordingly take steps to address the gaps, if any.
- The State Governments should particularly consider be directed to appointing full-time POs at each Block, with adequate supporting staff and. Necessary administrative and financial powers should be delegated to such Pos, even if they are appointed on contract basis, so that proposals are not routed through the already overburdened BDOs.
- In addition to other supporting staff, each PO should have a full-time dedicated computer assistant with a PC for data entry of NREGA records for the block.
- State Governments should be directed to ensure appointment of technical assistants as well as dedicated EGAs for each GP (separate from the GP Secretary). The requirement of accredited engineers at the District level,

and Technical Support Groups at the State and District levels must also be met.

- GoI may consider relaxing the funding norm of one technical assistant for every 10 GPs to one assistant for every 5 to 6 GPs in selected districts, depending on the number of works being undertaken.
- GOI may also consider amending the current pattern of funding administrative expenses as a percentage of total expenditure (which is variable over time) in the case of an identified subset of the 200 Phase-I districts which suffer from acute poverty , where employment demand is high, and consequently where there is increased pressure on the NREGA organizational setup4. In such selected districts, the requirement of salaries for the specified posts at the Block and GP levels (especially the EGA) may be funded (subject to controls for proof of actual payment etc.) so that such posts could be manned on a stable, ongoing basis for effective monitoring and implementation of NREGA. However, once such funding is provided, no leniency, whatsoever, should be shown in the matter of record maintenance and online data capture.

Planning

Planning is critical to the successful implementation of NREGA,The obligation and the need to act within a time limit, so as to provide employment within 15 days, necessitates advance planning. The basic aim of the planning process is to ensure that the District is prepared well in advance to offer productive employment on demand.

DISTRICT PERSPECTIVE PLAN (DPP)

Requirement

The NREGA Operational Guidelines stipulate the preparation of a five year District Perspective Plan (DPP) to facilitate advance planning and provide a development perspective for the District. The aim is to identify the types of REGS works to be encouraged in the district, and the potential linkages between these works and longterm employment generation and sustained development.

Audit Findings

Out of 68 districts test checked, DPPs were not prepared by 40 test checked districts in Assam, Bihar, Chhattisgarh, Gujarat, Haryana, Himachal Pradesh, Jharkhand, Karnataka, Kerala, Maharashtra, Manipur, Punjab, Tamil Nadu, Tripura, Uttar Pradesh, Uttarakhand and West Bengal (18 17 States).

Good Practices

In Andhra Pradesh, the watershed concept of ridge to valley treatment of natural resources had been adopted and Integrated Natural Resource Management (INRM) plans had been prepared for each GP. As a result, 7.5 lakh works had been identified for implementation over the next 5-6 years.

Responses of States

The Governments of Assam, Gujarat, Himachal Pradesh, Maharashtra, Punjab, Tripura, Uttarakhand and West Bengal had initiated action/ issued instructions for preparation of DPP as per the requirements of the Guidelines and orders of the Ministry.

Implication

In the absence of DPPs, a long-term shelf of projects is not available. This, in turn, affects the timeliness of project approval. Recommendation For ensuring a long-term shelf of projects, and ensuring timely preparation of Annual Plans, all Districts must sbe hould be directed to prepare DPPs so as to develop long-term shelves of projects. immediately.

Annual Plans

Requirement

The Annual Plan is a working plan that identifies the activities to be taken up on priority in a year. The process for preparation of the Annual Plan is as follows:

- Every year, the GPs shall convene a meeting of the Gram Sabha (GS) to estimate the demand for labour, and to propose the number and priority of works to be taken up in the next financial year. Based on the recommendations formulated in the GS, the GP will prepare an Annual Plan and forward it to the PO. This Annual Plan should indicate the existing demand for work, demand in the previous year, works taken up in the previous year, ongoing works, proposed costs, likely costs and proposed implementing agencies.

- The PO will scrutinize the Annual Plans of individual GPs for technical feasibility, and submit a consolidated statement of proposals at the block level to the Intermediate Panchayat (IP), which will discuss and approve the plan and forward it to the District Programme Coordinator (DPC).
- The DPC will scrutinize the plan proposals of all IPs, and consolidate them into a District Plan proposal with a blockwise shelf of projects (arranged GP-wise). This District Plan will indicate for each project (a) the time frame, (b) the person days to be generated, and (c) the full-cost. This plan will be discussed and approved by the District Panchayat (DP). At least 50 per cent of the works are to be executed by the GPs.
- The DPC will also coordinate the preparation of detailed technical estimates and sanctions, with project reports for each approved work specifying technical details, as well as the expected outputs and enduring outcomes.

Audit Findings

- While documented annual plans for 2006-07 were prepared in 318 GPs in 23 States. Such dDocumented annual plans for 2006-07 were was not prepared, or the plan plans were was not complete in 175 test checked GPs in Andhra Pradesh, Assam, Bihar, Chhattisgarh, Gujarat, Haryana, Himachal Pradesh, Jharkhand, Madhya Pradesh, Manipur, Orissa, Sikkim, Tamil Nadu, Uttar Pradesh and West Bengal (15 States).
- While Gram Sabha meetings for approving the Annual Plans were required to be convened, in 424 GPs in 25 States. Such Sabha meetings were not convened in 80 test checked GPs in Assam, Haryana, Himachal Pradesh, Jharkhand, Karnataka, Orissa, Uttar Pradesh and West Bengal (8 States).

- Works were not identified by the Gram Sabhas in 101 GPs in Assam, Bihar, Chhattisgarh, Gujarat, Haryana, Himachal Pradesh, Jammu & Kashmir, Jharkhand, Karnataka, Madhya Pradesh, Orissa and Punjab (12 states).
- The District Annual Plans were not prepared in 4 test checked Districts in Himachal Pradesh, Jharkhand and West Bengal (3 States).
- The District Plans in 4 Districts in Bihar, Jammu & Kashmir, Sikkim and Uttar Pradesh (4 States) did not comprise a block-wise shelf of projects.
- The District Plans in 47 Districts in Andhra Pradesh, Assam, Bihar, Chhattisgarh, Gujarat, Haryana, Himachal Pradesh, Jharkhand, Karnataka, Kerala, Madhya Pradesh, Maharashtra, Manipur, Nagaland, Orissa, Punjab, Rajasthan, Sikkim, Tamil Nadu, Tripura, Uttar Pradesh, Uttarakhand and West Bengal (23 States) did not indicate the timeframe for each project. Similarly, The District Plans in 25 Districts in Arunachal Pradesh, Assam, Bihar, Chhattisgarh, Gujarat, Haryana, Himachal Pradesh, Jharkhand, Karnataka, Kerala, Orissa, Sikkim and West Bengal (13 States) did not indicate the person days to be generated for each project, while the District Plans in 12 Districts in Arunachal Pradesh, Bihar, Haryana, Himachal Pradesh, Jharkhand, Sikkim and West Bengal (7 States) did not indicate the full cost for each project.
- The District Plans in 11 Districts in Arunachal Pradesh, Bihar, Himachal Pradesh, Jharkhand, Orissa, Sikkim, Uttar Pradesh and Uttarakhand (8 States) did not ensure that 50 per cent of the works were to be executed by the GPs.
- The Project Reports for approved works in the District Plans did not clarify the size of the physical assets (e.g. length of road, size of tank) in 14 Districts in Arunachal Pradesh, Bihar, Chhattisgarh, Himachal Pradesh, Jharkhand, Karnataka, Kerala, Manipur, Orissa, Tripura and Uttar Pradesh (11 States), and did not clarify the enduring outcomes (e.g. area irrigated, villages connected) in 22 Districts in Arunachal Pradesh, Assam, Bihar,

Chhattisgarh, Gujarat, Haryana, Himachal Pradesh, Jharkhand, Karnataka, Kerala, Manipur, Orissa, Tamil Nadu, Uttar Pradesh and Uttarakhand (15 States). Other deficiencies noted in the Annual Plans were as follows:

* In Orissa and Jammu & Kashmir, during 2006-07, participation in the GS meetings was poor – 2.3 per cent in 14 GPs in Orissa, and 1-2 per cent in 10 GPs in Jammu & Kashmir.
    * In Rajasthan, Annual Plans were not linked with DPPs, and approval of Gram Sabhas was not taken/ on record for the works executed.
    * In Maharashtra, no estimate was made of the demand for labour.
    * In Jharkhand, in Hazaribagh district, the Annual Plan was not prepared GP-wise and it did not specify the works to be taken up, the mandays to be generated, prioritization of works etc. In Ranchi district, the Annual Plan provided for only 2209 works, whereas 5918 works were taken up.
    * In Andhra Pradesh Uttarakhand (Chamoli District) the priorities assigned to the identified works in GP Annual Plan were not strictly adhered to, while executing the works.
    * In Jammu & Kashmir, in four test checked blocks, the POs did not scrutinize the annual plans of the GPs for technical feasibility. While approving Annual Plans for the year 2006-07, the GPs did not take into consideration the number of families registered, number of job cards issued, period for which households were willing to work, etc.
    * In Bihar, 242 works in spl. Divn. Darbhanga and 5 works in block Mohanpur during 2006-07 valued at Rs 8.72 crore were executed without inclusion in the AP. Annual plans prepared for NREGA in all test checked GPs were heavily loaded towards construction of brick soling roads, resulting in high material-labour ratio.

Response of States

- The Government of Andhra Pradesh indicated that the shelf of works of a GP was its annual plan. It had also indicated that since NREGS was a demand-driven programme, and time taken for project execution depended on labour reporting for work, timeframe for each project may not be required.
- Necessary instructions had been issued by the Governments of Assam and Chhattisgarh to the concerned authorities for preparation of documented Annual Plan after identification of works by the GS.
- Necessary instructions had been issued by the Government of Assam for wide publicity of GS meetings and identification of works.
- Instructions had been issued by the State Government of Uttarakhand, Tripura, Tamil Nadu, Uttar Pradesh for indicating the time frame for each work in the Annual Plan.Instructions had been issued by the Governments of Orissa, Tripura and Uttarakhand for indicating the enduring outcome for each work in the Annual Plan.

Implication

- In the absence of documented Annual Plans, there would be no shelf of projects for timely approval, thus adversely affecting the ability to meet demand for employment.
- Lack of participation, or inadequate participation by Gram Sabhas, and Gram Panchayats in the planning process would vitiate the process of people's participation, transparency and accountability, and also adversely affect the creation of productive assets benefiting the local community.
- In the absence of specification of physical assets and enduring outcomes in the District Annual Plans, no meaningful comparison of actual achievements vis-à-vis plans is possible.

Recommendations

- All Districts must be directed to ensure preparation of Annual Plans at the GP level to be consolidated at the Block and District levels.

- States should ensure more publicity at the grass root level, in particular through displays at Panchayat Ghars and Implementing Agencies so as to ensure adequate involvement of Gram Sabha.
- To simplify the workload at the GP level, the Annual Plan at the GP level could be limited to identifying works and estimating labour demand, with estimation of likely costs etc. being indicated at the PO's level.

Registration and Issue of Job Cards

Requirement

Before demanding employment under REGS, rural households have to register themselves, and get a job card. The process for registration of households and issue of job cards, as per the NREGA Operational Guidelines, is briefly as follows:

- Households may submit an application for registration, or submit an oral request.
- A Gram Sabha shall be convened when the Act commences, for the purpose of explaining the provisions of the Act, mobilize applications for registration and conduct verifications.
- A door-to-door survey may also be undertaken to identify persons willing to register under the Act.
- Job cards should be issued within a fortnight of the application for registration. Photographs of adult member applicants should be attached to the job cards.

Audit Findings

- While aWhile an introductory Gram Sabha meeting at the time of commencement of the Act was to be convened, in 340 GPs in 24 States, such a meeting was not conducted or no documentary evidence of such a meeting was available in 120 GPs in Andhra Pradesh, Assam, Bihar, Haryana, Himachal Pradesh, Jharkhand, Karnataka, Kerala, Manipur, Orissa, Uttar Pradesh and West Bengal (12 States).
- Door-to-door survey to identify persons willing to register was not conducted in 323 GPs in Andhra Pradesh, Assam,

Bihar, Chhattisgarh, Haryana, Himachal Pradesh, Jammu & Kashmir, Jharkhand, Karnataka, Kerala, Maharashtra, Manipur, Nagaland, Orissa, Punjab, Rajasthan, Tamil Nadu, Uttar Pradesh, Uttarakhand and West Bengal (20 States).

- While jJob cards were to be issued within 15 days of application for registration. in 261 GPs in 23 States, dDelays in issue of job cards were noticed in 196 GPs in Andhra Pradesh, Assam, Bihar, Chhattisgarh, Haryana, Himachal Pradesh, Jharkhand, Kerala, Maharashtra, Manipur, Orissa, Sikkim, Tamil Nadu, Uttar Pradesh, Uttarakhand and West Bengal (16 States).
- Photographs of the applicants were not attached to job cards in 251 GPs in Andhra Pradesh, Assam, Bihar, Chhattisgarh, Haryana, Himachal Pradesh, Jharkhand, Madhya Pradesh, Maharashtra, Orissa, Uttar Pradesh, Uttarakhand and West Bengal (13 States).

Other Statespecific findings

- In Orissa, 670 households of 16 GPs of Narla Block of Kalahandi District were not registered, despite submitting applications, on the grounds that their names did not feature in the 2002 BPL survey list.
    * In 6 GPs of 2 Blocks in Kalahandi District, job cards were not issued to 342 households, and 14 villages in one GP intimated non-supply of job cards despite applicationreceiving applications for registration.
    * One village (Kajumaska) of Santapur GP with a population of 90 (SC-11; ST-79) was not covered for registration of households.
    * In one GP, 13 job cards were found by DRDA officials to be lying with GP officials. In another GP, 21 cards were lying with the GP authorities, and were issued at the instance of audit.
    * In Haryana, in 5 test checked GPs, against 637 registered households, 968 households were reported to have been issued job cards; in addition, 72 minors

had also been registered for doing manual work. Also, in 16 test-checked GPs, photographs were not attached in 2,238 cases of job cards, out of 3467 registered households.

* In Himachal Pradesh, in Sirmour District, out of 13,695 BPL households, only 5389 households (39.3 percent) were registered and issued job cards. In Manipur, job cards were issued without identification. In Karnataka, in the two district of Davanagere and Gulbarga, out of the total registered households of 2.33 lakh and 3.89 lakh, only 1.55 lakh (66.5 percent) and 2.01 lakh (51.7 percent) households were issued job cards. In Tamil Nadu, in Cuddalore District, out of 2,24,000 applications registered, job cards were not issued to 1093 households as of March 2007.

Good Practices

- In Andhra Pradesh, for NREGA Phase-III districts, arrangements had been made for issue of job cards with photographs in all GPs.

Ministry's Response

- Convening of the Gram Sabha meeting at the time of commencement of NREGA was only an advisory instruction.

Responses of States

- The State of Andhra Pradesh stated that introductory mobilization was carried out in campaign mode.
- The States of Andhra Pradesh, Rajasthan, Tamil Nadu and Maharashtra stated that issue of job cards was an ongoing process and necessary instructions had been issued to the concerned Officers for proper maintenance of Job Cards.
- In Andhra Pradesh, photo affixing had been taken up in campaign mode, and was scheduled for completion by March 2008.

- Proper registration of beneficiaries i.e. timely issuance of job cards and fixing of photographs had now been initiated in Chhattisgarh, Jharkhand, Orissa and Sikkim.

Implication

- The NREGA Operational Guidelines mandatorily stipulate the convening of an introductory Gram Sabha meeting, in order to explain the provisions of the Act, mobilize applications for registration and conduct verifications. Since NREGA is termed a "People's Act", such a GS meeting is intended to promote public participation at the grassroots level.
- While audit notes the use of other mobilization methods like campaigns, Palli Sabha etc., a door-to-door survey (on the lines of the electoral registration process) ensures wider coverage of the population across all segments, and also ensures authenticity of the registration of the households.
- In the absence of other identifying documents for persons, photographs on job cards are the most important means to identify genuine beneficiaries, especially when payments are made through Muster Rolls, and not through postal and bank accounts. The absence of photographs weakens controls on allocation of employment and payment of wages to intended beneficiaries.

Recommendations

- State Governments should take steps to provide adequate publicity to the programme and to persuade as many ensure that all BPL households households as possible are persuaded to register under NREGA. In addition,The periodic door-to-door surveys, even at this stage, would be useful.
- State Governments should must be directed to take up a time bound programme to ensure affixing of photographs (at no cost to the beneficiaries) to the existing job cards.
- State Governments must ensure that under no condition are job cards retained by GP/ other departmental officials for any purpose.

WORKS

General

Requirements

According to the Act and the NREGA Operational Guidelines:

- To avoid duplication, a unique identity number should be given to each work.
- Administrative and technical sanction should be obtained for all works in advance, by December of the previous year.
- Worksite facilities (medical aid, drinking water, shade and crèche, if there are more than five children below the age of six years) are to be ensured by the implementing agency.
- Use of contractors is prohibited; as far as practicable, tasks shall be performed by using manual labour, and not machines.
- The ratio of wage costs to material costs should be no less than 60:40, preferably at the GP, block and district levels.

Audit Findings

- Out of 558 GPs test checked,Unique unique identity numbers were not allotted to works in 331 GPs in Assam, Bihar, Chhattisgarh, Gujarat, Haryana, Himachal Pradesh, Jammu & Kashmir, Jharkhand, Karnataka, Kerala, Maharashtra, Manipur, Nagaland, Punjab, Sikkim, Tamil Nadu, Uttar Pradesh, Uttarakhand and West Bengal (19 States).
- In 19 Districts in Bihar, Chhattisgarh, Haryana, Himachal Pradesh, Jharkhand, Orissa and Uttar Pradesh (7 States), the wages-material ratio of 60:40 was not maintained at the district level. Further, 39 test-checked blocks in Arunachal Pradesh, Bihar, Chhattisgarh, Himachal Pradesh, Jammu & Kashmir, Maharashtra, Nagaland, Orissa, Tripura, Uttar
- Pradesh and West Bengal (11 States) did not maintain a wage material ratio of 60:40 at the block level.
- Out of 558 GPs test checked, aAdministrative approval and technical sanction of works was not obtained in

advance in 95 GPs in Bihar, Haryana, Himachal Pradesh, Jammu & Kashmir, Jharkhand, Karnataka, Kerala, Madhya Pradesh, Maharashtra, Punjab, Uttar Pradesh and Uttarakhand (12 States).

- Out of 558 GPs testchecked, wWorksite facilities were not provided or only partly provided in 227 GPs in Andhra Pradesh, Assam, Bihar, Gujarat, Haryana, Himachal Pradesh, Jammu & Kashmir, Jharkhand, Karnataka, Manipur, Orissa, Uttar Pradesh, Uttarakhand and West Bengal (14 States).

Responses of States

- According to Andhra Pradesh, while drinking water and first aid box were generally provided, provision of shade and crèche was poor, and this would be regularly monitored.
- The Governments of Assam, Chhattisgarh, Haryana, Himachal Pradesh, Gujarat, Jharkhand, Maharashtra, Orissa, Uttar Pradesh and West Bengal had now issued necessary instructions for allotment of Unique IDs to works, maintenance of material wage ratio as per Guidelines, obtaining of administrative approval and technical sanction in advance and providing worksite facilities etc. wherever these were found lacking in Audit.

Implications

- Non-allotment of unique identity numbers to works leads to the possibility of duplication of works.
- Non-adherence to the stipulated wage: material ratio of 60:40 is a violation of the Act, and also leads to reduced provision of wage employment, which is the Act's primary objective.
- Non-obtaining of administrative approval and technical sanction in advance leads to delay in taking up the work, and non-timely provision of employment to households.

Recommendations

- The Ministry/ State Governments should ensure that a unique identity number is given to each work and also may be directed to ensure that administrative approval and technical sanction for works in the Annual Plan are obtained well in advance. by December of the previous year.

- State Governments may should also be directed to ensure compliance with the 60:40 ratio of wages: material costs not only at the District level, but also at the Block level, and also in respect of all implementing agencies.

Works taken up in test-checked GPs

Despite the fact that there was no shortage of funds for implementation of NREGA, audit scrutiny revealed that except in Tripura, none of the test checked GPs were able to take up all the works proposed in their Annual Plan for 2006-07. The average State-wise shortfall in works actually taken up vis-à-vis those contemplated in the Annual Plans ranged from 1 per cent (West Bengal) to 97 per cent (Maharashtra). The shortfall in execution of works affected the provision of the legally guaranteed 100 days of employment.

STATE-SPECIFIC AUDIT FINDINGS

Lack of Appropriate Approvals

Assam

- There was no formal allotment of work at GP level. Works were allocated verbally.

Haryana

- Expenditure of Rs. 1.53 crore was incurred in 2006-07 on all 129 works in Baraguda block in Sirsa District, without obtaining administrative approval and technical sanction.

Jammu & Kashmir

- In three blocks, (Poonch, Bhaderwah and Banihal) out of a total of 495 schemes executed during 2006-07, 116 schemes costing Rs. 111.79 lakhs had not been approved by the competent panchayats and did not form part of the approved annual works plan. An expenditure of Rs. 90.69 lakh was incurred on these schemes during the year.

- 14 works costing Rs. 33.55 lakh were executed in three blocks (Bhaderwah Banihal and Poonch) without obtaining administrative approvals in advance.
- 18 works costing Rs. 43.80 lakh were under execution in three blocks (Bhaderwah, Banihal, Mendhar) without obtaining technical sanctions from the concerned authorities.

Jharkhand

- In the absence of Annual PlanAP in Palamu, the DC instructed BDOs to take up " work of irrigation well" in villages without assessing the requirement. Consequently, 1112 wells were taken up (December 2006) at a cost of Rs. 9.93 crore for completion by February/ March 2007, which remained incomplete as of July 2007.
- In Gumla, schemes for construction of 159 irrigation wells, ponds and tree plantation were sanctioned by the DC, without holding the meeting of Gram Sabha, for Rs 8.32 crore for completion by September 2006 to May 2007. None of the above works were completed within by May 2007.
- On the recommendation of six MLAs, 71 schemes for Rs 5.14 crore were taken up (between March 2006 and May 2007) for execution, but these were neither in the Annual Plan nor approved by the Gram Sabhas.

Karnataka

- Two works (desilting of tanks) in Harasuru Gram Panchayat (69 acres) and Bheemalli GP of Gulbarga District costing Rs.50.33 lakh was taken up without administrative and technical sanction, and one road work of Rs. 8.75 Lakh was taken up in Gulbarga Taluk without technical sanction.

Orissa

- In one GP (Duarsuni of Bhawanipatna block), list of three works (estimated cost: Rs. 20 lakh) executed was not approved by the Gram Sabha.
- In Bhawanipatna block, one road work was executed at Rs 5 lakh during 2006-07 without technical sanction.

Punjab

- Technical sanction had not been obtained in advance for works due to non posting of Technical Assistants.

Incomplete Works

Bihar

- In Muzaffarpur, Samastipur, Darbhanga and Munger districts, despite availability of funds of Rs 11.12 lakh, no work was undertaken for the period 2006-07, leaving the entire allotted funds unutilized.

Gujarat

- Out of 8429 works taken up for execution during 2006-07 in the State, 5292 works (63 per cent) remained incomplete. None of the 1986 works taken up for providing irrigation facility on land of ST persons was completed.

Himachal Pradesh

- Completion of 22 works was delayed for a period ranging between one and eight months.

Manipur

- Out of 1615 works, 714 works with progressive expenditure of Rs. 8.06 crore remained incomplete as of 31 March 2007.

Meghalaya

- Against 11,446 works targeted for completion during 2006-07, only 867 works (8 per cent) were completed.

Orissa

- Out of 1835 works approved in the Annual Action Plans of 48 GPs test checked, only 444 works (24 per cent) were taken up.

Diversion and Misuse of Funds

Bihar

- The DDC, Darbhanga irregularly transferred Rs 2.69 crore to special division, Darbhanga during 2006-07 for construction of 34 protection walls of raised platforms constructed under Sam Vikas Yojana.

Haryana

- In Sirsa District, while the material consumed in the district from April 2006 to February 2007 for pucca works was Rs. 3.87 crore, expenditure on purchase of stores in March 2007 alone was Rs. 3.61 crore. Also, the cash books of 3 blocks of the district for 2006-07 had not been closed as of June 2007, as transactions relating to the purchase of the material had not been completed. Clearly, the material was purchased merely to show utilization of funds, without assessing the requirement on works.

Madhya Pradesh

- Rs. 12.05 lakh were irregularly incurred by PWD Dhar on repair of roads and renovation of meeting halls.

Punjab

- The One P.O. did not check the correctness of the final expenditure reported by the implementing agency at the time of authorizing final closure of work.

Tripura

- Rs.9 lakh was irregularly transferred (November 2006) to the account of Divisional Forest Officer, Manu for construction of 72 IAY type houses.

Uttarakhand

- Works of Jal Nikaas Naali, in one GP, amounting to Rs. 15220 was not commenced, but the expenditure was reported in the MPR.

USE OF CONTRACTORS/ MACHINERY

Madhya Pradesh

- Tractors and rollers were engaged on MRs for transportation of material and compaction of road and tank works.
- CEO, Zila Parisad Sidhi, incurred Rs. 20.80 lakh on spraying of hormones for zetropha plantation on contract basis.

Orissa

- In one block (Bhawanipatna) of Kalahandi District, 149 works were executed at a cost of Rs 7.55 crore between February 2006 and March 2007 through contractors in the guise of Village Labour Leaders (VLLs) (up to November 2006) and in the name of departmental execution through the Junior Engineers (from December 2006). The VLLs and JEs procured road metal and other materials out of their own resources and also in many cases indicated payment of wages without receiving any advance/ sufficient advance. Site account registers in respect of receipt and issue of materials to the work and temporary advance register in respect of advance availed from December 2006 for payment of wages had not been maintained, though they were mandatory., despite their mandated requirement for departmental execution. Materials were not purchased on tender/ quotation basis and purchase bills/ payment receipts were not treated as expenditure documents. Instead, work bills were paid to the VLLs/ JEs based on item and volume of works executed in a similar manner as allowed in the case of work done by the contractors. Measurement for these works was also made by the same JE, shown as departmentally executing the work. This is indicative of execution of works by the contractors in the guise of VLLs and in the name of departmental execution.

IRREGULAR EXECUTION OF WORKS

Bihar

- In Darbhanga and Supual Districts, due to absence of technical staff, work valued Rs 79.26 lakh was executed through non-qualified staff viz. peons, private persons during 2006-07.
- Works of Rs 1.49 crore under scheme were assigned by the DDC cum CEO of Madhubani District (June 2006) to two NGOs, who had not executed SGRY5 works amounting to Rs 46.22 lakh earlier allotted to them.

- Works valued Rs 1.76 lakh was shown as completed in Bahadurpur block, Darbhanga District before issue of work order.

Himachal Pradesh

- In respect of the selected works, detailed technical estimates were not prepared. The assessment of the works was done after completion of work and measurements were recorded in the MBs in such manner that the value of a work executed equalled the sanctioned cost.

Meghalaya

- No measurement of the works executed in the selected blocks was taken up, due to lack of technical manpower.

Orissa

- One executing agency in Bhawanipatna block, Kalahandi District utilized Rs 47.80 lakh to complete seven incomplete works taken up under NFFWP, without following the provisions of NREGA Guidelines.
- Similarly, the Assistant Soil Conservation Officer, Bhawanipatna utilized Rs 29.85 lakh during 2006-07 without following the NREGA Guidelines as registered labourers were not engaged and un-authorised (kutcha) muster rolls available in the market were used without the authority of the Programme Officer.

Tamil Nadu

- Measurement Books for the works executed under NREGS were not maintained in any of the sampled blocks and completion reports were also not recorded for the works completed so far.

West Bengal

- An expenditure of Rs.38.49 lakh was incurred in on 20 works, in 7 GPs, for due to execution of non-existent quantities of work, which was detected during joint physical verification.
- Unfruitful expenditure of Rs.6.13 lakh was also noticed in seven social forestry works due to damage of seedlings because of inadequate protection measures.

NON-ADHERENCE TO WAGE: MATERIAL COSTS RATIO

Haryana

- In Mohindergarh District, records showing segregation of expenditure on material and wages were not maintained.

Himachal Pradesh

- In two one (Bhatiyat and Mehla) out of four selected blocks, the wages-material ratio was 55: 45 and 42:58. respectively.

Jharkhand

- DC, Gumla sanctioned (March 2007) 100 units of "Safed Musli" cultivation for commercial farming for Rs 1.24 crore at Rs 1.24 lakh per unit, which had only 12 per cent (Rs 15.30 lakh) labour component.
- In West Singhbhum District, of 4,326 works executed (2006- 07) for Rs 52.13 crore, 2,373 were PCC Roads where labour component was as low as 19 to 24 per cent as against the norm of 60 per cent.

Tripura

- Rs. 52.44 lakh was incurred on construction of a motor stand where the wages-material ratio was 30:70. Similarly, in 62 projects under 2 Panchayat Samitis, Rs. 106.91 lakh was incurred where the wages – material ratio ranged from 9:91 to 31:69.

ABANDONED/UNFRUITFUL WORKS

Bihar

- 37 works estimated to costing Rs. 2.02 crore were abandoned in Supaul District after expenditure of Rs. 27.79 lakh, as they exceeded the stipulated material-labour ratio, resulting in unfruitful expenditure.

Haryana

- An expenditure of Rs. 4.31 crore was incurred on digging 257 ponds in Mohindergarh District, which is a drought prone area with scanty rainfall and where the soil is sandy and has no water retention power. Block and GP officials admitted that the ponds dug under NREGA were without water. One pond had almost become a swimming pool, as 80 per cent of expenditure was incurred on material and masonry works.

- Similarly in Sirsa District, expenditure of Rs. 7.31 crore was spent on digging of 237 ponds, for which factors like catchment area, source of recharging etc. were not conceptualized,assessed and works were executed without technical sanction and preparation of detailed estimates. Test check of records revealed lack of arrangements for filling the ponds with water, and complaints regarding absence of need.

Orissa

- NREGA Guidelines permit execution of road projects providing all weather connectivity in rural areas. However, joint physical inspection in September 2007 of three road works executed at a cost of Rs 15 lakh in Bhawanipatna block disclosed that the roads remained kutcha, even after improvement,improvement and were not able to provide all weather access. Further, recording of inflated measurement in the measurement books and Level section Graph sheets in all the three cases, and excess payment of Rs.1.80 lakh in one case was also noticed.

Photographs of Works Inspected by Audit Teams

Pond in Madhogarh Village, Ateli Block, Mohindergarh District, Haryana constructed like a swimming pool Pond in GP Panjuana in Block Baraguda, Sirsa District without water (NREGA Road work in Bhawanipatna Block, Kalahandi Distt., Orissa not providing all weather connectivity) (Ichapur to Bijepur Road, Bhawanipatna Block, Kalahandi Distt, Orissa not providing all weather access)

Other Irregularities

Haryana

- In 7 blocks of Sirsa District, while making purchases of Rs. 98.28 lakh for providing amenities, proper purchase procedures – invitation of tenders, quality assurance, inspection etc. were not followed.

Karnataka

- No details of measurements were recorded in the Muster Rolls in Gulbarga District and dates of payments were also not recorded. Assets created were not according to specification and quantities executed were not as per technical sanction.

Kerala

- In 3 test checked works, excess payment of Rs. 2.25 lakh due to application of wrong per unit rates was noticed.

Manipur

- A total of 843 works were executed on the basis of inflated estimates, resulting in avoidable expenditure of Rs.2.57 crore (inclusion of contractors' profit element- Rs. 1.19 crore and agency charges- Rs. 1.38 crore).

Orissa

- In Kalahandi district, due to delay in execution of 46 works by an executing agency (Assistant Soil Conservation Officer, Bhawanipatna), there was cost overrun by Rs 35.03 lakh.
- Excess payment of Rs. 7.98 lakh in 13 cases in Bhawanipatna block, due to non-deduction of voids and volume of sand and moorum utilized, was noticed.

Rajasthan

- In GPs test checked (in block Dhariyawad and Kherwara of Udaipur district) payment to labourers was made without measuring works and working out tasks; the reason indicated on the muster rolls was due to shortage of technical staff.

Responses of States

- The Government of Assam stated that the instructions had been issued to district authorities for formal allotment of work at GP level.

- The Government of Bihar stated that action has been initiated against the DDC, Executive Engineer for allotment of works to defaulting NGOs. Besides, directions had been issued to DPCs of Darbhanga and Muzaffarpur districts to look into the irregularities pointed out in Audit.
- The Government of Haryana admitted that the expenditure on digging of ponds in Sirsa and Mohindergarh Districts was wasteful, but contended that possibilities were being explored to connect these ponds with canals/ water channels.
- The Government of Madhya Pradesh had now initiated remedial action to rectify the irregularities pointed in audit and issued instructions to obtain administrative approval and technical sanction before start of work.

Recommendations

The Ministry/ State Governments should ensure that unique identity number is given to each work and also that administrative approval and technical sanction for works in the Annual Plan are obtained well in advance.

State Governments should also ensure compliance with the 60:40 ratio of wages: material costs not only at the District level, but also at the Block level.

State Governments should mandatorily ensure administrative and technical approval in advance of all works in the Annual Plan.

- *Audit scrutiny revealed execution of works like Shamshan* Ghats, Panchayat Ghars, school buildings and playgrounds, Community Centres, which are not listed as Permissible *Works under NREGA. GoI may consider adding* additional categories of works, and also consider empowering State Governments/ SEGCs to add other region-specific works, after keeping the Ministry informed.
- *State Governments may ensure better co-ordination with the* Line Departments so that NREGA works can be subsequently upgraded with additional mechanized work to create durable assets, e.g. metalling of REGS-constructed roads. In response, the Ministry stated that this

recommendation was outside the purview of NREGA and might lead to a violation of the Act, since the Act prohibited use of machinery, and this recommendation might open a window for serious diversions. Audit does not agree with this response, as the recommendation is, in no way, a violation of the Act, and refers to the subsequent improvement of works already constructed under NREGA. Further, such upgradation will help in creation of durable assets, which is an important objective.

- *In order to avoid duplication of NREGS works with other* schemes, especially in the absence of unique work IDs, durable signboards with cement concrete base may be preferred over temporary/ less durable signboards.

EMPLOYMENT AND WAGES

District Schedule of Rates

Requirements

The NREGA operational guidelines stipulate that:

- District Schedules of Rates (DSRs) should be prepared for each district, and should be posted at worksites in the local language.
- The States should prepare exhaustive and detailed list of tasks required for undertaking works under REGS in different geomorphological conditions, and the productivity norms for the District Schedule of Rates (DSRs) should be worked for each locale in such a way that seven hours of normal work earns minimum wages on a piece rate basis.
- State Governments should undertake comprehensive work, time and motion studies for observing out-turn and fixing rates; a matrix of rates for the same task needs to be drawn up for different ecological conditions.
- Implementing agencies may provide a description of daily work requirements to facilitate the fulfillment of productivity norms.

Audit Findings

The Governments of Arunachal Pradesh, Assam, Bihar, Chhattisgarh, Haryana, Himachal Pradesh, Jharkhand, Karnataka,

Kerala, Manipur, Meghalaya, Punjab, Sikkim, Tripura, Uttar Pradesh, and Uttarakhand (16 States) did not prepare separate District-wise Schedules of Rates (DSRs) specifically for NREGA works. , after listing tasks for REGS works in different geo-morphological conditions, and undertaking time and motion studies for observing out-turn and fixing rates. As regards the other States,

- In Jammu & Kashmir, in Doda District, DSRs for NREGA were prepared by modifying the approved schedule of rates
- In Maharashtra, separate Schedules of Rates were prepared circle-wise for 4 circles.
- In Orissa, separate rates for earth work in different types of soil had been notified.
- In Rajasthan, while time and motion studies were being conducted for tasks in different ecological conditions, a 20 per cent reduction from PWD rates in tasks for labour payments had been prescribed on the basis of interim studies.
- In Tamil Nadu, a rural schedule of rates was prepared, based on the tests conducted in the six NREGA implementing districts, with a separate schedule of rates for Sivagangai district.
- In West Bengal, time and motion studies for earthwork was conducted, and rates revised.

Good Practices

- In Andhra Pradesh, 158 works were taken up for conduct of time and motion studies by the Engineering Staff College of India, based on which a Rural Standard Schedule of Rates (RSSR) had been prepared and notified. Further, tasks were identified for various works under eight categories of NREGA, and productivity norms devised and circulated in the form of task sheets prepared in the local language. Salient features and rates were also painted on the Village Information Wall. According to the State Government, use of locally understood terminologies in the task sheets enabled labour to understand the payment structure for a given outturn better than displaying DSRs at the worksite.

State Responses

- The Governments of Assam, Kerala, Orissa, Rajasthan, Jharkhand and Tripura had now entrusted time and motion study.
- The Governments of Assam and Uttarakhand stated that the DSR had been prepared or were under preparation.
- The Government of Assam stated that instructions had been issued for preparation of exhaustive list of tasks under different geo-morphological conditions.

Implications

- In the absence of a detailed listing of tasks in different geomorphological conditions, and conduct of work, time and motion studies for fixing of productivity norms, and preparation of separate DSRs for NREGA works, the Schedule of Rates of the PWD, Rural Development Department etc. are being adopted. However it must be noted that the objective of NREGA is to provide livelihood security and any willing adult member can seek employment under NREGA, while construction works undertaken in other departmental works would place a premium on healthy and able bodied individuals. The use of PWD rates for NREGA works, thus, may not ensure provision of minimum wages and livelihood security to households.

Recommendation

- *The Ministry/ State Governments should be directed to* ensure preparation of separate District-wise Schedules of Rates for NREGA, after careful work, time and motion studies, and fixing of productivity norms for tasks in different geo-morphological conditions. Ultimately, seven hours of normal work must earn at least the minimum wage rate. Such rates should also be widely publicized in the local language.

Payment of Wages

Requirements

Every person working under REGS is entitled to wages at the minimum wage rate fixed by the State Government for agricultural labourers. Wages may be paid either on a time rate or piece rate basis. The NREGA Operational Guidelines further stipulate that:

- Wages should be paid on time. In the case of delay beyond 15 days, workers are entitled to compensation as per the provisions of the Payment of Wages Act, 1936.
- Measurements must be recorded transparently, whereby individuals may verify their measurement on a daily basis.

Audit Findings

- In 79 GPs in Andhra Pradesh, Bihar, Chhattisgarh, Jharkhand, Kerala, Madhya Pradesh, Maharashtra, Manipur, Orissa, Punjab, Rajasthan and Tamil Nadu (12 States), the workers, even after working for seven hours, were getting paid wages less than the minimum wage rate.
- In 213 GPs in Andhra Pradesh, Bihar, Chhattisgarh, Haryana, Himachal Pradesh, Jharkhand, Karnataka, Kerala, Madhya Pradesh, Manipur, Orissa, Rajasthan, Sikkim, Tamil Nadu, Uttar Pradesh, Uttarakhand and West Bengal (19 17 States), workers were not being paid wages on time i.e. within a fortnight of the date on which the work was done. No compensation was paid to them.REGS works were not measured daily in 383 GPs in Andhra Pradesh, Assam, Bihar, Chhattisgarh, Gujarat, Himachal Pradesh, Jammu & Kashmir, Jharkhand, Karnataka, Kerala, Madhya Pradesh, Manipur, Nagaland, Orissa, Punjab, Rajasthan, Sikkim, Tamil Nadu, Tripura, Uttar Pradesh and Uttarakhand (21 States).

State Specific Findings

A State-wise summary of audit findingsirregularities in the on payment of wages is as follows:

Andhra Pradesh

- No compensation was paid to labour in respect of 2,05,911 cases of delayed payments of wages in the State beyond the stipulated period of 15 days during 2006-2007.

Chhattisgarh

- Scrutiny of 63 works in selected GPs revealed delays uranging from onep to 355 days in payment of wages to workers, but no compensation was paid. The stated reason for non-payment of compensation was that it was not claimed.
- The minimum wage rate applicable during 2006-07 was Rs.61.37 per day (April to September 2006) and Rs.62.63 per day (October 2006 to March 2007). But during the period from April 2006 to September 2006, wages were paid at the rate of Rs.58.73 per day, resulting in non-payment of minimum wages to labourers.
- Due to non-rounding of wage rates to the nearest rupee, payment of full amount mentioned in MRs could not be verified.

Gujarat

- In the test checked works, delay in payment of wages could not be ascertained, as no dates of payment of wage were recorded in the MRs. However, the Sarpanchs of GPs checked informed audit that the measurements of the works executed were delayed for three to four weeks. No compensation for delayed payments was paid.

Haryana

- Arrears of Rs. 17.49 lakh(as worked out by audit) due to revision of minimum wage rates were neither calculated nor paid.

Himachal Pradesh

- Delay in payment of wages in test checked works ranged between 17 and 283 days. No compensation was paid.

Jammu & Kashmir

- In 19 works costing Rs. 22.87 lakh in two blocks (Mendhar, Bhaderwah), wages of Rs. 4.99 lakh to 458 workers pertaining to 2006-07 were unpaid not paid till July/August 2007.

Karnataka

- In one GP (Savaleshwar) in Gulbarga District, there was no acknowledgement for having credited the amount of Rs.5.42 lakh to Bank towards payment of wages involving 120 labourers during 2006-07.
- There were cases of delayed payment of wages of 3-4 months in 5 GPs amounting to Rs.62.04 lakh; however, no compensation was paid.

Madhya Pradesh

- In the test checked districts, the average daily wage rate paid was Rs. 45.
- Though wages of Rs. 62.69 lakh paid to 13868 labourers was delayed by 1 to 6 months, no compensation was paid.

Maharashtra

- Daily average wage in the three test-checked districts ranged from Rs. 8 to Rs. 187; this was due to non-determination of productivity norms by the Government.

Manipur

- Though the daily wage rates were enhanced from Rs. 72.40 to Rs. 81.40 from 1 January 2007, wages were paid at the old rates, resulting in denial of wages amounting to Rs. 46.89 lakh.

Orissa

- In 6 cases involving wage payment of Rs. 13.66 lakh, there were delays ranging from 17 to 53 days, but no compensation was paid.
- Due to issue of excess work orders for Rs. 2.96 crore beyond the allotted fund, the bills of 46 works were pending in Bhawanipatna block of Kalahandi District since June 2007. In two out of three test checked casesworks, wages of Rs. 0.96 lakh to 186 labourers engaged in April/ May 2007 had not been paid as of September 2007, and no MR was submitted in the third case. It was noticed that the

State had short-released its share by 27.96 crore upto 2006-07.

- Non-payment and delayed payment of wages in Kalahandi was also confirmed by the District Labour Officer.
- In 6 GPs, there was underpayment of wages vis-à-vis the minimum wage rate of Rs. 0.48 lakh to 866 labourers.
- Beneficiary interviews of 142 households in 21 villages of Kalahandi and Bolangir Districts in the presence of the Sarpanch/ PRI member and BDO revealed that in 98 cases, the beneficiaries disputed their engagement, and in 117 cases, they stated receipt of wages of only Rs. 3.41 lakh against Rs. 5.76 lakh shown in the online job cards and Muster Rolls.
- In 13 muster rolls (Bhawanipatna block), 64 ineligible labourers (30 unregistered labourers and 34 labourers belonging to households already provided with 100 days employment in a year) were engaged on work and paid Rs.0.77 lakh as wages.

Rajasthan

- Delayed payment of wages ranging between 1 andupto 209 days was was noticed in test checked GPs, but no compensation was paid.

Tamil Nadu

- The average number of days for which work was provided in the sampled blocks of Tiruvannamalai district ranged between 22 and 43 days.Delay in payment beyond 15 days was noticed in, ranging from 1 to 112 days in 43 instances in 12 out of 16 sample villages in two sampled districts. However, no compensation was paid.

Uttar Pradesh

- There was non-payment of wages to labourers in two test checked blocks for want of funds.

Uttarakhand

- In one test checked GP, extra expenditure of Rs. 0.61 lakh on account of payment from GoI Funds of more than 100 days employment, ranging between 110 – 219 days, was detected.

West Bengal

- Delay in payment of wages beyond 14 15 days was noticed in 14 out of 24 test checked GPs, but no compensation was paid.

Good Practices

- Andhra Pradesh was now making all payments to NREGA wage seekers through individual postal savings accounts. 66 lakh postal accounts have been opened, with separate accounts for women and men. Wage seekers were issued pay slips (indicating the period of work, no. of days worked and authorized pay) by village-level EGS functionaries. Payment of wages through postal accounts was also noticed during audit in Karnataka and Jharkhand (one GP in Hazaribagh District), while payment through bank accounts was noticed in Karnataka and Kerala.
- In Andhra Pradesh, work-wise computer generated measurement sheets were used for recording measurements; each payment has a corresponding measurement sheet. According to the State Government, the measurement book concept was not appropriate as payments were to be processed every week.
- In West Bengal the payment of wages in Dakshin Dinajpur District was now being made entirely through Bank and Post Offices and the system had been started in Birbhum and Bankura Districts.

Responses of States

- Instructions had been issued by the Governments of Jharkhand, Madhya Pradesh, Rajasthan, Tamil Nadu, Uttar Pradesh and West Bengal to ensure timely payments of wages to the workers.
- According to Government of Andhra Pradesh, delays in some places did occur in view of the massive spread of the programme; however, these would be minimized within the next six months.

- The States of Andhra Pradesh and Orissa stated that measurement of works on daily basis was not practicable.
- The Government of Rajasthan stated that payments through Post Offices may be considered, if the administrative charges of 5 per cent were reimbursed by GoI.
- The Government of Haryana stated that the arrears of wages would now be paid to the workers.

IMPLICATION

- Both the Act and the Operational Guidelines stipulate that under no circumstances shall the labourers be paid less than the minimum wages. Non-payment of minimum wages, and delayed payment of wages is illegal, and also defeats NREGA's objective of providing livelihood security.

Payment through postal or bank accounts is essential to minimize chances of leakage and payments to fictitious workers.

Recommendations

- *Both the Act and the Operational Guidelines stipulate that* under no circumstances shall the labourers be paid less than the minimum wages. Non-payment of minimum wages or delayed payment of wages is a violation of the NREG Act. The offenders need to be identified and punished in terms of provisions of the Act.
- *Payment through postal or bank accounts is essential to* minimize chances of leakage and payments to fictitious workers. Work norms should be prepared such that any person working at a normal pace for seven hours earns no less than the minimum wage rate.
- *GoI may explore a nation-wide agreement with the* Department of Posts for all REGS payments through postal accounts (except where State Governments have ensured payment though banks). Further, a per-account payment by GoI to the Department of Posts as handling charges may be considered, to ensure that no minimum account balances are stipulated for REGS postal account holders.
- *It was noticed that REGS works were not being measured on* daily basis. Andhra Pradesh and Orissa stated that it was

not practicable to measure works on daily basis. GoI may consider amending the NREGA guidelines for measurement of works on a weekly basis, keeping in view the availability of technical staff and other practical considerations.

Employment Generation in test-checked GPs

The primary objective of NREGA is to enhance livelihood security by providing at least 100 days of guaranteed wage employment on demand. Audit conducted a review of the employment provided (as per the Monthly Progress Reports (MPRs) of March 2007) in 465 GPs in 111 blocks in 26 States. Details of employment generated in the test-checked GPs are available in Annexure-D.

Data in respect of households demanding work could not be calculated for 373 test checked GPs in 95 blocks of 16 States, out of 558 GPs, as detailed data, at the GP level, on number of households demanding employment and provided employment was not available. A chart showing the average number of mandays provided to each household in the test checked GPs who had demanded work (in respect of the 9 10 States where the data of households demanding work was maintained GP wise) is given below:

In its response, The Ministry stated that:

- Registration of households did not automatically lead to employment, which would be provided only to those households applying specifically for employment.
- The average days of employment generated per household should be calculated on the basis of total number of households provided employment (and not the total number of registered households).
- The percentage of households receiving 100 days of employment should also be calculated on the basis of total number of households provided employment.
- However, the, the fact that the data in respect of employment demanded could not be verified, in the case of nearly 67 per cent of the sampled GPs, the data in respect of employment demanded could not be verified,

clearly demonstrates the lack of reliability, and authenticity of the reported figures of average employment provided to each households demanding work. Further, tThis strikes at the root of the process of providing employment on demand. Audit came across specific discrepancies in the case of Jharkhand and Orissa as mentioned below

- State Specific Findings

A State-wise summary of audit findings on employment demanded and generated is as follows:

Demand for Employment

In the States of Andhra Pradesh, Assam, Chattisgarh, Jharkhand, Karnataka, Manipur and Uttarakhand, (7 States) the actual demand for employment could not be verified as either no applications demanding employment were received or the applications received were undated. Work was apparently provided on verbal consent of the workers. As a result, the proportion of mandays of employment provided with reference to the demand could not be verified.

Generation of Employment

Andhra Pradesh

- During 2006-07, 51,84,952 Job cards were shown as issued, out of which only 79,642 households got 100 days of employment

Assam

- Percentage of achievement of targeted mandays was 27 percent. On an average, 26 mandays were provided to each registered household in the test checked GPs.

Gujarat

- Against 6.32 lakh Job Cards issued during 2006-07, 2.26 lakh (36%) household demanded and were provided employment. Of these, only 0.12 lakh (5 per cent) had completed 100 days employment.

Haryana

- Against the registered 106772 households in the State, only 50765 demanded employment and only 5626

(5 *per cent* of registered households) completed 100 days employment. Average mandays earned per household in all the sampled panchayats was 17.

Himachal Pradesh

- In the State, 100 days of wage employment was provided in 2006-07 to 26 per cent of households demanding employment, and the overall average mandays per household demanding employment was 47.
- Only 9 per cent women workers were provided employment under NREGS.

Jharkhand

- In five districts, only 671 out of 8.05 lakh registered households were provided 100 days of employment.
- In 10 districts, 6.10 lakh applicants were reported to have been provided employment against 0.70 lakh households, while in three districts, 0.10 lakh applicants against 0.90 lakh households were reported to have been provided employment. These figures are clearly unreliable.For the State as a whole, 5.20 crore mandays were generated under NREGA during 2006-07, as against 8.09 crore mandays generated under SGRY and NFFWP in 2005-06.

Karnataka

- In two selected districts viz. Davanagere and Gulbarga, out of the total registered households numbering 232869 and 389317, job cards were issued to 155057 (67 per cent) and 200688 (52 per cent) households respectively. Further, the number of households provided 100 days of employment in the selected districts was only 29 per cent and 3 per cent respectively.

Kerala

- Actual generation of employment was 8 per cent and 9 per cent of the targeted employment generation as per AP in Palakkad and Wayanad districts respectively.
- Out of 101304 registered households in 4 test checked GPs, employment was provided to 43068 households

(43 per cent) at an average rate of 18 days per household and 100 days of employment was provided to only 299 households (0.3 per cent).

Madhya Pradesh

- In the State, against 44.26 lakh registered households, 28.69 lakh households had actually demanded jobs. However, 100 days of employment was provided to only 19 per cent of households demanding employment.

Maharashtra

- Out of 630607 total job cards issued in three test checked districts the percentage of households demanding work ranged from 22 to 31 per cent. In these districts, the average mandays provided to each household who demanded work ranged from 36 to 51 mandays.

Meghalaya

- In the selected blocks, out of 33,470 registered households who had been issued job cards and had demanded work, only 257 households (0.77 per cent) had been assigned 100 days of employment during 2006-2007.

Orissa

- In 48 test checked GPs, against 37, 630 households registered only 13,778 households were provided employment during 2006-07.
- In the 12 test checked blocks, against the targeted generation of 194.50 lakh person days as per the Annual Plan, only 44.27 lakh person days (23 per cent) were generated. Average employment provided was 24 days per household. Out of 1.80 lakh registered households, only 5158 households were provided 100 days or more of employment. Providing 100 days of employment was also not free from doubt, as physical verification of job cards of 13 out of 14 test checked households revealed only 10 to 96 days of employment, as against 100 days or more shown in the online job cards. Further, out of 121 households reported by 4 GPs to have completed 100 days of employment, only 3 households were found to have

completed 100 days of employment as per the GP Employment Registers.

- Out of 142 job cards test checked, in 55 cases the employment provided as per the physical job cards ranged from 9 to 99 days – totaling 2615 days, while the online job cards showed employment provided from 13 to 108 days – totaling 4313 days. In the remaining 87 cases, the employment provided as per the physical job cards ranged from 18 to 335 days – totaling 8272 days, while the employment provided as per the online job cards ranged from 3 to 108 days. Thus, the job cards were unreliable.

In response, the Government of Orissa clarified that as far as entry of excess days in the job card was concerned, many non-job card holders also worked and in order to make their payments early their work out-put had been shown against existing job card holders, due to which the number of days shown in the job card varied from the actual number of days the said job card holders had been engaged in the work. The response of the State Government is not tenable, as the sanctity of the process of registration, demand and allotment of work is completely destroyedvitiated. Further, there is no assurance on the authenticity of the employment stated to have been provided.

In the 48 test checked GPs, against the targeted generation of 47.79 lakh mandays for 2006-07, only 7.09 lakh mandays (15 per cent) were generated.

Rajasthan

- In the State, 11.75 lakh households (78 per cent of registered households) demanded employment, and 100 days of employment was provided to only 6.36 lakh households. Thus, the claim of the State Government of generation of 999 lakh mandays at an average of 85 days per household demanding employment appears unrealistic.

Tamil Nadu

- The number of households provided with 100 days of employment in selected districts of Tiruvannamalai and Cuddalore were 0.11 *percent* and 0.29 *percent* respectively. The average mandays provided for the remaining households was only 28 and 31 days in the sample districts during 2006-07.

Tripura

- Test check of 8 GPs of the 2 Blocks (Ambassa and Salema) revealed that only 5.16 and 0.46 per cent respectively of the registered households were provided with 100 days employment. Average mandays generated per household in the test checked GPs of the selected Blocks viz. Ambassa and Salema was 6 days and 5 days respectively.

Uttar Pradesh

- In the six selected districts, 7.6 percent of households were provided 100 days employment.

In five of the six selected districts, only 7 percent of the total employment generated was taken by women.

Uttarakhand

- As per MPRs for the period ending March 2007, against 84700 mandays (projected as per AP) the man-days generated were 24947, leaving a difference of 59763 mandays (71 per cent). The average man-days provided to each household with reference to man-days generated as per MPR for March 2007 and total registered households in test checked GPs ranged from 7 to 43 and out of 847 households in the test checked GPs, only 33 households (4 per cent) got 100 days of employment during 2006-07.

West Bengal

- In Dakshin Dinajpur, Paschim Medinipur and Purulia districts, 0.50 percent, 0.04 percent and 2.97 percent of households respectively were provided with 100 days work, and 16, 16 and 13 persondays per household respectively were created.

Demand for Employment

Andhra Pradesh

- The actual demand for employment could not be verified in audit as no applications were received from the wage seekers who demanded employment.

- The proportion of mandays of employment provided with reference to employment demanded could not be verified due to absence of any information / records in this regard.

Assam

- Actual demand could not be verified for partial maintenance of records. The proportion of employment provided with reference to employment demanded could not be verified for want of data with the GPs in this regard.

Chhattisgarh

- Out of the total number of registered households, the number of households which actually demanded employment could not be ascertained at GP level. Further, there was no exact data in respect of households which demanded work. The demands for work were undated and dated receipts were not given.

Jharkhand

- Actual position of demand for work and employment provided could not be verified due to non-availability of updated data in this regard.

Karnataka

- Undated applications for works were received, and the number of days of employment demanded by the workers was neither recorded nor available to justify the demand for work.

Manipur

- No written applications for work were on record. Work was provided on verbal consent of workers.

Orissa

- In 18 GPs in Bolangir, Gajapati and Keonjhar District, out of 26,055 registered households as of March 2007, only 7038 persons (27 per cent) had applied for work.

Tamil Nadu

- In two sample blocks of Tiruvannamalai district, against 39,038 BPL households registered under the scheme, only

21,641 (55 *per cent*) households were reported to have demanded work and were provided with jobs during 2006-07.

Tripura

- In 4 GPs each at Salema and Ambassa Blocks, 99 and 86 per cent of the registered households respectively applied for and were provided with jobs.

Uttarakhand

- In Chamoli district, the actual demand for employment could not be verified in audit for want of availability of updated relevant details with GPs.

West Bengal

- In 24 test checked GPs, against 0.74 lakh households, only 0.33 lakh households (44.23 per cent) demanded wage employment.

Other Irregularities relating to payment of wages

Chhattisgarh

Though DPC allocates the works to OIA (Other Implementing Agencies), it was noticed that OIA neither sent any information to blocks/ GPs nor to the district panchayats regarding expenditure and employment provided.

Orissa

In 13 muster rolls (Bhawanipatna block), 64 ineligible labourers (30 unregistered labourers and 34 labourers belonging to households already provided with 100 days employment in a year) were engaged on work and paid Rs.0.77 lakh as wages.

Out of 142 job cards test checked, in 55 cases the employment provided as per the physical job cards ranged from 9 to 99 days – totaling 2615 days, while the online job cards showed employment provided from 13 to 108 days – totaling 4313 days. In the remaining 87 cases, the employment provided as per the physical job cards ranged from 18 to 335 days – totaling 8272 days, while the employment provided as per the online job cards ranged from 3 to 108 days. Thus, the job cards were unreliable.

In response, the Government of Orissa clarified that as far as entry of excess days in the job card was concerned, many non-job card holders also worked and in order to make their payments early their work out-put had been shown against existing job card holders, due to which the number of days shown in the job card varied from the actual number of days the said job card holders had been engaged in the work.

The response of the State Government is not tenable, as the sanctity of the process of registration, demand and allotment of work is completely destroyed. Further, there is no assurance on the authenticity of the employment stated to have been provided.

Beneficiary interviews of 142 households in 21 villages of Kalahandi and Bolangir Districts in the presence of the Sarpanch/ PRI member and BDO revealed that in 98 cases, the beneficiaries disputed their engagement, and in 117 cases, they stated receipt of wages of only Rs. 3.41 lakh against Rs. 5.76 lakh shown in the online job cards and Muster Rolls.

Tamil Nadu

In 16 villages of 4 blocks in the 2 test checked Districts, audit observed that the persons who demanded jobs were provided employment in turn in both sample districts. In the Social Audit conducted by the members of the Central Employment Guarantee Council at Villupuram district, it was pointed out that employment was rotated between different wards in successive weeks.

West Bengal

Employment provided under N.F.F.W.P. was not recorded in the employment register and relevant job cards, but mandays generated under N.F.F.W.P. were shown in the Progress Report as an output of N.R.E.G.A.

UNEMPLOYMENT ALLOWANCE

Requirement

- Under NREGA, the State Government is required to provide employment to a registered applicant within 15 days of demand, failing which unemployment allowance at stipulated rates is payable.

- Unemployment allowance is to be paid from State Government funds, and not from GoI funds.

Audit Findings

- In 282 GPs in 21 States, dated receipt of applications for demand for work were not given, and in 329 GPs in 19 States, Employment Registers were not maintained, as described in paragraph 8.8.1 . In the absence of recorded date of demand, the entitlement to unemployment allowance could not be easily established.
- However, audit scrutiny in 58 blocks in Arunachal Pradesh, Bihar, Chhattisgarh, Himachal Pradesh, Jharkhand, Karnataka, Kerala, Manipur, Meghalaya, Nagaland, Orissa, Punjab, Rajasthan, Sikkim, Tripura, Uttar Pradesh and Uttarakhand (17 States) revealed that unemployment allowance was not paid to those workers, who could not be provided with employment within 15 days from the date on which work was requested for.

Detailed Statewise Findings

- In Andhra Pradesh, Assam, Uttarakhand and Tamil Nadu though no unemployment allowance was paid, there was a possibility of work not being provided within the stipulated period, as undated applications were being received.
- In Chhattisgarh, scrutiny of 63 works in selected GPs revealed that in nine cases, though there was delay in providing job ranging from one upto 384 days, unemployment allowance was neither claimed nor paid. In 19 cases, the demand for work was undated, and in 35 cases the demand for work was not available. Further, dated receipts were not given to any of the 28 demands for work in the sample.
- In Himachal Pradesh, in four test-checked GPs, unemployment allowance to 198 persons, who had applied for wage employment between April 2006 and January 2007 and were not provided employment within the prescribed period, was not paid

- In Jammu & Kashmir, the State Government had not prescribed any procedure for payment of un-employment allowance nor authorized any authority which would pay the un-employment allowance.
- In Jharkhand (Palamau and Sahebganj districts) though work was provided to only 0.97 lakh workers out of 1.04 lakh workers who demanded work, no unemployment allowance was paid.
- In Madhya Pradesh, unemployment allowance of Rs. 4.75 lakh was paid to 1574 households for 18 days in Janpad Panchayat Pati and Pansemal of Barwani district. The entire amount was paid from NREGA funds and no funds were demanded from the State Government.
- In Orissa, no budget provision was made by the State government for payment of unemployment allowance. Resultantly, in 12 test checked blocks, no unemployment allowance was paid to 5143 registered households who were not provided with employment during 2006-07 despite demanding the same.
- In Rajasthan, though State Government had released (2006-07) Rs.20 lakh to the six identified NREGA districts for payment of unemployment allowances, the amount remained unutilized.
- In Uttar Pradesh, in four of the six districts covered in audit, 40,587 households demanding employment were neither provided employment, nor was any unemployment allowance paid to them.

Responses of States

- The Governments of Assam, Himachal Pradesh, Chhattisgarh and West Bengal had issued instructions to the implementing agencies to issue dated receipts for the application for employment.
- After being pointed out in Audit, the Government of Madhya Pradesh had now debited the amount of Unemployment Allowances, paid out of NREGS funds, to the State Fund.
- After being pointed out in Audit, the Government of Orissa

had now made payments of Unemployment Allowances from the State Funds.

- The Government of West Bengal stated that, in order to address the issue of low demand for employment, lack of women participation etc. a massive awareness programme was being carried out and efforts were being made to sensitize the women through self help groups.

Implication

- Undated applications and non-maintenance of employment registers leads to a situation where the right to unemployment allowance cannot be verified; this is compounded by lack of awareness. Further, payment of unemployment allowance is to be done suo moto by the State Government; no claim needs to be preferred.

The main reason for lack of documentation, and consequently, non-payment of unemployment allowance appears to be that it is to be funded entirely by the State Governments.

Recommendations

- *Undated applications and non-maintenance of employment* registers leads to a situation where the right to unemployment allowance cannot be verified defeating the very purpose of the Act to provide employment guarantee. Record maintenance at GP level needs to be given serious priority. State Governments should consider appointing EGAs must be appointed in each GP to ensure record maintenance. They EGAs should ensure that all applications are dated and dated receipts of applications are given to the job applicants.
- *Payment of unemployment allowance is to be done suo moto* by the State Government; no claim needs to be preferred. Ministry should suitably take up with the State Governments for suo moto payment of unemployment allowance to the eligible labourers.
- *GoI may consider amending NREGA for partial* reimbursement (out of GoI funds) of payment of unemployment allowance, while instituting controls to minimize chances of persons drawingneed for payment of

unemployment allowance without demanding employment or working.

In response (February 2008), the Ministry stated that this recommendation was contrary to the legal provisions. However, in the entire sample, audit found payment of only Rs. 4.75 lakh as unemployment allowance; clearly, this cannot be taken to mean that in all other cases, employment was provided within 15 days of demand. In audit's view of larger interest of rural poor, the Ministry may consider proposing suitable amendment to the Act., this situation arises because the unemployment allowance has to be funded entirely by the State Government, and hence audit's recommendation for considering amendment of the Act follows.

MUSTER ROLLS

General

Requirements : According to the NREGA Operational Guidelines, Muster Rolls (MRs) issued from the Block level, each with a unique identity number, were to be maintained by the GPs and other implementing agencies, in a proforma suggested by the Ministry. Further, photocopies of the MRs were to be kept for public inspection in every GP / Block. MRs were also to be digitized at the PO level.

Audit Findings Audit scrutiny revealed the following:

- MRs maintained by 269 GPs in Assam, Bihar, Chhattisgarh, Gujarat, Haryana, Himachal Pradesh, Jharkhand, Karnataka, Kerala, Maharashtra, Orissa, Rajasthan, Sikkim, Tamil Nadu, Uttar Pradesh, Uttarakhand and West Bengal (18 States) did not bear Unique Identity Numbers.
- In 134 GPs in Andhra Pradesh, Bihar, Gujarat, Himachal Pradesh, Jharkhand, Karnataka, Kerala, Madhya Pradesh, Manipur, Orissa, Uttar Pradesh and West Bengal (12 States) it was observed that the MRs did not contain requisite details viz. the name of the person on work, job card number, days worked/ absent and wages paid.
- In 246 GPs in Assam, Bihar, Haryana, Himachal Pradesh, Jharkhand, Karnataka, Kerala, Manipur, Nagaland, Orissa,

Punjab, Uttar Pradesh, Uttarakhand and West Bengal (15 States), copies of MRs were not available for public scrutiny in the GPs.

State Specific Findings

A State-wise summary of audit findings on Muster Rolls is as follows:

Andhra Pradesh

- Tampering of muster rolls by using white fluid and marking absent as present and also overwriting the number of days worked was noticed in general during examination of muster rolls pertaining to the works selected in certain selected GPs

Arunachal Pradesh

- An amount of Rs. 33.47 lakh was paid to 2336 non eligible households for their 26 days work.

Assam

- Attendance of workers was not verified by any authorized official. The certificate of the inspecting official was not recorded. There were cases where the names of some of the workers were entered and counted more than once, resulting in overpayment.

Bihar

- Rs 2.77 crore was paid during 2006-07 to unregistered labourers.
- Rs 8.99 lakh was paid as wages to fictitious labourers in respect of 7 works, as the name of the same labourer was recorded twice or thrice for the same period in the same or other MRs.
- Rs.12.05 lakh was paid for 24846 mandays in 17 schemes on muster rolls without having date and work order numbers.

Chhattisgarh

- Summary of muster roll and classification of labour viz. total number of workers, women, men, SC, ST, physically handicapped etc. was not recorded/ drawn to verify exact representation of these sections. Signature of person taking attendance, signature of inspecting authority and certification by officials was not found. Attendance on 15 August, 26 January and 31 April in Other Implementing Agency (OIA) works and continued attendance of workers for more than 14 days without a weekly break was noticed. Job card numbers were not mentioned in about 75 per cent cases of works executed by OIA.

- There were cases where signature of workers was not found against payment and cases where excess signature was found in comparison to actual workers getting the payment. Over-writing, corrections and use of muster rolls other than those issued by DPC/PO were noticed in OIA works. Further, it was noticed that instead of separate muster rolls, the OIA used inner sheets in violation of the guidelines. Measurement book was not cross-referenced on muster rolls (particularly in works executed by GPs). Further, payment for transportation of material was also shown and paid through muster rolls.

Haryana

- Over-payment due to wrong calculation of working days, double payment due to payment for the same person , payments without signature/ thumb impression of workers were noticed.
- MRs without counter-signature, reference of Measurement Books, inspection of work, dates of payment, details of workers etc. were noticed in audit.

Himachal Pradesh

- Job card number, dates of payment of wages etc. were not indicated on the muster rolls.
- Wages were shown as paid up to 31st November in one case.

Jammu & Kashmir

- In eight panchayats of 2 blocks (Banihal, Bhaderwah), date of disbursement of wages was not recorded in any muster roll.

Jharkhand

- Muster rolls were not certified by any official, and there was no counter signature of JEs/ AEs. Details of measurement books/ running bills/ quantum of works were not indicated in muster rolls.
- Irregularities like preparation of false MRs, difference in figures of labourers between MBs and MRs, purchase of materials after completion of works, payment of wages to labourers prior to commencement of NREGS etc. were noticed in 19 works involving payment of Rs 8.01 lakh
- In Hazaribagh, 20,995 muster rolls, without Unique Identification Numbers (UIN), were utilized. Of this, in Ichak block, Rs 5.22 lakh was paid as wages through 5,000 Muster Rolls bearing no UIN.
- There were several cases of cuttings, over-writings, applying whitener on muster rolls without attestation by any officials etc.

Karnataka

- In Channagiri block of Davanagere district, new muster rolls were purchased locally by the GPs instead of getting it issued from the offices of the programme officer and executed works and paid Rs.79.24 lakh as wages.

Kerala

- There were cases where the muster rolls did not have job card numbers of the households, work number, signature of concerned officers etc.

Madhya Pradesh

- Work-wise muster rolls were not issued and code numbers not given to them. Muster Rolls in test checked districts were issued on dates later than the start of works.
- Wages of Rs. 15.38 lakhs were paid even before the issue of muster rolls.
- 214 minors were employed for 1833 days and paid wages of Rs.1.13 lakh.
- Job Cards of 3248 labourers were not mentioned on MRs.

- Names of 96 labourers appeared simultaneously in various muster rolls at different worksites for the same period. The Government of Madhya Pradesh stated that the matter would be investigated and action taken against the defaulters.

Manipur

- Necessary certificates regarding actual engagement of labourers to whom payments were made were not recorded.

Orissa

- In all 12 test checked blocks, original copies of the muster rolls were not treated as expenditure documents of the concerned executing agencies.
- In Bhawanipatna block of Kalahandi district and Loisinga of Bolangir district, 5316 muster rolls in support of payment of wages for Rs 5.91 crore were not treated as expenditure documents. Instead, payment was released to the executants/ Junior Engineers based on items and volume of work executed in similar manner as payable to contractors.
- In seven cases (Bhawanipatna block), names and wages paid as per original copy of the muster rolls did not agree with online muster rolls, due to engagement of ineligible labourers and tampering of muster rolls.
- In three cases (Patnagarh block), the dates of engagement of 45 labourers mentioned in original copies of the muster rolls were found to have been manipulated and changed at the time of online entry.
- In case of one executing agency (Bhawanipatna block), the muster rolls for the period 16 March to 30 March 2007 in support of payment of wages for Rs 1.76 lakh were tampered with by pasting another sheet of paper over the original entries. Similarly, in four other GPs, wage payment to 114 labourers for 684 mandays were manipulated on the higher side (Rs 0.67 lakh) in relation to the online muster rolls.

- Test check of muster rolls, public complaints and cross verification with villagers revealed that wages were shown as disbursed to deceased beneficiaries showing engagement even after their death as well to daughters of labourers living outside after marriage, students undergoing studies in towns, businessmen, employees etc who never worked.
- As per the statement of beneficiaries recorded by the District level officers in Keonjhar and Bolangir districts, 21 labourers were engaged for 155 mandays in three works, whereas 762 mandays were shown in the muster rolls and online job cards.
- In two GPs of Narla block, the same eleven labourers were shown as engaged in different works on the same days.

Rajasthan

- The Executive Engineer, Jakham Irrigation Project, Dhariyawad had paid Rs 18.34 lakh on NFFWP muster rolls by irregular employment of un-registered labourers between April 2006 and June 2006.

Tripura

- The muster rolls were not maintained in the prescribed format, as a result of which the SC/ST populations provided with employment could not be ascertained in audit.

Uttarakhand

- The muster rolls were first prepared in kutcha form and thereafter their particulars entered in the pucca muster rolls; the date of issue of muster rolls was not indicated; the measurement book numbers were not referenced on the muster rolls; the inspection of works were not carried out by the concerned officers; muster rolls were not countersigned by the concerned officers; and the dates of payment of wages were not found recorded on all the paid muster rolls.
- There was no signature of three workers in token of receipt of their wages on one muster roll. The entries of the work done by three workers were not found recorded in their job cards.

- In one test checked GP, for the same work, one muster roll was paid on piece rate basis while all other muster rolls for the same work were paid on time rate basis. The dates of work indicated on job cards of workers did not match with the dates mentioned in their muster rolls.

West Bengal

- Period of work and absence during the work were not available in the muster rolls. Attendance of labourers working in the scheme was not attached to the muster rolls. Measurement sheet of the work done was not attached to muster rolls.

Good Practices

- In West Bengal, a 9 digit code was being used as Unique ID for muster rolls with the first two digits for block code, the next two digits for GP code, the next two digits for sansad code and the last 3 digits as the serial number of the muster roll.

Responses of States

- The Governments of Assam, Bihar, Chhattisgarh Haryana, Himachal Pradesh, Jharkhand, Uttarakhand, Sikkim and Tripura and had since issued instructions to the concerned DPCs to maintain the MRs properly.

In respect of 96 labourers which appeared simultaneously in various MRs at different worksite, the the Government of Madhya Pradesh stated that the matter would be investigated and action taken against the defaulters.

Implication

- MRs form the single most important document under NREGA. Improper maintenance of MRs makes identification of genuine beneficiaries difficult, especially in the absence of bank/ postal payments.

Recommendations

- *StateMRs form the single most important document under* NREGA. Improper maintenance of MRs makes identification of genuine beneficiaries difficult, especially in the absence of bank/ postal payments. State Governments should be directed to ensure compliance with the necessary rules and procedure so as to ensure properfor maintenance of MRs.

- *To ensure unique identity of the MRs across the Block,* merely using serial numbers as printed on the MRs is not enough. A MR must be serially numbered for the entire block with the Block code enfaced on it.
- *Full efforts should be made to ensure that MRs are entered* online, and are thus available publicly, in addition to being available at the PO and GP offices.

RECORD MAINTENANCE AND REPORTS

Maintenance of Registers at GP and Block Levels

Requirements

- Maintenance of records under NREGA is critical to ensure ing verifiable compliance with the legal guarantee of 100 days of employment on demand and payment of unemployment allowance. The NREGA Operational Guidelines have specified details of records and registers to be maintained at different levels.
- In particular, the most important records are:

Application Registration Register – which records applications/ requests for registration of households;

Job Card Register – which gives details of job cards issued to households;

Employment Register – which records (for each registered household) details of employment demanded, employment allotted and employment actually taken up;

Asset Register – which is a register of all works sanctioned, executed and completed;

Muster Rolls – which is a record of attendance and payment of wages for individual works;

MR Issue/ Receipt Registers – which record issue and receipt of Muster Rolls (from the PO to the GP/ implementing agency); and Complaint Register – which records details of complaints made, and action taken.

Audit Findings – GP Level

- In 200 GPs in Andhra Pradesh, Assam, Bihar, Chhattisgarh, Haryana, Himachal Pradesh, Jammu & Kashmir, Jharkhand, Karnataka, Kerala, Madhya Pradesh, Maharashtra, Manipur, Nagaland, Orissa, Punjab, Uttar Pradesh, Uttarakhand and West Bengal (19 States), the Application Registration Register was not maintained, or was not properly maintained (i.e. it did not contain, at the very least, the names of the applicants, date of receipt of application/ request and date of issue of job card).
- In 253 GPs in Andhra Pradesh, Assam, Bihar, Chhattisgarh, Haryana, Himachal Pradesh, Jharkhand, Madhya Pradesh, Maharashtra, Orissa, Rajasthan, Uttar Pradesh, Uttarakhand and West Bengal (14 States), the photographs of applicants were not found attached to the job cards, as per the job card register.
- In 293 GPs in Andhra Pradesh, Assam, Bihar, Chhattisgarh, Gujarat, Haryana, Himachal Pradesh, Jammu & Kashmir, Jharkhand, Karnataka, Kerala, Madhya Pradesh, Maharashtra, Manipur, Orissa, Punjab, Rajasthan, Tamil Nadu, Uttar Pradesh, Uttarakhand and West Bengal (21 States), the Job Card Register was not found properly maintained.
- In 329 GPs in Andhra Pradesh, Assam, Bihar, Chhattisgarh, Haryana, Himachal Pradesh, Jammu & Kashmir, Jharkhand, Karnataka, Madhya Pradesh, Maharashtra, Manipur, Nagaland, Orissa, Punjab, Tamil Nadu, Uttar Pradesh, Uttarakhand and West Bengal (19 States), the Employment Register was not maintained, or did not indicate the details of employment demanded, employment allotted and employment actually taken up.
- In 327 GPs of Andhra Pradesh, Assam, Chhattisgarh, Gujarat, Haryana, Himachal Pradesh, Jammu & Kashmir, Jharkhand, Karnataka, Kerala, Madhya Pradesh, Maharashtra, Manipur, Nagaland, Orissa, Punjab, Sikkim, Tamil Nadu, Uttar Pradesh, Uttarakhand and West Bengal (21 States), dated receipts of applications for demand for work were not given to the applicants.

- In 223 GPs in Andhra Pradesh, Assam, Bihar, Chhattisgarh, Gujarat, Haryana, Himachal Pradesh, Jammu & Kashmir, Jharkhand, Karnataka, Madhya Pradesh, Maharashtra, Manipur, Nagaland, Orissa, Punjab, Uttar Pradesh, Uttarakhand and West Bengal (19 States), the applications for employment did not have the job card registration number, date from which employment was required, and the number of days of employment required.
- In 319 GPs in Andhra Pradesh, Assam, Bihar, Chhattisgarh, Gujarat, Haryana, Himachal Pradesh, Jammu & Kashmir, Jharkhand, Karnataka, Madhya Pradesh, Maharashtra, Manipur, Nagaland, Orissa, Punjab, Rajasthan, Sikkim, Uttar Pradesh, Uttarakhand and West Bengal (21 States) the Asset Register was not maintained or was incompletely maintained.
- In 206 GPs in Andhra Pradesh, Assam, Bihar, Chhattisgarh, Gujarat, Haryana, Himachal Pradesh, Jharkhand, Karnataka, Maharashtra, Manipur, Orissa, Rajasthan, Uttar Pradesh, Uttarakhand and West Bengal (16 States) the Muster Roll Receipt Register was not maintained or was incompletely maintained
- In 312 GPs in Andhra Pradesh, Assam, Bihar, Chhattisgarh, Gujarat, Haryana, Himachal Pradesh, Jharkhand, Karnataka, Kerala, Maharashtra, Manipur, Orissa, Punjab, Rajasthan, Sikkim, Tamil Nadu, Uttar Pradesh, Uttarakhand and West Bengal (20 States) the Complaint Register was not maintained or was incompletely maintained.

Audit Findings – Block Level

- Employment Registerc& was not maintained/ prepared in 104 block offices in Andhra Pradesh, Assam, Bihar, Chhattisgarh, Himachal Pradesh, Jharkhand, Karnataka, Kerala, Madhya Pradesh, Maharashtra, Nagaland, Orissa, Punjab, Rajasthan, Sikkim, Tamil Nadu, Uttar Pradesh, Uttarakhand and West Bengal (19 States).
- Muster Roll Issue Register was not maintained in 8 block offices in Andhra Pradesh, Bihar, Himachal Pradesh, Karnataka (4 States).

- Asset Register, in computerized form based on the date of asset registers furnished by Gram Panchayat and Implementing Agency, was not maintained/ prepared in 103 block offices in Andhra Pradesh, Assam, Bihar, Chhattisgarh, Haryana, Himachal Pradesh, Jharkhand, Karnataka, Kerala, Madhya Pradesh, Maharashtra, Nagaland, Orissa, Punjab, Rajasthan, Tamil Nadu, Uttar Pradesh, Uttarakhand and West Bengal (19 States).
- Complaint Register was not maintained/ prepared in 62 block offices in Andhra Pradesh, Assam, Bihar, Himachal Pradesh, Jharkhand, Karnataka, Madhya Pradesh, Maharashtra, Nagaland, Orissa, Punjab, Rajasthan, Sikkim, Tamil Nadu, Uttar Pradesh and West Bengal (16 States).

Requirement

- The NREGA Operational Guidelines prescribe detailed monitoring formats for Monthly Progress Reports (for both physical and financial) performance to be compiled and sent by the State Governments. In addition to ensuring transparency and accountability at the local level, the information furnished by the States is consolidated for public information through the Ministry's Internet web site.
- The NREGA Operational Guidelines also require that procedures be framed to ensure that data on work requested and allotted by the PO and GP are properly maintained, and also for sharing of information on employment allotments between the PO and GP on a weekly basis.

Audit Findings

- In 89 blocks of Andhra Pradesh, Arunachal Pradesh, Assam, Bihar, Chhattisgarh, Haryana, Himachal Pradesh, Jammu & Kashmir, Jharkhand, Karnataka, Kerala Madhya Pradesh, Manipur, Nagaland, Orissa, Punjab, Rajasthan, Sikkim, Uttar Pradesh, Uttarakhand and West Bengal (21 States), procedures had not been framed to ensure sharing of information on employment allotments between the PO and GP on a weekly basis.

- It was noticed that in most cases, the information between PO and GP was not being shared on a weekly basis. Mostly, the information was being shared on a monthly basis or during meetings.
- Deficiencies were noticed in furnishing of MPRs by blocks and districts. Some instances are mentioned in the following paragraph.

Sharing of Information between PO and GP

In other blocks where procedure had been framed for sharing information between PO and GP, it was noticed that in most cases the information was not being shared on a weekly basis or it was done without proper documentation. Mostly the information was being shared on a monthly basis or during meetings. The details of the discrepancies noticed in the States are indicated in Annexure-

Andhra Pradesh

In the test checked blocks, audit was informed that information was being shared between the PO and GP through discussion in weekly meetings at the Block Offices. Details on deployment of labour at particular works were collected daily on phone

Assam

No documentary evidence of sharing of information on employment allotment between PO and VCDC (GP) could be produced to audit.

Haryana

Sharing of information on employment allotment between PO and GP on a weekly basis was not being adopted.

Himachal Pradesh

Information on employment allotment between PO and GP was being shared on a monthly basis.

Jharkhand

No such records were being maintained by the BDO in 4 blocks, while in 2 blocks, the information was reportedly shared on a monthly basis.

Karnataka

No procedure had been framed to ensure sharing of information on employment allotment between the PO and GPs on a weekly basis. However, as and when the GP Secretaries met the PO in a monthly meeting, this information was being shared.

The MPRs contained details of SC/ST/Female labourers/ households, but no records were found to be maintained in test checked GPs in respect of these categories of labourers.

Kerala

Information on employment allotment by GPs was furnished to PO in MPRs, or weekly reports.

Madhya Pradesh

Though procedures had been framed for sharing information on employment allotments between PO and GP on a weekly basis, this was not done.

Tamil Nadu

Weekly reports prescribed for monitoring were not generated from GP level, but compiled at block level from oral information received from GPs.

Tripura

Information was being shared in a monthly meeting.

Uttar Pradesh

In the test checked blocks, audit was informed that information was being shared in a weekly meeting, but no documentary evidence was made available.

Uttarakhand

In District Champawat, weekly reports were being sent by GPs to POs. However, in District Chamoli, audit was informed that information was being collected telephonically or through verbal discussions in a meeting.

In District- Chamoli; Block- Karanprayag, the figures of labours employed, mandays generated, cost of material and labours in the MPR of the Block were not consistent with the figures depicted in the related muster rolls in two Gram Panchayats as detailed in Annexure – F.

West Bengal

Procedures had been framed for sharing of information on a fortnightly/ monthly basis.

INFORMATION SHARING AT BLOCK AND HIGHER LEVELS DEFICIENCIES IN MPRS

Arunachal Pradesh

- MPRs were not submitted by the blocks and district to the Directorate/Central Government.

Bihar

- Katihar, Darbhanga and Supaul districts reported less generation of mandays by 15.60 lakh compared to expenditure on unskilled labour, whereas Munger, Samastipur and Muzaffarpur showed excess generation by 37.66 lakh mandays in comparison to expenditure on unskilled labour.
- The State report of NREGA for the year 2006-07 disclosed that in Darbhanga district not a single job card was issued to SC/ST households, but as per the district report, 71810 SC/ST households were provided jobs.
- Excess reporting of 3614 job cards in 12 gram panchayats of four blocks under three districts was noticed

Chhattisgarh

- The Monthly Progress Reports (MPRs) compiled at selected Blocks and Districts was fabricated as: neither MPRs nor any other report which could reflect the exact demand for work, employment provided, mandays generated and expenditure (including wages) incurred were prepared and sent to blocks. The blocks were preparing the MPRs on the basis of valuation of works and total expenditure.

Most of the muster rolls did not contain the job card numbers, classification of labourers (viz. SC, ST, Women etc.), and the basis of calculation of representation in MPRs could not be verified. Other Implementing Agencies (OIAs) did not report the demand for work, employment provided, mandays generated and expenditure (including wages) incurred etc. either to the blocks or to the districts. In their absence, the basis of progress in respect of works executed by OIA could not be verified. It was noticed that GPs did not send the copies of paid MRs to blocks. Similarly, OIA neither sent the copies of paid MRs to blocks nor to the districts.

Jammu & Kashmir

- The figures of employment generation were reported either without maintaining the basic Panchayat wise data at Block level, or higher figures were reported at Block/District level.
- As against issue of only 4,630 job cards to house-holds in Bhaderwah block during 2006-07, 4,910 households were reported to Government as demanding/provided employment during the year by D.P.C. Doda.
- As against 3.43 lakh person days of employment reported by the POs to DPC Doda, 3.66 lakh persondays were reported by DPC Doda to the State Government.
- Other cases of incorrect reporting of data by POs to DPC and by DPC to Government as noticed in audit are indicated in Annexure-F.

Karnataka

- There were cases of incorrect reporting for the year ending March 2007, as the Districts Authorities had reported higher figures of physical and financial achievements to the State Authorities as compared to what had actually been reported by the Blocks, as indicated in Annexure-F.

Punjab

- The figures shown in the monthly progress report of the District/State as reported to the Ministry do not seem to be correct as there was a difference between the figures of the District/State and the figures reported by blocks in their monthly progress reports, as detailed in Annexure – F.

Uttarakhand

- Monthly Progress Reports (MPR) from the POs for the month of March 2007 was based on anticipated figures and not on actuals.

Further Limited Scrutiny of Record Maintenance

Subsequent to the original audit, a limited scrutiny of record maintenance for one month (November 2007) was conducted between February and March 2008, covering 24 GPs in 12 blocks in 12 districts in 6 States from within the original audit sample. The objective of this exercise was to assess the improvement in maintenance of records as a result of the performance audit.

The focus was on:

1. Reconciliation of MPRs with the data of basic records submitted at various levels i.e GP/Block and District.
2. Preparation of Annual Plans for 2007-08.
3. Checking the maintenance of important records viz. Employment Register, Applications for Employment, Asset Register, Job Card Register, Muster Rolls etc.

While details of the results of scrutiny are given in Annexure E, the main findings were as follows:

- At district and block level there were either instances of excess reporting in mandays generated, household demanding employment, household provided employment, and funds utilized or there were no sufficient records to verify the details, except in Uttar Pradesh, where records were maintained properly.
- Annual plan was found to have been prepared and approved by GS in most of the GPs, except Bihar where data was not available.
- In most of the GPs of West Bengal, photographs of the workers were not found in the Job card register. Uttar Pradesh had all the photographs in place while in Rajasthan 10-20 per cent photographs were missing.
- Employment register was not maintained in Maharashtra and Bihar. While other states GPs maintained the register, the crucial data on employment demanded was missing in both West Bengal and Jharkhand

- In Maharashtra, Jharkhand and Bihar records of application demanding employment were poorly maintained. West Bengal had 50 per cent records, while Rajasthan had all the details.
- Reconciliation of households demanding work, households provided work and households with 100 days of employment could not be ascertained from the employment register of the GPs in 5 test checked states, except in Uttar Pradesh.
- In Maharashtra and Bihar and 3 out of 4 GPs of West Bengal, asset registers were not maintained properly.
- Photographs of work were missing in most of the states, except Jharkhand.
- Muster rolls had few details of Job Card Number, classification of labour (SC/ST, women) in most of the states, except in Uttar Pradesh and Maharashtra where no work was in progress in November 2007.

The scrutiny revealed that while there was a definite some improvement in record maintenance especially in Uttar Pradesh, after the conduct of initial audit, the maintenance of basic records at the GP level, in particular the employment register was still deficient and there was considerable scope for improvement. Further, the reliability of MPRs from the block and district levels was in serious doubt, as they could not be reconciled with the relevant basic records.

Good Practices

- The State Government of West Bengal had now made provision for outsourcing of maintenance of different registers at GP level.
- In Orissa, every GP had since been provided with a digital camera for pasting of photographs in JCs.

Ministry's Reply

- In response, the Ministry stated that the GoI already funded the cost of administrative expenses, which had been raised from 2 per cent to 4 per cent; this included deployment of persons dedicated to NREGA at the block level, inclusive of computer assistants and operational expenses.

Responses of States

- The Governments of Assam, Chhattisgarh, Gujarat, Haryana, Jharkhand, Madhya Pradesh, Maharashtra, Rajasthan, Tamil Nadu, Sikkim, Uttarakhand and Uttar Pradesh had subsequently issued necessary instructions for proper maintenance of all registers at each level. According to the Government of Bihar, properly trained staff had now been provided to ensure proper maintenance of Records/ Registers.
- The Government of Orissa had agreed that the situation of maintenance of records was not good; however, it had now improved after the appointment of GRSs and instructions had also been issued for proper maintenance of records/ registers.
- The Governments of Assam, Chhattisgarh, Haryana, Jharkhand, Orissa and Uttarakhand had now initiated action for framing procedures to maintain records of employment generated etc. and ensuring sharing of information on weekly basis between PO and GPs.
- The Government of Punjab stated that the 'sensitization' of the BDPOs and their staff had been done to avoid such lapses in future.

Implication

- There are deficiencies in the process of reporting from the GPs to POs, and onwards, and documentary records of transmitting of information was, in many cases, not produced to audit. In the absence of such information, the reliability of information being furnished to Ministry is adversely affected.
- In the absence of maintenance of critical registers, especially at the GP level, it is impossible to authentically verify:
  * How many households demanded employment?
  * How many households were provided employment, and for how many days?

  * How many households got 100 days of employment?
  * What was the break-up of SC, ST and women beneficiaries, and how much employment did they demand and receive?
  * What was the entitlement of individual households to unemployment allowance?
- Thus, the compliance with the legal guarantee of 100 days of employment on demand is not verifiable, based on available documents. In addition, transparency and accountability is adversely affected.

RECOMMENDATIONS

- *For proper record-keeping at the GP level, appointment of* EGAs for each GP should be considered. is essential.
- *Online data entry of the following documents is essential to* increased transparency and accountability and minimize fictitious/ duplicate entries, besides providing a basis for physical verification:
  * Muster Rolls (with job-card numbers and other details)
  * Job Card Register
  * Employment Register (to indicate employment demanded)
  * Asset Register
- *State Governments should be funded to employ a dedicated* computer assistant for NREGA data entry at the block level, along with a PC. In addition, the GoI could consider "incentivizing" online data entry, by giving a small percentage – say 0.5 per cent of total expenditure – for data entry of these registers to a specified level of completeness, within a specified time frame.

National Quality Monitors may, during their visits, be asked to cross-verify compare MPRs furnished by POs with documents furnished by GPs to POs for specified months, specifically for households demanding and provided employment (with an SC/ST/ women/ Others breakup) and also for households receiving 100 days of employment, and certify the correctness of information.

Ministry's Reply

In response, the Ministry stated that the GoI already funded the cost of administrative expenses, which had been raised from 2 per cent to 4 per cent; this included deployment of persons dedicated to NREGA at the block level, inclusive of computer assistants and operational expenses. However, unless the Ministry is able to ensure through other persuasive or punitive measures that online data entry is complete in all districts in the first phase (particularly in view of the poor record maintenance at the GP level), audit recommends that the Ministry consider use of an incentive mechanism for completeness of online data entry.

FUND MANAGEMENT

General

Requirements

- The GoI releases funds through the National Employment Guarantee Fund directly to Districts. State Governments are required to set up revolving funds at the District, Block and GP levels.
- State share of funds should be released within 15 days of the release of the Central funds.
- The State Government should design a complete Financial Management System for the transfer and use of funds, for ensuring transparency and accountability.
- Separate bank accounts for funds under the Scheme should be opened at the District, Block and GP levels.
- After utilizing 60 per cent of the earlier funds released, the DPC may apply for the next installmentinstalment, along with Utilisation Certificate (UC), certificate regarding receipt of State Share etc. Similarly, the PO will be eligible for the next installmentinstalment after utilizing 60 per cent of available funds. Likewise, after 60 per cent of the allocation given to a GP has been spent, the GP may apply to the PO for release of additional funds, with a statement of work-wise expenditure and the report of the Vigilance and Monitoring Committee (VMC) approved by the Gram Sabha.

- Monthly squaring of accounts – verifying that all money released under NREGA is accounted for under (a) bank balance (b) advances (c) expenditure vouchers – should be introduced.

Audit Findings

- In 51 districts in Arunachal Pradesh, Andhra Pradesh, Assam, Bihar, Gujarat, Himachal Pradesh, Jharkhand, Karnataka, Kerala, Manipur, Meghalaya, Nagaland, Orissa, Punjab, Rajasthan, Sikkim, Tripura, Uttar Pradesh, Uttarakhand and West Bengal (20 States), the State Share was not released within 15 days of the release of the Central funds
- In 58 blocks in Arunachal Pradesh, Assam, Bihar, Gujarat, Himachal Pradesh, Jammu & Kashmir, Jharkhand, Karnataka, Kerala, Manipur, Orissa, Punjab, Rajasthan, Sikkim, Tamil Nadu, Tripura, Uttar Pradesh, Uttarakhand and West Bengal (19 States), the PO/ BDO did not submit UCs for utilization of at least 60 per cent of funds at their disposal, while applying for the next instalment.
- While demanding additional funds, 364 GPs in Andhra Pradesh, Assam, Bihar, Haryana, Himachal Pradesh, Jammu & Kashmir, Jharkhand, Karnataka, Kerala, Madhya Pradesh, Manipur, Nagaland, Orissa, Punjab, Rajasthan, Sikkim, Tamil Nadu, Tripura, Uttar Pradesh, Uttarakhand and West Bengal (21 States) did not furnish the report of the VMC duly approved by the Gram Sabha.
- 24 GPs in Gujarat, Haryana, Jammu & Kashmir, Jharkhand, Karnataka, Madhya Pradesh and Uttar Pradesh (7 States) had spent funds on REGS without obtaining administrative approval and technical sanction.
- Monthly squaring of accounts under three heads viz. money held in bank accounts at various levels, advances to implementing or payment agencies, and vouchers of actual expenses, was not done by 151 GPs in Andhra Pradesh, Chhattisgarh, Himachal Pradesh, Jammu & Kashmir, Jharkhand, Kerala, Madhya Pradesh, Orissa, Uttar Pradesh and West Bengal (States).

STATE SPECIFIC FINDINGS

A State-wise summary of audit findings on fund management is as follows:

State Share and Transfer of Fund

Arunachal Pradesh

During 2006-07, State Government did not release its share. The funds released as state share (Rs 19.09 lakh) during 2006-07 included Rs.17.00 lakh, which was the state share of SGRY for 2005-06 released during 2006-07. Out of its due share of Rs 121.09 lakh, only Rs 50.00 lakh was released during 2007-08.

Bihar

The DRDAs of Katihar and Samastipur failed to draw State share of Rs 0.30 crore, due to negligence of officials.

Gujarat

On two occasions, the release of State share was delayed by 4 months 21 days and 1 month.

Himachal Pradesh

Delay in release of State share ranged between three and 188 days.

Jharkhand

In three test checked districts, there was a delay in releasing the state share of Rs. 9.44 crore for 2006-07 for periods ranging from 10 to 268 days.

Karnataka

Delay in release of state share ranged from two to three months in selected districts.

Manipur

There was a short release of State share of Rs.87.20 lakh.

Meghalaya

There was a short release of State share of Rs.178.22 lakh.

Orissa

Against Rs 103.42 crore payable towards State share, only Rs 75.46 crore was released, resulting in short release of State share of Rs 27.96 crore. State share of Rs 1.55 crore for 2005-06 payable on the initial installment released in February 2006 by the Centre (Rs 15.48 crore) under NREGA to DRDA, Kalahandi had not been released as of September 2007. Delay in release of State share of Rs 4.03 crore for DRDA Bolangir ranged between 37 and 74 days.

Punjab

State share amounting to Rs. 3.58 crore for 2006-07 was not released.

Tamil Nadu

State share of Rs.18.30 crore corresponding to the GoI release for 2005-06 and first installment of 2006-07 was released after a delay of 4 to 8 months.

Tripura

The delay in release of State share for the first installment for 2006-07 was 9 months.

Uttar Pradesh

In five out of the six selected districts, against an expenditure of Rs. 82.06 crore incurred on material and wages of semiskilled and skilled labourers, the State Government released only Rs. 7.26 crore instead of Rs. 20.52 crore (25 per cent of Rs. 82.06 crore). There was thus a short release of Rs. 13.26 crore.

West Bengal

There were delays of one and half months to six months in release of State share in 10 districts.

Irregularities related to non-submission of Utilisation Certificates and, details of expenditure and VMC reports

Arunachal Pradesh

- Expenditure details of Rs 22 lakh were awaited as of July, 2007 in DRDA Daporijo from the Director of Rural

Development, Itanagar against the amount of Rs. 25 lakh paid to them in March 2006.

Bihar

- The state government did not send the utilization certificate of DRDAs of Katihar and Samastipur to the GOI, resulting in curtailment of central share by Rs 10.00 crore during the year 2006-07.

Jharkhand

- The expenditure shown as incurred included advances of Rs. 4.29 crore to Implementing Agencies but not spent.
- Interest accrued of Rs. 1.22 crore in two districts was short reported in the MPR for March 2007.

Orissa

- Against an actual expenditure of Rs. 49.80 lakh, the DRDA Kalahandi had submitted Utilisation Certificate for the entire release of Rs. 70.02 lakh during March 2006.

Tripura

- Utilisation Certificate furnished by the DPC, Dhalai indicated an unspent balance of Rs. 389.62 lakh as of May 2007, while check of Cash Book, Bank Pass Book along with other relevant records of the Project Director, DRDA, Dhalai revealed an unspent balance of Rs. 377.48 lakh; thus there was under-reporting of expenditure by Rs. 12.14 lakh.
- Test check of records of the PD, DRDA, Dhalai, Zilla Parishad, Dhalai and other Implementing Officers (IOs) revealed that most of the UCs were pending submission by the IOs up to August 2007, but further funds were being released to these defaulting IOs.

Cases of Diversion and Irregular Expenditure

Haryana

- Rs. 8.50 lakh was diverted during 2006-07, and spent on other schemes.

Bihar

- The DDC, Darbhanga irregularly transferred Rs 2.69 crore to special division, Darbhanga during 2006-07 for construction of 34 protection walls of raised platforms constructed under Sam Vikas Yojana.

Haryana

- Rs. 8.50 lakh was diverted during 2006-07, and spent on other schemes.
- In Sirsa District, while the material consumed in the district from April 2006 to February 2007 for pucca works was Rs. 3.87 crore, expenditure on purchase of stores during the month of March 2007 alone was Rs. 3.61 crore. Clearly, the material was purchased merely to show utilization of funds, without assessing the requirement on works. Also, the cash books of 3 blocks of the district for 2006-07 had not been closed as of June 2007, as transactions relating to the purchase of the material had not been completed.

Himachal Pradesh

- NREGA funds of Rs. 11.15 lakh were utilized on salary and contingent advance to the ministerial staff of DRDA, Chamba.

Jharkhand

- Expenditure of Rs. 8.74 crore was incurred in the State on inadmissible items – contingencies on fuel, stationery, repairing of vehicles, payment of salaries of DRDA staff not associated with NREGA, and procurement of diesel generator sets. DRDA Sahebganj released Rs. 34.06 crore in 2006-07 to 166 GPs without selecting any approved works, resulting in an unspent balance of Rs. 22.42 crore as of March 2007.

Madhya Pradesh

- Rs. 12.05 lakh were irregularly incurred by PWD Dhar on repair of roads and renovation of meeting halls.

Meghalaya

- Rs.28.36 lakh was diverted from REGS fund to DRDA Administration towards the pay and allowance for the staff of DRDA Tura during 2006-07.

Orissa

- Scheme funds of Rs 29.67 lakh were diverted during 2006-07 in Loisinga block (Rs 10.60 lakh), Bhawanipatna block (Rs 19.07 lakh) and three GPs (Rs 0.93 lakh) for purposes not connected with NREGA viz. payment of staff salary, Calamity Relief Fund etc., of which Rs. 11.16 lakh remained unrecouped.
- BDO Bhawanipatna , Kalahandi District irregularly charged Rs. 11.37 lakh as works contingency for miscellaneous use.
- Although the State Government prescribed submission of vouchers in support of advances within 7 days of receipt of cash advances, such vouchers in respect of advances of Rs. 71.74 lakh were outstanding from 13 officials/ ex-officials for periods ranging from six to nine months.
- In 2 GPs, the Executive Officers, despite being transferred, had not handed over the unspent cash balance of Rs. 1.77 lakh to their successors

Rajasthan

- The proportionate increase in expenditure during the last quarter of 2006-07 indicated that advances given to Panchayat Implementing Agencies were treated as final expenditure in MPRs.

Punjab

- One P.O. did not check the correctness of the final expenditure reported by the implementing agency at the time of authorizing final closure of work.

Tripura

- Rs.9 lakh was irregularly transferred (November 2006) to the account of Divisional Forest Officer, Manu for construction of 72 Indira Awas Yojana houses.

Uttarakhand

- Works of Jal Nikaas Naali, in one GP, amounting to Rs. 15220 was not commenced, but the expenditure was reported in the MPR.

Unspent Balances of SGRY and NFFWP and Maintenance of Accounts

Bihar

- The unspent balances of SGRY and NFFWP of March 2006 amounting to Rs 38.99 crore of 3 districts were not transferred to NREGS account up to June 2007.

Karnataka

- Instead of operating a single bank account for REGS works, in the test checked blocks and GPs, separate bank accounts had been maintained for unskilled wages, material component, unemployment allowance and administrative expenses.

Manipur

- The balance of Rs. 2.24 crore left under NFFWP and SGRY was used for NFFWP and SGRY works, evidently without following NREGA Guidelines.

Rajasthan

- In block Dhariyawad (district-Udaipur) NFFWP balance (Rs 28.67 lakh) as on 1 April 2006 was not deemed as resources under NREGA account, and out of Rs 136.59 lakh released by ZP, Udaipur during 2006-07 under NFFWP, Rs 55.14 lakh was the closing balance as on 31 March 2007. Similarly, in block Kherwara (district-Udaipur) SGRY (30 *per cent*) balance (Rs 14.99 lakh) as on 1 April 2006 was not deemed as resources under NREGA account, and out of Rs 18.69 lakh sanctioned (31 March 2006) for 26 works under SGRY (50 *per cent* by 26 GPs) Rs 14.59 lakh was spent during 2006-07. Resultantly, these funds were utilised without confirming to the NREGA guidelines.

West Bengal

- Cut off date (2 February 2006) for transfer of N.F.F.W.P. fund into N.R.E.G.S. account was not adhered to by 16 out of 24 GPs test checked. The Gram Panchayats were still maintaining the separate Cash Book and Bank Pass Book for N.F.F.W.P. and N.R.E.G.A.
- A sum of Rs.61.21 lakh from N.F.F.W.P. fund was spent for the works under N.R.E.G.A. without observing the norms of N.R.E.G.A.

Implication

- Non-compliance with the guidelines on funding leads to misutilisation / non-utilisation of NREGA funds, and lack of transparency and financial accountability.
- Delay/ non-provision of State share adversely impacts implementation of NREGA

Responses of States

- The Governments of Assam, Jharkhand, Tripura, Tamil Nadu, Maharashtra, Sikkim and Uttar Pradesh have issued instructions to the DPCs to adhere to the requirements of the NREGA Guidelines for management of NREGA funds.
- The irregular expenditure pointed out in audit had now been recouped by the the Government of Himachal Pradesh.
- The Government of Orissa had now issued strict instructions not to charge any work contingency for NREGA works. The state Government had also initiated action against the erring officers for not handing over unspent balances of NREGA funds.
- The Government of West Bengal stateds that corrective measures had been initiated for transfer of NFFWP funds to NREGA as per the guidelines of the Ministry.

Recommendations

- *State Governments should ensure timely release of their* share and issue necessary directions to ensure that NREGS All funds are not diverted or misutilised. should be recovered immediately from the State Governments.

- *In order to guard against any manipulation, the GoI may* consider levying interest commensurate with the delay in release of State share, to deter such delays.
- *State Governments should be directed to ensure that* separate bank accounts at all levels are maintained, and monthly squaring of accounts is mandatorily regularly conducted. , or else future GoI funding should be withheld.

SOCIAL AUDIT, TRANSPARENCY AND GRIEVANCE REDRESSAL

Requirements

- NREGA gives a central role to "social audits" as a means of continuous public vigilance. The Guidelines indicate two types of social audit: Periodic assemblies in the Gram Sabha for scrutinizing details of projects (which is referred to as "Social Audit Forum"); and Social audit as a continuous process of public vigilance involving potential beneficiaries and other stakeholders, which covers verification of 11 stages of implementation right from registration of families through to evaluation and the Social Audit Forum.
- Updated data on demand received, registration, number of job cards issued, list of people who demanded and had been given/ not given employment, funds received and spent, payments made, works sanctioned and works started, cost of works and details of expenditure on it, duration of work, person-days generated, reports of local communities and copies of muster roll should be made available in a predesigned format outside offices of all agencies involved in implementing REGS.
- Social Audit Forums must be held twice a year at the Gram Sabha level for all works done in the preceding year.

AUDIT FINDINGS

- In 354 GPs in Andhra Pradesh, Assam, Chhattisgarh, Haryana, Himachal Pradesh, Jammu & Kashmir, Jharkhand, Karnataka, Kerala, Maharashtra, Manipur, Nagaland, Orissa, Punjab, Rajasthan, Tamil Nadu, Tripura,

Uttar Pradesh, Uttarakhand and West Bengal (20 States), a Gram Sabha once in every six months to conduct a Social Audit Forum was not held.

- The updated data on demand received, registration, number of job cards issued, list of people who demanded and been given/ not given employment, funds received and spent, payments made, works sanctioned and works started, cost of works and details of expenditure on it, duration of work, person-days generated, reports of local communities and copies of muster rolls were not made public in 376 GPs in Andhra Pradesh, Bihar, Chhattisgarh, Gujarat, Haryana, Himachal Pradesh, Jammu & Kashmir, Jharkhand, Karnataka, Kerala, Maharashtra, Manipur, Nagaland, Orissa, Punjab, Rajasthan, Sikkim, Tamil Nadu, Tripura, Uttar Pradesh and Uttarakhand (21 States).

Other Statespecific findings

- In Arunachal Pradesh, the grievance redressal forum was not in place.
- In Jammu & Kashmir, a grievance redressal system had not been devised.
- In Jharkhand, wide publicity had not been undertaken;, as the villagers were not fully aware about NREGA as observed during interaction with villagers.; noNo grievance redressal cell was set up at any level.
- In Karnataka, no summary of data was prepared and placed before the Gram Sabha.
- In Rajasthan, the State Government had not specified the grievance redressal mechanism;
- In Uttar Pradesh, in 29 out of 48 test checked GPs, no meetings of the social audit forum were organized. Whenever these meetings were organized, no minutes were available, due to which it could not be ascertained if the forum performed its prescribed role.

Responses of States

- The Governments of Assam, Haryana, Jharkhand, Orissa, Rajasthan, Tripura and Uttar Pradesh had now issued necessary directions to conduct Social Audit Forums at least twice in a year.

- In Orissa, the work of conducting 100 per cent social audit had been assigned to NIRD Hyderabad.
- The Government of Bihar stated that the necessary instructions had been issued to ensure all aspects of social audit, however, no improvements were noticed by audit during the limited scrutiny of 2 districts during March 2008.
- The Government of Madhya Pradesh had issued directions/ taken necessary action for conducting social audits.
- Instructions had been issued by the Governments of Jharkhand, Chhattisgarh, Sikkim, Tripura, Uttar Pradesh and West Bengal to make available updated data on registration, JCs issued, demands for employment received, employment provided etc. to the public.
- The Governments of Rajasthan, Jharkhand and West Bengal were now developing Grievance Redressal Mechanism.

Implication In the absence of proper maintenance of records, social audit and the Social Audit Forum in Gram Sabhas remain the only methods for ensuring a degree of transparency and accountability at the GP and GS level. Non-conduct of social audit adversely affects demand-driven bottom-up approach of NREGA.

Recommendation Social audit and Social Audit Forum in Gram Sabha are important means of ensuring transparency and accountability at the GP level. The State Governments should be advised to ensure conduct of Social Audits Forum in all Gram Sabhas twice a year.

MONITORING

Requirements NREGA Operational Guidelines stipulate the following procedures for monitoring and reporting

- Block-level officials shall inspect 100 per cent of works every year, District-level officials 10 per cent of works, and Statelevel officials 2 per cent of works.

- Financial audit of all districts is mandatory.
- District Internal Audit Cells shall be constituted to scrutise the reports of the Gram Sabhas.
- Verification and quality audit by external monitors must be undertaken at the Central, State and District levels through National, State and District Quality Monitors. Terms of reference for quality monitors have been fixed separately by the Ministry.
- Local Vigilance and Monitoring Committees (VMCs), consisting of members elected by the Gram Sabha, should monitor the progress and quality of work while it is progress.

Audit Findings

- State-level inspection of works was not conducted, or documented in respect of Arunachal Pradesh, Andhra Pradesh, Assam, Chhattisgarh, Haryana, Himachal Pradesh, Jammu & Kashmir, Jharkhand, Kerala, Maharashtra, Manipur, Orissa, Punjab, Rajasthan, Tamil Nadu, Tripura, Uttar Pradesh, Uttarakhand and West Bengal (19 States.)
- In 43 districts in Andhra Pradesh, Bihar, Chhattisgarh, Haryana, Himachal Pradesh, Jharkhand, Karnataka, Kerala, Madhya Pradesh, Maharashtra, Manipur, Nagaland, Orissa, Punjab, Rajasthan, Sikkim, Uttar Pradesh, Uttarakhand and West Bengal (19 States), the district level officials did not conduct 10 per cent inspection of the works.
- In 105 blocks in Arunachal Pradesh, Andhra Pradesh, Assam, Bihar, Chhattisgarh, Haryana, Himachal Pradesh, Jharkhand, Karnataka, Kerala, Madhya Pradesh, Maharashtra, Manipur, Nagaland, Orissa, Punjab, Rajasthan, Sikkim, Tripura, Uttar Pradesh, Uttarakhand and West Bengal (22 States), the block level officials did not conduct 100 per cent inspection of the works.
- Financial audit was not carried out in 39 districts in Arunachal Pradesh, Andhra Pradesh, Assam, Bihar, Chhattisgarh, Gujarat, Haryana, Himachal Pradesh,

Jharkhand, Kerala, Madhya Pradesh, Nagaland, Orissa, Punjab, Rajasthan, Sikkim, Uttar Pradesh, Uttarakhand, West Bengal (19 States).

- In 57 districts in Arunachal Pradesh, Andhra Pradesh, Assam, Bihar, Chhattisgarh, Gujarat, Haryana, Himachal Pradesh, Jharkhand, Karnataka, Kerala, Maharashtra, Manipur, Meghalaya, Nagaland, Orissa, Punjab, Rajasthan, Sikkim, Tamil Nadu, Tripura, Uttar Pradesh, Uttarakhand, West Bengal (24 States), District Internal Audit Cells were not constituted.
- Both State and District Quality Monitors had not been designated by the State Governments of Andhra Pradesh, Arunachal Pradesh, Assam, Chhattisgarh, Gujarat, Haryana, Himachal Pradesh, Jammu & Kashmir, Jharkhand, Kerala, Maharashtra, Manipur, Meghalaya, Nagaland, Orissa, Punjab, Rajasthan, Sikkim, Tamil Nadu and Tripura (20 States), while District Quality Monitors had not been designated in West Bengal.
- Local VMCs were not constituted by 141 GPs in Andhra Pradesh, Bihar, Haryana, Himachal Pradesh, Jammu & Kashmir, Jharkhand, Karnataka, Kerala, Madhya Pradesh, Maharashtra, Manipur, Orissa, Uttar Pradesh and Uttarakhand (14 States).

Responses of States

- The Governments of Assam, Bihar, Chhattisgarh, Jharkhand, Rajasthan, Sikkim, Tripura and Uttar Pradesh had now issued directions to the concerned officials to conduct the stipulated inspections periodically.
- Local VMCs had since been constituted in each district in Jharkhand. In Uttar Pradesh, instructions had been issued for constitution of VMCs.
- The Governments of Assam, Jharkhand, Punjab, Tripura, Maharashtra and Sikkim had now issued instructions to constitute District Internal Audit Cells and conduct financial audit periodically.
- The Governments of Assam, Chhattisgarh Jharkhand, Orissa, Punjab, Rajasthan, Sikkim and Tripura had now initiated the process of designating District and State level

Quality Monitors.

- The Government of Madhya Pradesh stated that Financial Audits were now being carried out through Chartered Accountants, while the Government of West Bengal stated that the Audit of accounts for the year 2006-07 had now been completed.
- The Government of Rajasthan had now issued orders for evaluation of the scheme.
- The Government of West Bengal stated that the required manpower had now been appointed to increase the inspections/ monitoring of works, at each level, to the desired norms.

Implication

- The lack of adequate monitoring mechanisms affects the groundlevel implementation of NREGA.

3

NATIONAL RESOURCE CENTRE OF NATIONAL RURAL EMPLOYMENT GUARANTEE ACT

BACKGROUND

National Rural Employment Guarantee Act – 2006 came into force on 2 February, 2006 and was initially launched in 200 of India's most backward districts. From April 2008 the Act has extended to cover all the districts of the country. The objective of the scheme is to provide for the enhancement of livelihood security of households in rural India. At least one hundred days of guaranteed wage employment in a financial year is to be provided to every household whose adult members volunteer to do unskilled manual work.

The Act was framed to give legal guarantee of wage employment to anyone who is willing to do casual manual labor at the statutory minimum wage, thus making it the most expansive public employment programme anywhere in the world. It provides for a universal and enforceable legal right to employment. Under NREGA the state is under commitment to provide employment within 15 days to any adult who applies for work.

The major highlights of the programme are:

- Development Initiative
- Public Investments for creation of durable assets
- Demand Driven
- No Specific Allocation for a Village Panchayat

- Participatory Planning
- Decentralized Implementation

The major safeguards are:

- Ban on Contractors
- Labour intensive works, hence labour oriented
- Prevention of Pilferage
- Increase in Agricultural Wages
- Prevention of Distress Migration
- Social Security

Objectives

For the potential of NREGA to be realized, major reforms need to be initiated in its implementation, as the power of the Act is derived from the fact that it creates a right to work, is demand driven, and has an inbuilt targeting mechanism. The National Institute of Administrative Research has been given the responsibility to act as the National Resource Centre for NREGA. Keeping the above framework in view, the following objectives have been highlighted.

- To build the capacity of functionaries and officials at various levels to handle NREGA implementation effectively.
- Conduct research and evaluation in different districts to identify the best practices being followed and also the shortcomings which may provide lessons to other districts which are lagging behind.
- Need for fully trained and committed personnel to handle NREGA implementation at the panchayat, block and district level. In this constext it was considered necessary to impart training on the implementation of the Act to the All India Service Officers at the initial stage of their entry into the service since they will also carry forward the task of implementing the act at various levels. Other key personnel and agencies from PRIs, district and state departments as well as committees and groups formed for the purpose of vigilance, monitoring and social audit need to be trained to discharge their responsibilities effectively.

- Documentation of the practices for collecting and dissemination of good practices.
- Publication of the outcomes of the training and research activities both internal and external.

NIAR has already conducted Five workshops on NREGA for the modalities involved in NREGA.

The key task and activities to be initiated and undertaken are:-

Building Resources and Networks at Various Levels

The National Resource Centre will create a national network involving state training institutes and rural development institutions including universities and individuals to build capacities of state, district block and sub block level functionaries to implement NREGA.

A zone wise network will be created in which zone wise nodal centre will be selected and identified namely: for North, South, East, West, Central and North Eastern Zone. The Govind Ballabh Pant Institute of Social Sciences, Allahabad has already been selected as the Zonal Centre for North Zone and others will also be identified soon.

The zonal centres will be involved to coordinate and train state/ district level officials and agencies in estimation, quality parameters, monitoring systems and evaluation systems. They will also undertake quality appraisals in different areas and devise ways to remove deficiencies.

Capacity Building and Training Programmes

(i) NIAR in collaboration with the regional resource centres identified will conduct at least 2 capacity building workshops every month for NREGA officials of various districts. The slots for the coming months have already been allotted in the tentative training schedule.

(ii) Training of the All India Service Probationers on matters relating to the Act at the LBSNAA. The mandate will also cover reviewing different state schemes and practices through the field attachments during phase II of the training.

Training Material, Modules and building of resource group

I. Training materials and need based training modules for NREGA officials will be developed.

II. Training of master trainers for different training modules will be undertaken. A group of experts in the field will be involved both at the national and state level to finalize the modules and training material. Experiences of the institutes involved, and CSOs (Civil Organizations) working in the field will also be incorporated in the training modules. Process for formation of core group of experts which will be part of the resource group will soon be initiated and finalized. The resource group will design material for training which will assist in planning, designing, monitoring and quality assessment of various initiatives

Documentation of Training and Research activities

Documentation, inventorisation and dissemination of good practices and conduct of research including action research in NREGA to be taken up after mutual agreement with the MoRD. Executives will be hired for the purpose of documentation, inventorisation and dissemination of the good practices and other issues identified and raised in the training sessions.

Research

I. Researchers will be engaged and encouraged to undertake fieldbased action research in related areas. These research activities will be conducted at the national, state and district level.

II. In addition Impact Evaluation Studies will be undertaken.

III. It is envisaged that the above research findings feed into policy oriented research studies.

Publication

NIAR will publish, internally and externally, the proceedings of workshops as well as the reports of the research studies undertaken. A reputed publisher will be contacted for the entire publications pertaining to the NREGA.

Conclusion

Overall the National Resource Centre will be involved with preparation of reading material, preparing, developing and imparting academic input, developing tools and techniques of training and developing of professional skills. Conduct joint research or field of study and sharing data. Also the resource centre will be responsible for publication and circulation of reading material and sharing of library resources. If any research or study requires outsourcing the same shall be jointly administered and approved by the nodal officers of the two organizations. The above themes would be covered through joint discussions. The outcome would be to develop programs and policies through an understanding on concepts as well as current strategies and challenges in program implementation.

Daily Reporting System through SMS - improving quality of NMR under National Rural Employment Guarantee Scheme (NREGS) at viluppuram District - Tamil Nadu

NREGA is a flagship programme of Government of India and Government of Tamil Nadu. This scheme assures 100 days of work in a year with minimum wages to poor workers on self selection basis.

Success of this programme mainly depends on proper execution of works, correct entries in Nominal Muster Roll (NMR)s, correct and timely payment of wages.

For the success of any wage employment programme, quality of entries in NMR should be improved. To ensure this, at Viluppuram district, we tried to put in a system (at work sites in Village) in place which will reflect timely closing of NMR by the authorised person by 11.00 a.m. The information regarding this is passed on from Village to Block level and subsequently to District level by taking advantage of good network of communication in the Telecom Sector in the state of Tamil Nadu through telephone message.

We felt that timely closing of NMR and reporting to Block level and District level eliminates the scope of bogus entries in the NMRS. It is very difficult to fudge the NMR, once the total number of workers has been informed to the monitoring office.

This system has worked well in this district for quite some time now.

The Officer, who are going to inspect the site are directed to take the details of number of workers at the work site which has been already reported from the Village and are available at Block Level and District Level by 11' O' Clock. The inspecting official does the headcount and verifies the figures with the NMR at work site, thereby it almost works as concurrent audit for entries in NMR on daily basis.

This has created moral fear among the people who are maintaining the NMR at Village level. There is always a fear that someone is monitoring the maintenance of NMR on daily basis and if bogus entry or ghost workers are there, they will be caught on the same day and there is no scope for fudging entries in the NMR after 11.a.m

After successful implementation of this system, we tried to improve the daily reporting through SMS by cell phone. Through this system the details in works being executed in all the Panchayat can be collected and consolidated through a simple software and minimum hardware.

The authorized person from Village Panchayat can send SMS through CELL PHONE or WLL PHONE from the village to the respective Block. In turn, the block message can automatically be forwarded to the district office.

Thereby, the report can be generated at Block level and District level. This report will show the details of labourers from each Village Panchayat with male and female workers breakup at a work site on the particular date.

This system helps not only in eliminating the wrong entries in NMR and thereby reducing the scope for ghost workers, but is also useful as feedback tool for getting the data of labourers engaged in a Village Panchayats on continuous basis for taking corrective measures to improve the over all performance of each Panchayat to provide the ensured 100 days employment, to the households demanding employment under this scheme.

The Panchayat report is being sent through the (model) SMS in the format below.

Format : B00.V00.M000.F000.W0.D00.00.00

B00	–	Block Code
V00	–	Village Code
M000	–	No. of Male workers
F000	–	No. of Female workers
W0	–	Work Number
D00.00.00	–	Date, Month and year (DD/MM/YY).

The above reports from Panchayat will be consolidated in the computer as below.

Block wise Report Dated:

SI. No	Name of the Block	Total.No.of Village Panchayat	No.of Village Panchayat where works going on	Total No of Works in a Village Panchayats	Male	Female	Total No.of Workers
1							

Village Panchayat wise Report Dated:

SI. No	Name of the Village Panchayat	Name of the Habitation - Hamlet	Total No.of Works in a Panchayat	Male	Female	Total No.of Workers
1						

TOLL FREE HELP LINE – GANJAM DISTRICT

One of the important requirements for implementing NREGA in letter and spirit is an effective grievance redressal mechanism. Towards this objective Ganjam district administration has started a toll free help line for receiving complaints on NREGA.

How it works

- Districts have a four digit toll free number 1077 for receiving information during natural calamities and disasters. This number is also being used to collect complaints on NREGA.
- The entire process has been out sourced to Nehru Yuva Kendra. NYK volunteers man the help line and they also

provide man power for the quick response teams located in every block to enquire in to complaints.

- NYK volunteers have been trained adequately on NREGA and also on manning the help line documentation etc.
- The help line functions from 6.00 am to 8.00 pm and we are in the process of making it round the clock.
- When a complaint is received, the details are entered and a reference number is given to the complainant. Based on the nature of complaint it is passed on to the QRT for enquiry or to the supervisory officer. The complainant using the reference number can ask for details of action taken after 48 hrs.
- A daily report on complaints along with action taken is given to the DPC every evening. A simple soft ware has been developed locally for effective documentation of complaints and monitoring.
- Adequate publicity about the toll free number has been made through news papers and also through wall writings in work sites, GP offices, Block offices and prominent places like banks.

Advantages

- People don't have to come all the way to district head quarters or block to lodge their complaints. They can make a call from their village and lodge their complaints.
- Because it is toll free there is no problem of people spending money to make a call and lodge their complaints.
- Four digit toll free number is easy to remember and also to dial
- The entire process of manning the help line and preliminary enquiry has been out sourced to an independent agency (NYK). This adds credibility to the entire process.
- With the help of reference number the complainant can track his complaint and get details of action taken.
- Some complaints may require immediate action for eg. Use of labour displacing machines etc. in these cases the QRT of that block area can rush to the spot and enquire in to it immediately.

- There is fear amongst implementing agencies about this toll free help line and this is helping in effective implementation of the provisions of the act.
- The toll free help line has become so popular now people are also using the same lodging complaints about drinking water, and PDS related problems. This has helped in visibility for the toll free help line which will also make people use the same during natural calamities and disasters.

THE ROAD AHEAD

On February 2, 2006, amid great hype and hope, the National Rural Employment Guarantee Act (NREGA) came into force in 200 of India's most backward districts. Last year it was extended to cover another 130 districts and with effect from April 1, 2008, the Act is to cover all of rural India. This is the largest ever public employment programme visualised in human history. But even before it has had a chance to take off, its detractors, led by the chief minister of one of India's most populous and backward states, want it to be scrapped. While those who worked hard to get NREGA enacted into law are bound to call this a premature overreaction (which it undoubtedly is), there can be no denying that the disappointments of NREGA come as no surprise to any student of the history of rural development, especially public works programmes, in India. It is clear that as far as implementation of public works programmes is concerned, there has been no discernible improvement since independence. If anything, progressive deterioration has occurred, especially in the most backward regions, where such interventions are needed and matter the most. How did we then expect NREGA to do any better when we entrusted its implementation to the same ossified, decaying structure that has deeply institutionalised corruption, inefficiency and non-accountability into the very fabric of Indian democracy at the grass roots?

In this chapter, we will try to show why NREGA has raised expectations like no other rural development programme and how it can and must be made to deliver on its massive, if yet unrealised, potential. In doing so we draw upon the experience of a National Consortium of Civil Society Organisations (CSOs) that is working closely with panchayat raj institutions (PRIs) across 30 districts in seven states to help them plan, implement and social audit NREGA works [SPS 2008]. We also incorporate the insights provided by the recent report of the Comptroller and Auditor General [CAG 2007] on NREGA.

A NEW PROGRAMME

The most important change NREGA represents is that it gives rise to programmes that spring not from its wilful benevolence, but as a legally binding response by the state to a right to work that is, after NREGA, enshrined in law. This also means that a constraint of resources cannot be cited by the government as an excuse for not providing work and its attendant entitlements, all of which are now also safeguarded in the Constitution. This is a commitment by the state that is unprecedented in the history of independent India – both as a legally enforceable right and in terms of financial resources.

NREGA is also supported by an extraordinary set of guidelines issued by the ministry of rural development, government of India [MoRD 2005a]. These guidelines are unique in the emphasis they place on planning of works and mechanisms of social audit. In this way, the official guidelines reflect the understanding that quality of works is of central importance. Thus, it is abundantly clear that this is not a welfare programme dishing out doles. It is a development initiative, chipping in with crucial public investments for creation of durable assets, without which the growth process will not get the requisite momentum in the most backward regions of rural India.

The emphasis on water conservation, drought- and flood-proofing is also critical as it underscores water security as the pre-requisite and foundation for rural transformation. Perhaps the most novel and remarkable feature of NREGA through which it makes a decisive break with the past is the complete ban on the use of contractors. It is not very widely known but most government programmes in rural areas over the last 60 years have been implemented through the agency of local contractors, who have emerged as major sources of exploitation of the rural poor, especially women. They have run roughshod over basic human rights, paying labour a pittance and doing most work through labour-displacing machinery. NREGA bans the use of such machines, places central emphasis on payment of statutory minimum wages and provides legal entitlements to labour on working hours, rest, drinking water, medical aid and crèche facilities. There is also provision for unemployment allowance being paid to workers in case the state is unable to provide the guaranteed days of work. All of this is obviously incompatible with programmes where the main goal becomes maximisation of profits of the contractor.

NREGA visualises a programme where the local people are centrally involved at all stages – planning, implementation and social audit. The official guidelines outline in meticulous detail completely new mechanisms for social audit, which reflect the influence of civil society in the formulation of NREGA. It is recognised that corruption is a major contributor to lack of quality in rural works (roads that get washed away every monsoon and earthen dams that are unable to stand peak run-off, being the most frequently encountered examples), apart from its negative impact on the rights of labour. Great emphasis has been placed on transparency and accountability at every stage of the programme. There is also an unprecedented emphasis on the use of information technology (IT). This is meant to facilitate the right to information, more intensive monitoring of the programme, as also greater speed of execution.

All these features put together signal the possible inauguration of a wholly new chapter in rural governance in India. One of the key factors endangering the very roots of democracy is the falling apart at the seams of systems of service delivery and programme implementation.

The failure of the public sector in rural development is one of the least understood but most threatening features of life for the poor in post-independence India [Shah 2007]. And this is not a mere consequence of the advent of the so-called "reforms" era in the 1990s. It has been an enduring feature of rural life over the last 60 years, which has only got worse over time. NREGA can change this for all time to come, if that is, its provisions are implemented in right earnest.

LACK OF PROFESSIONALS

The central proposition of this commentary is that there is no way NREGA can realise its full potential if implemented within the same moribund structure of governance that has characterised rural India since independence. A bureaucracy that is both unmotivated and corrupt and which, in any case, has its hands full with a whole host of pre-existing responsibilities, can hardly be expected to muster the imagination and energy required by NREGA.

A radically new programme also makes dramatically new demands from the system, requirements that the public sector in rural development, as it exists today, is completely unprepared for. Every state government was required to appoint, in each block, a full-time programme officer (PO), exclusively dedicated to the implementation of NREGA, with necessary support staff. However, the CAG report finds that 19 states had not appointed these officers in 70 per cent of the blocks it surveyed. The existing block development officers (BDOs) had been appointed POs and given "additional charge" of NREGA. Unfortunately, NREGA is not a programme that can work on an "additional charge" basis. An employment guarantee assistant (EGA) was to be appointed in each gram panchayat, in view of the pivotal role of PRIs in NREGA implementation. According to the CAG report, 52 per cent of the 513 gram panchayats it surveyed had not appointed EGAs.

The state governments were also required to constitute panels of accredited engineers at the district and block levels. Without timely and transparent costing of works and their measurement and valuation by such a panel, neither sanction of works nor payment to labour can happen on schedule. CAG found the panel missing in as many as 20 of the states it studied. The state governments were also to appoint Technical Resource Support Groups at the state and district levels to assist in planning, design, monitoring, evaluation, quality audit, training and handholding.

The CAG report finds that 23 states had not set up such groups at the state or district levels. According to the report, non-appointment of a full-time dedicated PO, who is pivotal to the successful implementation of NREGA, and giving the additional charge of PO to BDOs, who were responsible for other developmental schemes at the block level, strikes at the root of effective implementation of NREGA.

In the absence of dedicated technical resources, the administrative and technical scrutiny and approval of works was, thus, routed through the normal departmental channels burdened with existing responsibilities. This was further compounded by the failure to specify time frames for processing and approval of proposals at different levels. This was reflected in the poor progress in taking up works. The CAG report summarises "significant deficiencies" and their impact on NREGA implementation:

The main deficiency was the lack of adequate administrative and technical manpower at the block and GP levels. The lack of manpower adversely affected the preparation of plans, scrutiny, approval, monitoring and measurement of works, and maintenance of the stipulated records at the block and GP level.

Besides affecting the implementation of the scheme and the provision of employment, this also impacted adversely on transparency, and made it difficult to verify the provision of the legal guarantee of 100 days of employment on demand. Planning was inadequate and delayed, which resulted in poor progress of works.

Systems for financial management and tracking were deficient, with numerous instances of diversion/ misutilisation, and delay in transfer of state share. Monthly squaring of accounts at different levels to maintain financial accountability and transparency was also not being done. Maintenance of records at the block and GP levels was extremely poor, and the status of monitoring, evaluation and social audit was also not up to the mark.

All of this meant that of the 2.10 crore households who were employed under NREGA during its first year, only 0.22 crore received the full 100 days promised under the Act. The average employment per household was 43 days in 2006-07 and 35 days in 2007-08 [MoRD 2008]. Field reports of the partners of the national consortium provide more details, confirming the picture presented in the CAG report.

Under-Staffing

In Bolangir and Nuapada districts of Orissa, BDOs are doubling up as NREGA programme officers. In Dahod and Panchmahals districts in Gujarat, officers are being sent on deputation from other government departments, particularly the irrigation department, as POs. In Pohri block of Shivpuri district in Madhya Pradesh, the panchayat inspector is also the PO of NREGA. In Tikamgarh and Khandwa districts of MP, the CEOs of block panchayats have been given additional charge of NREGA. In Raigarh, Sarguja and Rajnandgaon districts of Chhattisgarh, uncertainty of tenure and resulting discontinuity have had an adverse impact on NREGA work. POs are demoralised and unmotivated and feel that the work done by them has come to nothing. In Orissa's Bolangir district, engineers of line departments have been given additional responsibility of NREGA. For a block of 140 villages, there are only four to five junior engineers (JEs), two of whom are given additional responsibility for NREGA, while the others continue with their normal departmental work. These two JEs in-charge of NREGA also look after other schemes such as the Backward Region Grant Fund, Indira Awas Yojana, Revised Long Term Action Plan for KBK, Biju-KBK Scheme, MPLAD and DPAP.

The documentation and procedural requirements of NREGA often make it an unattractive proposition as compared to these other schemes where financial leakages are seen to be easier. Thus, the whole process of planning and design of works, implementation, measurement and payment is marked with poor attention to quality and long delays. In Chhattisgarh, the situation is no different. In Wardrafnagar block of Sarguja district, for instance, four technical assistants are shared across 72 gram panchayats. There is no pool of engineers available at the district either. In Raigarh and Jashpur districts, where fresh JEs have been appointed, their tenure is again for a period of one year, after which it has to be renewed. The number of such JEs falls far short of what is required. Similar shortages of technical staff are reported from the Dahod and Panchmahals districts in Gujarat. In Tikamgarh and Shivpuri districts of MP, the Regional Engineering Services (RES) and other line department engineers have been given additional charge of NREGA. In Tikamgarh, some appointment of engineers at the block or district level have been made, but under contract for a limited tenure. In Khandwa, there have been some contractual appointments but too few to make any difference. In Anuppur, also there is a shortage of technical personnel at the disposal of the GPs, as a result of which they are dependent on engineers of line departments posted at the block level.

DELAYS IN ADMINISTRATION

This shortage of staff leads delays in execution of works and payment of wages. This is the experience in all our consortium districts but the most vivid illustration of the process comes from Bolangir and Nuapada districts of Orissa. The JE prepares the work plans and estimates. This itself takes time, since the JE is also overloaded with other responsibilities. Once the plan is made, it is submitted to the assistant engineer (AE) for approval. Since each AE is at times given the responsibility of more than one block, approval at the AE level also takes extra time. When the AE approves it, the proposal is sent to the PO (BDO) who has powers to approve a plan up to Rs 2 lakh. If the proposal is for more than Rs 2 lakh, it is sent to the district headquarters. Once the work is approved and funds released for it, the cheque is signed by the sarpanch, the panchayat EO and the PO-BDO. The BDO's signature is an additional requirement under NREGA; normal non-NREGA panchayat works do not need this signature. This further delays withdrawal of funds and execution of works. Once work reaches a certain stage, the work done has to be valuated and payments made to workers based on this valuation. This requires technical people who are in short supply. This means that measurement itself can sometimes take several months, although it is supposed to be done within a week. A utilisation certificate (UC) has to be submitted by the panchayat to the PO-BDO, for release of the next instalment.

After measurement is done, the UC is prepared and sent to the PO-BDO. The PO-BDO then waits for all GPs to submit their UCs so that they can be pooled together and sent to the district panchayat (DP) for the next tranche. If one or two GPs delay submission of their UCs, onward submission to the DP is delayed. In parts of Shivpuri district, Madhya Pradesh, delays of as much as two to three months in payment of wages have been reported. Wage payments are delayed because of long gaps between execution and valuation of work due to paucity of engineers. In Rajnandgaon, delays in wage payments are reported by PRI leaders as one of the major problems facing NREGA works. In Sarguja, a shortage of technical personnel to do the valuation work is reported to cause delays in wage payments of up to three months.

LACK OF PEOPLE'S PLANNING

Another serious consequence of shortage of professional staff is that there is little effort at social mobilisation without which there is no chance of NREGA emerging as a people-centred programme. In Rajnandgaon, Raigarh, Sarguja and Jashpur districts of Chhattisgarh, works are focused mainly on activities for which standardised estimates are available. Plans are made and approved at the "top" and sent downwards for implementation by the GPs. For instance, in the entire Wardrafnagar block of Sarguja, 75 per cent of funds have been utilised on roads of different types. Since this area is one of the poorest tribal pockets of the country, with a long history of droughts, the focus should naturally have been on drought proofing. The topography is naturally suited to watershed works too. But these are not the priority of NREGA plans. In Mandla district, MP there is an absence of annual plans.

The shelf of projects exists but it is very broad in nature and the activities are not well defined. The general practice is that funds are first released by the DP and then activities are identified. In Shivpuri, the focus continues to be roads. The gram sabha is not aware of the plans nor do people know that without their approval, works cannot start or be completed. The perspective plans are photocopies of those prepared for the National Food for Work Programme (NFFWP). A list of such works compiled together has formed the perspective plan. The annual plans also are prepared in the form of lists culled out from previously prepared "plans". Activities may be subtracted from these lists or added to them by the PO and the RES engineers on their own. In Tikamgarh district there are no annual working plans ratified by the gram sabha. The plans are prepared by the CEO block panchayat and GP secretary and forwarded for fund release to the DP.

In Anuppur, plan ratification by the gram sabha was a mere formality since people were reportedly excluded from the whole process. The panchayats are forced to implement action plans made by the district. In Khandwa district too, gram sabhas are not actively involved in the process of planning. Focus seems to be on rural connectivity and wells to the exclusion of other works. In Gujarat, the planning process again does not involve the people directly. While records suggest that the gram sabha was involved, field checks belie this claim. There has been very little effort to mobilise the people to take active part in plan formulation.

Poor Quality

Given the low level of support infrastructure provided for NREGA works, it is not surprising that quality of works undertaken is uniformly reported to be poor. In Rajnandgaon, the emphasis is more on spending a larger amount of money than on ensuring quality in works execution. In Sarguja, shortage of technical staff is reported as adversely impacting quality. Also poor and thoughtless implementation strategies result in low quality work – planting is done but no provision is made for watering, nor is any protection (mechanical or human) planned against grazing. The plantations are thus destroyed fast. In Jashpur and Raigarh districts, the poor quality of works is widely reported, particularly given the paucity of technical manpower resources at the disposal of NREGA projects. In Gujarat, the rates of work are an issue, due to which quality of work is adversely affected. In Madhya Pradesh, in Shivpuri, it is reported that quality of works is very poor. Farm bunding has been initiated without any proper technical planning because of which the quality of work is shoddy. In Tikamgarh, plants have already died because no arrangement was made for water. The condition of roads is variable and only a few may survive.

Sabotage

The field experience of our consortium partners shows that shortage of dedicated personnel is not the only problem. It appears that the existing bureaucratic machinery is just not willing to play ball with the strict provisions of NREGA and are at times actively sabotaging its implementation. Where PRI leaders are keen to implement NREGA work, secretaries and executive officers of gram panchayats are seen to be working overtime to convince these leaders of the "perils" of getting entangled with NREGA. In Bolangir, Orissa, executive officers of panchayats routinely dissuade sarpanchs from putting up a demand for work under NREGA by raising the bogey of getting caught under the strict provisions of the law. NREGA is apparently seen as a programme where making money is not only "unnecessarily complicated" but might also be "fraught with danger". While critics of the Act have expressed fears that this scheme too will go the normal route of leakages, ironically many field-level functionaries perceive NREGA as a programme where corruption is very difficult, due to the numerous procedures that have been introduced.

In Rajnandgaon district, Chhattisgarh, there are reports that sarpanchs fear that getting work done under NREGA is tantamount to going to jail and that the unemployment allowance will have to be given out of the sarpanchs' pockets. In Dahod and Panchmahals districts of Gujarat, the talatis are also being seen as putting the fear of NREGA into the sarpanchs and dissuading them from raising work demand. An elaborate mechanism has been evolved in Bolangir and Nuapada districts in Orissa to escape doing NREGA work by suppressing such demand if it arises. When an applicant demands work in writing by submitting Form B-1 (work application or demand form) to the panchayat, the application has to be acknowledged in writing by the GP through a notice to the applicant for reporting to work (Form B-2 in Orissa). What the panchayat does is to duly fill up Form B-2 for each applicant but the form is never actually given to the applicant. It is kept with the panchayat.

This is done so that work under NREGA does not start, but in case of an official inquiry, the sarpanch and the EO can claim that the job cardholders concerned were issued a written notice to appear for work vide Form B-2, but that they never turned up at the work site. To discourage POs from keeping job applications pending, they are threatened that any unemployment allowance paid will be recovered from their salaries. This suppresses the demand for work, especially in the absence of time bound sanction and release procedures.

Inappropriate Rates

Work done on rural employment programmes in India is measured through the schedule of rates (SoR). This schedule provides rates at which work done by labour is valued. Workers are paid according to the value placed on their work by the SoR. What the government has overlooked is that the present SoRs are meant for a system that uses contractors and machines to carry out public works. These contractors, as a rule, do not pay statutory minimum wages to labour and get most of their work done through machines like the JCB.

Deploying the same SoRs under NREGA makes it impossible for workers to earn minimum wages. This is also because existing SoRs make inadequate provisions for variations in geology and climate, discriminate against women, tend to underpay workers by lumping various activities together and do not revise rates in line with increments in statutory minimum wages. Deploying the old SoRs also makes it impossible for implementers like gram panchayats to correctly cost works undertaken by them. The result is a varying combination of a series of malpractices – more work is shown than actually undertaken on the ground, poor quality of work takes place, works are left incomplete as actual costs exceed sanctions, labour is underpaid, bogus workers are shown as paid while machines actually do the work, etc.

In Mandla, wage payments of as low as Rs 37 per day are also being reported because of the valuation as per the task rate. Here people are unwilling to work on a task rate basis because they get less than the minimum wage under the system. In Rajnandgaon, while minimum wages are being paid, the work actually extracted from workers is reported to be more than that mandated by the wage rate. In Panchmahals and Dahod districts of Gujarat, the use of JCBs for excavation has been reported. In Orissa, village labour leaders appointed as EGAs were widely reported to be working as contractors. In Sarguja district, Chhattisgarh, 50 per cent of NREGA works that are to be implemented by line departments, are invariably found using machinery. But in Raigarh and Jashpur, the use of both contractors and machines has come down following public outcry against the same.

MOCKERY OF SOCIAL AUDIT

All partners of our consortium report that there is no real social audit process taking place in any location nor is there any system in place to do so. Provision for mandatory availability of muster rolls on work site is also not followed. In Gujarat, while the administration in Panchmahals and Dahod claims that social audit has been conducted, actually no report of the proceedings of these audits is available for scrutiny. Nor has the necessary mobilisation been carried out before organising such events. Talatis also resist divulging any information, despite threats of using the RTI Act. In Chhattisgarh, monitoring and vigilance committees have been largely inert in Raigarh and Jashpur. In Rajnandgaon, social audits have been done to complete a formality.

Monitoring and vigilance systems are either not present or inactive. In Sarguja, the social audits conducted have been far from satisfactory. Field reports indicate that the frequency of these audits needs to be increased from the present once every year to once a quarter.

In Madhya Pradesh's Tikamgarh district, only one social audit is reported, that too in October 2006. Even for this reports are not available for public scrutiny. In Mandla, no social audit is reported to have been conducted. The data on work done and payments is kept tightly under wraps. In Khandwa there does not seem to be any social audit arrangement in place. In Shivpuri reports clearly point to a lack of social audit and no village level vigilance committees. Panchayat secretaries have floated vigilance committees by entering a few names from the GP in their records. These names are also used for "ratification" by gram sabhas of various decisions.

However, these members do not themselves know either of their membership of these committees or about their duties or powers. The worst thing that could have happened to social audit is the process of inviting tenders for conducting them. In Shivpuri, it is reported that some agencies have tendered as low as Rs 27 per gram panchayat to do a social audit. In Khandwa, owners of photography shops, printing presses and manufacturing units had also submitted tenders to conduct this audit. Here the lowest bid was for Rs 100 per GP. Social audit is a qualitative process, needing tremendous efforts at grass root mobilisation and preparation of the community to understand what the audit process means and how they can use it to ensure that they direct development interventions in their own villages.

Thus, the process leading up to the social audit event and persistent follow-up after the event are as important as the event itself. Unfortunately, many so-called NGOs have also been unable to resist the temptation of bidding for social audit tenders at ridiculous rates, ending up making a mockery of one of the most radical and critical provisions of NREGA.

It is evident that both the number and quality of human resources deployed so far are completely inadequate for shouldering the complex and manifold responsibilities of NREGA implementation. It is obvious that governments have failed to recognise the enormous diversity of tasks involved and the skills required to execute the same with speed and quality.

Workload and Personnel Required

We have carried out a careful work study of NREGA and the staff currently deployed to identify precisely the additional personnel required at each level of implementation. Our key recommendations (summarised and explained in Table 1 (p 46)) are:

(1) Appointment of a full-time District Programme Coordinator dedicated only for NREGA.

(2) Constitution of Technical Resource Support Group at the district-level.

(3) Appointment of full-time Programme Officer at the block-level, dedicated only for NREGA.

(4) Appointment of three civil engineers in each block (not visualised in the official guidelines).

(5) Appointment of one Technical Assistant for a group of five gram panchayats as suggested by CAG (as against 10 GPs in the official guidelines).

(6) Appointment of one assistant programme officer for a group of five gram panchayats to undertake the task of social mobilisation (not visualised in the official guidelines).

(7) Appointment of Employment Guarantee Assistants in each village (as against each GP in official guidelines).

Costs

From April 2008 onwards, the NREGA will be extended to the whole country. In our own view, this is a decision that should have been taken only after the lessons of the first two years had been absorbed and necessary correctives put into place. Be that as it may, we have to now estimate the cost of the support structure we are suggesting, assuming that the employment guarantee will extend to the whole country from April 2008.

According to the Seventh Report of the Rural Labour Enquiry, there were 13.71 crore rural households (RH) in the country in 1999-2000, of which 5.51 crore (40 per cent) were rural labour households (RLH). Projecting the number of RLH to grow at an annual compound rate of 1.93 per cent (the national rate of growth of population between 1991 and 2001), we get a figure of 6.42 crore RLH in the country in April 2008. If we assume that 80 per cent of them offer themselves for employment, the number of RLH for whom the 100-day job guarantee would have to be extended comes to 5.14 crore, (say, for the sake of convenience 5 crore households).3 Assuming a daily minimum wage rate of Rs 70 (which is the weighted average of minimum wages across states reported by the MoRD 2008), the total wage cost of the programme is Rs 35,000 crore. The average wage: non-wage cost ratio of NREGA over the last two years has been around 70:30 [MoRD 2008]. Thus, the total cost of NREGA works comes to Rs 50,000 crore, if the programme is to be extended to the whole country by April 2008.

A quick cross-check with actual NREGA expenditure so far validates our figure of Rs 50,000 crore for NREGA works. The cumulative expenditure in 330 NREGA districts in financial year 2007-08 comes to Rs 10,133 crore as on January 31, 2008. This expenditure was sufficient only to provide an average of 35 days of employment per household.

Thus, we would require nearly Rs 29,000 crore if we were to provide 100 days of employment to all households seeking work across 330 districts. Extending this guarantee to all 604 districts of India in 2008-09 would, therefore, require an expenditure of nearly Rs 53,000 crore. As we have argued above, NREGA needs an appropriate human resource support structure for it to truly deliver on its potential. The last two years have witnessed a fierce struggle within the government and the Central Employment Guarantee Council (CEGC) over the so-called "administrative costs" of NREGA. These were fixed at 2 per cent when NREGA was enacted and subsequently raised to 4 per cent of total costs in 2007-08 after pressure from within the CEGC. But this is a debate couched in false terms. The expenses required to infuse NREGA implementation with quality are not so much administrative, as costs of professionalising the programme and introducing the critical inputs of capacity building as also monitoring and evaluation, with all the seriousness that these tasks demand. Without these inputs NREGA appears almost programmed to fail. A very small investment could make a big difference in truly transforming NREGA outlays into enduring outcomes. These inputs must be regarded as "investments" and not as administrative overheads or contingencies, as currently understood.

In order to cover the costs of the Central Employment Guarantee Council and the State Employment Guarantee Councils, as also to support a system of regular monitoring and evaluation of NREGA, we suggest fixing 1 per cent of the total cost of works to meet these expenses. These are illustrative exercises intended to establish the reasonableness in cost terms of our proposed structure of professional support for NREGA. By spending an additional 10 per cent, we are in a much better position to ensure quality in the money spent on NREGA works.

CAPACITY BUILDING

There is a need to continuously upgrade the capacities of the massive support structure of human resources needed for NREGA. An inadequate emphasis on capacity building has been a characteristic failure of rural development programmes in India

[GoI 2006]. Indeed, we need to first recognise that this order of magnitude of trained people are just not available in rural India. This means that a major new initiative is required to build capacities of rural people in NREGA related work. For example, we need nearly 6 lakh Employment Guarantee Assistants and over 50,000 each of Assistant Programme Officers and Technical Assistants.

Government should seriously consider recognising a one-year diploma course on NREGA, conducted by the whole range of government and nongovernment training institutions spread across the country. This is the kind of preparatory work that was required even before NREGA was launched. But it is still not too late to initiate such a programme, in which institutions like CAPART can play a special role.

It comes to only 2 per cent of the total cost of NREGA works. Even though we believe that capacity building must be a continuing process, there is no doubt that these costs would also come down as a fully trained cadre emerges over time.

CRITICAL ROLE OF IT

Information technology (IT) must be seen as a key player in NREGA reforms. The use of IT can effectively make possible: – reduction in time taken for tasks such as estimation, planning and managing fund flows as also standardisation of procedures. – reducing or eliminating the scope of "discretions" and "judgments" exercised to disguise malpractices. – reduction in time taken over administrative decisions, particularly on sanction and releases by proactively offering information. – making data transparently available on a network for monitoring, thus enabling concurrent vigilance and audits.

As the software deployed for NREGA in Andhra Pradesh [MoRD 2006] has shown, all stages of NREGA work, from registration of workers to issue of job cards, preparation of estimates for works, muster rolls and transfer of payments to workers can be very effectively computerised, leading to reduction in time taken and administrative costs. Modules in the software related to estimation and planning make it possible for technical survey readings for a standard basket of activities,4 taken by a Technical Assistant or EGA, to be fed into the system and a work estimate generated on this basis. Works to be executed at any village can be identified by the gram sabha and data entered into input sheets. The identified work will have necessary measurements along with the leads. With the help of input sheets, work estimates are generated in the computer system and sent to the gram panchayat for scrutiny and prioritisation. Depending on its nature and type, every work has a given set of tasks. All the above details for a particular work are estimated task-wise and the total estimated work and material requirements for that work are computed. The estimate is given a unique ID, which is used to track the work, prepare muster rolls from the MIS system and also prepare orders for payments. The system also has modules for material management, maintaining a list of authorised suppliers, and integration of accounts.

Scope for MIS

The MIS has already ensured that most or all stages of NREGA implementation cannot bypass it. Thus, work estimates, pay orders, muster rolls, etc, must be generated from the system for work to continue. There is scope to take the NREGA MIS [MoRD 2005b] even further. Given an integrated network with uninterrupted online access, the MIS has the ability to make proposals pending for sanction at various levels transparent over the network, as also the ability to accord sanctions online or to make observations on proposals available on the network. By also generating required note-sheets, the system has the capacity to lead the workflow rather than be an addon for data storage, retrieval and post-facto monitoring. Such a feature can be effectively deployed to rule out standard transmission and distribution losses associated with paper-work pipelines. These include delays in dispatch and receipts, long pendancy of files, difficulties in more senior lines of authority getting to know about pending decisions, resultant delays in sanctions and finally, zero accountability.

Take for instance field reports regarding huge delays in receiving a sanction order for work. In a typical scenario this happens because a proposal is made on paper, signed and physically dispatched to the sanctioning authority. It may or may not be put up to the sanctioning authority on time. Even when it does, there may be a delay because the person in-charge simply does not sign the sanction order, either because of a lack of time or because he wants to delay the order, and uses the fact that the files are buried deep in his office to "duck", as it were.

In a paper system, unless a senior official asks this sanctioning authority why the sanction order was not made, he may not even come to know that this was indeed the case. So there is no effective check on the sanctioning authority. Contrast this with a computer network where the same data is available to everyone concerned online. The time taken for the physical passage of paper files is removed. The proposal is "put up" online and sanctioned "on line" too. Moreover, the data on proposals pending for sanction are available to the sanctioning authority as well to his seniors up the line. The fact that this information is speedily available and the transparency this induces leaves fewer channels for escape and ensures that the task is done. The fact that different users have different accesses and privileges in the system also deters possibilities of misuse.

In today's age of core banking and money transfers across computer networks, the ability to take and communicate decisions online must be seen as an idea whose time has definitely come. The other major contribution of this MIS is that it opens up NREGA for public scrutiny, thus engendering greater transparency and better public audit. Since each job card issued, each work undertaken and every payment made anywhere in the state has a unique identification code, and since all this information is just a click away on the web, anyone interested in doing so can access this information, identify the person and actually conduct an evaluation to see whether what is reported is true or not. A great impediment to effective public audits – the lack of access to information – is thus taken care of. To fully realise the potential of IT, there is an urgent need to:

(i) Put a proper infrastructure in place so that the network is tightly integrated and uploads/downloads of data and decisions are as concurrent as connectivity allows. This means investments in connectivity. In the interest of rural governance reforms, extension of such communication highways to the most backward areas of the country must be a priority.

(ii) Select and train personnel in data entry and posting, so that quality is ensured.

(iii) Customise the software, wherever necessary, especially in estimation processes, in order to accommodate ground-level variations 8.5 Potential with Support How much difference such a support system can make to the quality of NREGA implementation is illustrated by the work of the National Consortium of Grassroots Civil Society Organisations for NREGA initiated in 2007 by Samaj Pragati Sahayog. The consortium is a coming together of CSOs working across 30 districts of 7 states of the country.

These CSOs have committed themselves to supporting PRIs in their areas to make NREGA a success. Many of these CSOs include panchayat leaders in their ranks. These CSOs have all been formally invited by the PRIs to help them plan, implement and social audit NREGA work. Consortium partners have worked to create awareness among people about the Act and its provisions, built a dialogue with PRI leadership, filled lacunae in the planning process and ensured greater participation of rural people in the functioning of the employment guarantee. In Raigarh, Jashpur and Sarguja districts of Chhattisgarh, CSOs have identified and supported rozgar mitaans (friends) who perform the role of EGAs. Door-todoor campaigns for registration of workers and applications for job cards have resulted in significant increases in job card holders. More work is being demanded by people under NREGA. There has been an increased demand by people to diversify the type of works undertaken to include watershed activities.

For example, gram sabhas held in seven villages after a systematic campaign on NREGA by a consortium partner in Raigarh led to work proposals worth Rs 1.30 crore, of which a majority are water conservation works. Qualitative changes include an increase in attendance in gram sabhas, particularly of women, more active local vigilance committees, who question use of poor quality material in construction work undertaken by the panchayat, information sharing on NREGA in gram sabhas, better worksite facilities and transparent payment procedures. In Madhya Pradesh too, encouraging results are reported. In Tikamgarh, job demand and registration of workers have gone up in panchayats where the consortium partners are working. There is now a greater awareness among people of their entitlements under the Act. In these panchayats work demand has increased and people are insisting on this work being provided at minimum wages. Some reduction in migration is also reported. Mobilisation campaigns in Shivpuri district have also led to increased awareness about the rights under NREGA. There is greater pressure on PRIs and the bureaucracy to deliver. In other blocks of the same district, thousands of people who were left out of the job card process were registered and their job cards issued after systematic mobilisation campaigns. In Khandwa district, at the specific request of the district administration, a consortium partner undertook an awareness drive across 50 villages with the aim of increasing work demand. Works valued at Rs 9 crore were demanded as a direct consequence of this drive. In Orissa, one consortium partner convinced the district administration that plans be made for a variety of activities other than roads, with a clear sustainable livelihoods focus, such as water harvesting structures and plantation. This resulted in a sixfold increase in allocation to one GP alone. This clearly brings out the fact that it is the absence of proper planning that results in low offtake and utilisation of funds. Everywhere consortium partners are helping panchayats by placing technical personnel at their disposal, who help GPs estimate, valuate and measure work and also directly help in work execution. Partners have also convinced the administration to integrate simple water harvesting technologies into NREGA. In such cases, consortium partners are providing their engineers to help GPs and the block administration to plan, cost, layout, execute and measure works. In recognition of the power of this approach, the ministry of rural development, has provided pilot support for some partners of the consortium. The way forward is for the government to provide a clear mandate and support for CSOs to work with PRIs to effectively implement NREGA. This would help institutionalise the CSO-PRI partnership, putting pressure on both CSOs and PRIs to build such relationships.

CONCLUSIONS

We would like to end with a brief reflection on the politics of NREGA. For it cannot be overlooked that the very enactment of NREGA is the product of a sustained struggle led by civil society and supported by left-leaning politicians across the political spectrum. The significance of this movement cannot be overstated as it represents one of the very few successful campaigns in favour of the rural poor in India, whose voice is almost unheard on the national scene. This is, of course, truly ironic for it is these "dumb millions" who fashion the destinies of those seeking to rule this country. But their cries for reform of the public sector in rural areas, which is often their sole lifeline, have gone completely unattended. Over the last 20 years, governments so committed to an agenda of reforms for the corporates, appear to have absolutely nothing to offer to their main constituency, the rural poor.

On the contrary, with the pressure on the state to shrink, expansion in scale of programmes is increasingly attempted using under-paid, poorly qualified "worker-volunteers". Corners must be cut when it comes to the rural poor. Anything for them, it appears, can be of the lowest quality. Of course, we must also recognise that even during the Nehru-era, rural development was never seen as a professional activity. The legacy of Gandhian anti-state anarchism, where people know best and can manage their affairs on their own, without any external help, only reinforced this tendency. The left, fighting for the very right of the public sector to survive, appears to have become so defensive as to completely overlook the need for reforms, long overdue in a sector marked by massive corruption and complete non-accountability towards the "public".

Our advocacy of reforms must not, of course, be seen as a stand-alone magic bullet, a kind of techno-managerial quick fix. We must recognise that without continuous public vigilance the most efficient of systems will inevitably be corrupted. Civil society activism has, therefore, tended to focus on perfecting the mechanisms of social audit. But it is also true that if we do not have the strength and imagination to demonstrate the possibility of positive results through an initiative like NREGA, there is a real danger that disaffection will express itself in frustration, cynicism and violence. This will lead to a spiral of negative outcomes, which will always return to hurt the most vulnerable. Neither a vigilant public nor a professional system is by itself sufficient in guaranteeing an accountable democracy, delivering development to the poor. Both must grow organically in tandem with each other. The NREGA ranks among the most powerful initiatives ever undertaken for transformation of rural livelihoods in India.

The unprecedented commitment of financial resources is matched only by its imaginative architecture that promises a radically fresh programme of rural development. However, for NREGA to realise its potential, it must focus on raising the productivity of agriculture in India's most backward regions. This can then lead further to the creation of allied livelihoods on the foundation of water security. This is also the only way we can envision a decline in the size of the work guarantee over time, as public investment under NREGA leads to higher rural incomes, that in turn spurs private investment and greater incomes and employment. At the same time, there has to be a continuous mobilisation of the rural poor so that NREGA can be powerfully social audited. For works to be productivity enhancing and for effective social accountability, major reforms need to be introduced in NREGA implementation. These include:

(1) Deployment of full-time professionals dedicated to NREGA at all levels, but most crucially at the block level, which is at the cutting-edge of implementation;
(2) Intensive effort at building up a massive cadre of fully trained "barefoot professionals" required at the gram panchayat level through a nationwide movement for capacity building, engaging government and non-government training institutions;
(3) Provision of adequate resources and setting up systems for continuous monitoring and evaluation at every stage of the programme to ensure quality;
(4) Greater use of information technology to infuse more transparency, accountability and speed at all stages, from sanction of works, release of funds, wage payments to social audit;
(5) Revising the Schedule of Rates so that they (a) are in line with a programme that bans machines and contractors, (b) are gender-sensitive, (c) more accurately reflect variations in climate and geology (d) valuate separately

the different activities that comprise works, and (e) move in tandem with changes in statutory minimum wages;

(6) Mandating a role for civil society organisations to work as support agencies for panchayat raj institutions in NREGA planning, implementation and social audit.

The NREGA programme, reformed on these lines, holds out the prospect of not only transforming livelihoods of the poorest people of our country but also heralding a revolution in rural governance in India.

BANK PAYMENTS: END OF CORRUPTION IN NREGA?

Recent reports of lurking corruption in public works initiated under the National Rural Employment Guarantee Act (NREGA) have led many observers to advocate the payment of wages through bank accounts, instead of cash payments. The main advantage of this approach is that it reduces the likelihood of any fudging of the muster rolls on the part of the implementing agencies (e g, the gram panchayats), since the actual wage payments are beyond their reach. It can be seen as an example of "the separa-tion of payment agencies from implement-ing agencies", adopted by several states (in various forms) as a safeguard against the embezzlement of NREGA wages.

Bank payments of NREGA wages have already been introduced in a number of districts, and are likely to be used more widely in the near future. Against this background, this paper presents a few observations on this arrangement, based on a field visit to Mayurbhanj district (Orissa). The investi-gation was carried out in October 2007, on the sidelines of a larger survey of NREGA in Orissa. A small team visited three blocks of Mayurbhanj district (Joshipur, Betnoti and Suliapada). It covered four randomly-selected gram panchayats (GPs) within each block and one worksite in each GP. One worksite in each block was select-ed for detailed muster-roll verification and a questionnaire was filled at each worksite.

Within Orissa, the system of paying NREGA wages through bank accounts was pioneered by Mayurbhanj. Beginning from late 2006, by May 2007 most blocks in Mayurbhanj had initiated the practice of paying labourers through bank or post office accounts. Today all but a few of the remotest GPs in Mayurbhanj disburse NREGA wages through bank accounts.

Rationale of Bank Payments

The NREGA attempts to make the process of wage payment (even in cash) as trans-parent as possible. There are a series of safeguards mandated by the Act. Muster rolls are supposed to be maintained at the worksite and displayed at the GP office. Payments are to be made in public in front of all the labourers, with the details of attendance and wages being read aloud from the muster rolls, so as to reduce the risk of fudged entries being made. Job cards are intended to act as a record kept with the labourers themselves of the wages they have received and the number of days they have worked. Through these there has been an attempt to create a new model of accountability in public works, eliminating corruption through the vigi-lance of workers themselves.

Unfortunately, from the larger survey mentioned earlier, it appears that a number of these transparency safeguards have been systematically undermined in Orissa. Muster rolls are almost never present at worksites. The muster rolls that were examined by the survey teams were often found to have fake names or inflated entries, suggesting a siphoning of funds by the middlemen. The job card design was faulty to the point of being useless (e g, it had no column to record wage payments). Contractors, who are banned under the Act from implementing NREGA works, were found at nearly half of the sample worksites. Accompanying them was an elaborate "PC system" ("percentage sys-tem") of bribes to government officials at various levels of the official hierarchy. In-deed, one of the reasons cited for the in-troduction of bank payments in Orissa is that it would eliminate contractors from the system.

The fundamental attraction of the use of bank accounts for NREGA wage pay-ments in Orissa is twofold. First, as men-tioned earlier, it separates the payment agency from the implementing agency, thus making corruption far more difficult. Second, it ensures that money sanctioned for wage payments can be received only by the labourer listed on the muster rolls. It eliminates the possibility of any intermediaries – whether a contractor or a government official – getting their hands on the money without the knowl-edge of the labourer. Once this possibility is eliminated, other records like muster rolls and job cards should fall into place, since there is little incentive to fudge them if you cannot get the money at the end of it.

Bank payments also have a useful trans-parency role. They extend the trail of transparency all the way down to the money actually reaching the hand of the labourer. In addition, it can be argued that bank payments of NREGA wages encour-age savings and help to initiate people to modern banking arrangements.

The System

This section discusses the system of main-taining bank accounts and the instru-ments of transfer.2.1 Bank Accounts

In Mayurbhanj, accounts have been opened in a variety of banks – rural banks, cooperative banks, nationalised banks and, in a few cases, post offices. The dis-tance between the GP and the bank has been the key criterion for selecting the bank. The effort has been to open accounts in institutions that are as close as possible to the village where work is being carried out. For some of the more inaccessible tribal pockets which are not yet using bank payments, there are even proposals to introduce mobile banks. This is the case in Betnoti.

In terms of opening bank accounts for labourers, a variety of procedures have been followed. In Suliapada and Betnoti blocks, most bank accounts were proactively opened en masse for the labour-ers, with GPs facilitating the entire process. However, very often, long periods of time would elapse between the time when application forms are completed and the receipt of passbooks. In fact, in most cases, passbooks were received only after the first payments had been made. In Joshipur, on the other hand, there was evidence that the opening of accounts was left to the individuals. The labourers either took the initiative or were made to open accounts so as to access the payment which was compulsorily made through account payee cheques. In most cases, these accounts were found to be zero balance or "no frills" accounts. The Reserve Bank of India directive for "no frills" accounts for

NREGA purposes has been clearly helpful here. In the post office accounts, a minimum bal-ance of Rs 50 is a requirement and there is a cap of Rs 2,000 on maximum withdrawal, per account, per day.

However, most of the accounts have been opened as operable by one individual. Ordinarily, this is the male head of the household. One of the significant aims of the NREGA is to ensure that women are paid equally and are able to exercise some control over their earnings. To this end, it would be preferable to have at least jointly operated accounts if not individual accounts for each NREGA worker.

Individual accounts for each worker would also double up as a transparency measure. In the current set-up where wage funds are simply credited to the account, there exists no record, including passbook, to identify the particular family member for whom the wage has been deposited. Introducing individual accounts would resolve this problem. On the other hand, there is a case for having a 1:1 ratio of job cards and passbooks, in which case, as will be discussed below, new ways of entering wage information into the pass-book should go hand-in-hand with a joint account system.

INSTRUMENTS OF TRANSFER

There are slight variations in the methods followed by each of the three blocks vis-à-vis bank payments, but all are based on the same basic flow of funds. Once a project is sanctioned, the money for it is sent to the account of the GP. As and when payments are due on the conclusion of muster rolls at the worksite, the funds are transferred from the GP account to the labourers' bank accounts. This is done in one of four ways: letters of credit from the GP account to the labourers' bank, cash deposits in the labourers' bank, bearer's cheques and account payee cheques to the labourers.

Letter of Credit: This is, at the moment, the most common instrument of transfer. In this system, the sarpanch and panchayat executive officer (PEO) draft a letter of credit detailing the accounts of the labour-ers to which the funds are to be credited. The funds are then transferred directly from the GP's account into the bank accounts of the labourers. Delays during the course of the transfer of funds from the GP account to the labourers' have been a major problem where the two accounts are not in the same bank (more on this later). One inherent flaw in this arrange-ment is that the labourer receives no inti-mation as to when the wages are credited to his or her account. An intimation proce-dure needs to be put in place.

Cash Deposits in the Labourers' Bank: Given that such delays were adding to those that already exist (e g, linked to record-keeping and work measurement) some GPs have found it more convenient to use the second method: to simply with-draw the funds from the bank physically and deposit them at the bank where the labourers' accounts are kept. In such cases, on a given day, the sarpanch and PEO will go to the bank together, withdraw the money, carry it to the other bank and deposit it there along with a list of the accounts into which the money is to go.

Account Payee Cheques: In many GPs, bank accounts were opened as a result of payment made through account payee cheques. In order to compel workers to open accounts, they were paid through account payee cheques drawn on the GP account. Otherwise also, payment through account payee cheques is a widely used method to disburse wages in Mayurbhanj. One advantage of this method is that a receipt or acknowledgement can also be taken when the cheque is given to the labourer, unlike the letter of credit method where there is no interaction with the labourer before the actual payment is credited to the account of labourer. This also facilitates the regular maintenance of job cards.

Bearer's Cheques: In some places in Joshipur, instead of account payee cheques, bearer's cheques were issued. While still maintaining some of the ad-vantages of the system of bank payments, this arrangement is vulnerable to manipu-lation. Any middleman who can manage to catch hold of the bearer cheque would be able to withdraw the money.

Reception

There is a pronounced pattern to the way in which the elaborate system of bank payments has been received. District or block level officials are fairly sanguine about the possibilities of the bank system. Extravagant claims about the efficacy of the system in eliminating corruption are often made. It is not uncommon, however, to see GP level officials rather more circumspect about the system. They maintain that it has added to their work and they speak of the time that it takes to complete bank payments.

In a sense, however, these responses are difficult to interpret given the evidence that officials at a variety of levels often participate in the embezzlement of NREGA funds in Orissa. At least as important as the official responses is the way in which bank payments are received by the labourers themselves. The first few questions to block or district level officials about how labourers have received the bank payment system often yield formulaic declamations about its convenience and efficiency, how it eradicates corruption and encourages the saving habit, and so on. It is only after a little probing that the responses begin to suggest various acceptance problems in the "transition period".

The most common elaboration of this theme is something along following lines: "You know, these tribal people, they want to work in the morning and receive payment in the evening... Actually there is a local market on Friday and they demand to have their wages before that. They don't understand that this cannot be done..."

Quite apart from showing a casual contempt for labourers, this statement is empirically questionable. At SS Nahandasole, labourers said that they would be happy if they received their bank payments within 10 days, and, if needed, even two weeks. However, anything more than that, they said, made it very difficult for them to sustain themselves. This suggests that labourers can both understand the fact that delays happen as well as cope with them, as long as they remain within reasonable bounds. The Act itself provides for the payment of wages within 15 days of the date on which the work was done as a basic entitlement of workers. Quite obviously, the 15-day requirement applies to payments made through banks as well.

Stray evidence suggests that where this has been done, labourers are prepared to accept it. Respondents from Renugaon (in Betnoti GP) claimed that they much preferred the system of bank payments to payments in cash. They understood that bank accounts helped to ensure that they received the correct amount of wages. At a worksite using the cash payment system, they claimed, contractors could get away with paying them half the wages for half a day of work (the worksite was only kept open for half a day).

Renugaon was one of the villages where the labourers' bank was very close to the village. Where this is not the case, as at Anla in Betnoti block, labourers could be quite unhappy. The complaints were not simply about the fact that the bank was 8 km away. It was also because they would have to sacrifice an entire working day (if not more) to withdraw money from the bank. Often, they might make the trip to the bank only to find that it would be impossible for them to withdraw money on that day.

Quite worryingly, most labourers seemed unfamiliar with most of the basic banking procedures and documents. Many were unable to read their passbook, and there was strong evidence that some had been made to sign withdrawal slips without realising the implications. Nor had there been any effort by panchayat or block authorities to acquaint labourers with these practices.

It is only in a few places like Renugaon and Bilash (Suliapada block), where labourers were relatively familiar with banking practices, that all the expected benefits of bank payments seemed to be visible. As mentioned, labourers in Renugaon testified that corruption had come down since the introduction of these payments. A few of the labourers in these two villages even said that they were beginning to save some money – a source of some hope that the system of wage payments through banks, if introduced with due consideration of all these factors, can take popular root.

BANK PAYMENT HURDLES

Wage payment through banks is a recent innovation. Bank payment also means interaction of an external system with NREGA processes, which is bound to present some policy challenges as well as compatibility issues. Some of these hurdles are here.

- *Excess Burden and Bank Reluctance*: It appears that banks (and even more so post offices) are reluctant partners to the scheme as a whole. This is somewhat surprising, given the untapped potential rural India holds for the banking sector. Two concerns were usually cited by bank officials. First was the fact that large numbers of individuals were likely to transact business at the bank simultaneously. This would entail holding amounts of cash that the bank was not, in the past, required to keep. A second related concern is that the branches near the GPs are small and ill-equipped (staff- and infrastructure-wise) to deal with the large numbers of people involved. Opening large numbers of accounts and making entries on a given day is extremely difficult in a poorly staffed local branch (or for a single postmaster).

- *Delays*: As mentioned earlier, in cases where the GP account is held in a bank which is different from that of the labourers' bank, delays often ensue.6 Some branches of local banks refuse to accept letters of credit transfers unless they have been approved by their regional offices. Thus, the process of clearing this transfer of funds often involves sending the letter of credit from the panchayat's account to the branch where the labourers' account is held, and from there to the regional headquarter of the bank, where the letter will be approved. The funds will then be released from the regional headquarters to the local branch and finally credited to the accounts of the labourers themselves. We were informed that such a process would take 15-20 days at a minimum. Many labourers said that their main problem in the bank payment system was the hardship caused by frequent delays. In most places it was common to find that wages were being paid around a month after the conclusion of work. In Khanddeula village of Betnoti block, labourers were paid in September for work that had begun at the end of May and ended in the middle of June. In SS Nahandasole, labourers' post office accounts were credited with their wages for two fortnights on July 3, 2007. The work had commenced on June 1 and ended on June 24. It appears that, because of complications in the flow of funds, there is a temptation to wait till work is finished and then credit large amounts all at once, instead of regular weekly payments. This tendency adds to other delays, such as those due to work measurement and record keeping. Furthermore, in the absence of any intimation arrangement, the money reaches the accounts of labourers without them knowing about it. As a result, most labourers are informed about the money reaching them through some middleman (usually a contractor who has greater access to the panchayat officials than they do). These delays and lack of intimation open up spaces within the system into which contractors and other middlemen insert themselves, claiming, then, that they form an indispensable link in the chain.

- *Distance*: While the question of distance from the village was one that the block officials were relatively sensitive to, many labourers interviewed did complain about the distance of the bank from the village. In Anla, labourers claimed that the bank was far away (they said that it was 9 km away) and that it was extremely inconvenient to use it.
- *Complication of Records*: Muster Rolls, Job Cards and Passbooks: In the enthusiasm to introduce the system of bank payments, insufficient attention has been paid to the status of the documents already involved in the NREGA. Where bank payments have been introduced, a degree of ad hocism has appeared with respect to maintaining muster rolls and job cards. The Operational Guidelines envisaged a system where the maintenance of muster rolls and job cards is built around the distribution of wages in public: details on the muster rolls would be read out, wages distributed, signatures/thumb impressions of labourers collected and job card entries made. Since (in most places) letters of credit mean that money is directly transferred to the labourers' bank accounts, there is no designated point in the process at which signatures on muster rolls and entries in job can be made at all, let alone publicly. Different officials choose to complete these documents at different points of time, though most make people sign muster rolls before payments are received and fill in job cards by and by. The uncertain status of two of the most essential transparency safeguards in the NREGA is an unacceptable situation; more so because a simple policy directive can

clarify matters tremendously. A pessimistic, if only partial, view of the system of bank payments might hold that it has ended up merely adding another document to the numerous records that are supposed to be maintained under NREGA. In some places, the bank passbook has become a requirement for being employed at worksites. As elsewhere in Orissa, where an incomplete distribution of job cards has led to dangerous "adjustments" in the muster rolls to accommodate workers without a job card, an inadequate distribution of passbooks is having a similar effect.8 Officials and labourers claim that people who do not have passbooks are being paid through other people's passbooks, with the money being divided up between labourers later. In such a situation it is difficult to know where "adjustment" ends and corruption begins. In essence, the system of adjustment runs completely counter to the aim of introducing the passbook system in the first place – to extend the trail of transparency right down to the labourer's pocket. In other words, if a system of bank payments is to be put in place, it is essential to ensure complete distribution of job cards, and importantly, passbooks as well. One convenient way of doing this might be to have the job card application "double up" as an application for a bank account. Both documents, then, can run in tandem.

- *Continued Vulnerability to Deception*: The most disturbing finding, however, was that in a number of villages labourers did not have their passbooks with them. In four out of the 11 villages that we visited, labourers either did not have their passbooks or these had been recently returned to them because of the news of an impending survey. In the case of Nahandasole, when we examined the dates of the withdrawal of money, the labourers claimed that the passbooks had been with someone else at the time of withdrawal. In other cases, labourers said that they were with the bank for updating (though a month or more might have passed since the time they received the money). In one instance, a contractor claimed that he had collected the passbooks, "as collateral for loans given to the labourers". Given such evidence that middlemen had collected passbooks, it is difficult to interpret the pattern of deposits and withdrawals found in the survey villages. In four villages where we were able to see the passbooks the pattern was that all the money would be withdrawn on the first visit after deposit. If, for instance, Rs 2,400 was deposited in a post office account on July 10, 2007, Rs 2,000 would be withdrawn on July 10, 2007 itself (this was the maximum withdrawal limit) and the remainder on the very next day. Therefore the money withdrawn was immediately visible in each of these four villages. However, in each of these, there was also evidence that a contractor or suspected contractor had collected the villagers and accompanied them to the bank. In the one village where we could see the passbooks and there was no suspicion of a contractor, the pattern of withdrawals was more mixed.

- *Incomplete Separation of Implementing and Payment Agency*: One question that must be posed is how effectively the implementing and payment agencies have been separated in Orissa so far. The idea of separating implementing and payment agencies is that, since the implementing agencies would not have the money at any point of time, there would be less of an incentive to fudge the muster rolls. However, the system of payment, as it stands in Orissa, does not achieve this separation to a satisfactory degree. In practical terms, it is panchayat officials who prepare the muster rolls. The same officials then write the cheques on the basis of the muster rolls and sanction payments from the bank.

A more effective separation of these would entail, at one end, some amount of effort at training "mates" (worksite supervisors) to maintain muster rolls and oversee work in conjunction with the junior engineer. In this way, the muster roll preparation would not be in the hands of the GP officials. At the other end, it would mean re-examining the way in which the funds are released to the panchayats.

In Andhra Pradesh (AP), the muster rolls are passed directly to the block which sanctions payments and sends it directly to the post office at which the labourers' accounts are held. The PEOs and sarpanches in Orissa can direct and manipulate the flow of funds in a way that is impossible for panchayat level officials in AP to do. This opens up many possibilities of collusion and misappropriation of funds. A PEO could, for instance, in tandem with a contractor, arrange to have money sent into accounts of people close to the contractor with the money being shared later. The possibility of such collusion is not ruled out in the AP system. It is, however, made less likely since the responsibility of the panchayat officials ends at the point of preparation of muster rolls. They do not deal with the money at all.

As can be seen, the system of bank payments is not free of hurdles. Some of these, for instance bank reluctance, have been negotiated over time. Others threaten to get entrenched if they are not addressed immediately. At any rate, it must be acknowledged that an unqualified enthusiasm about bank payments is unwarranted. Banks in Mayurbhanj cannot be thought to have eliminated fundamental problems, like the presence of contractors or the possibility of corruption. Even some of the more procedural matters – policies with respect to clearances across banks and guidelines about completion of records and measures to ensure prompt payment – appear to have been inadequately tackled. If there was more clarity on these policies, performance of banking system could have palpably improved. As things stand, over half a year since the introduction of bank payments in

Mayurbhanj, one can, at best, express a cautious approval of the banking system in principle, but the details of the system fail to impress.

COMPARISON WITH ANDHRA MODEL

The system of bank payments in Orissa took inspiration from AP's experience. We have already dealt with the issue of separation of implementing agencies and payment agencies. It is worthwhile to examine some of the other aspects of the Andhra system with respect to the payment of wages through the post office, which have a potential to be fruitfully emulated in other places.

Andhra Pradesh has worked out a method of integrating bank or post office payments with intimation of labourers and records maintenance. When the muster rolls are being paid from the block to the bank, a computerised pay slip is also printed at the block office. These are sent for distribution in public to the village. At the time of their collective distribution, the muster roll details are read out and job card entries can be made. This is a fairly innovative approach that can resolve the two basic problems that affect the banking system in Mayurbhanj: lack of transparency during payment of wages and absence of intimation arrangement.

A second interesting innovation has attempted to address the issue of delays. In some districts of AP, this is being done through advance payments. A payment of Rs 60 (out of a minimum wage of Rs 80 per day) is credited to labourers' accounts immediately after the end of the week and the rest is credited later according to the work measurements, thus ensuring that labourers do not have to turn to contractors or moneylenders for their immediate needs.

There is much to be gained from understanding these alternative models of payment, particularly with respect to the solution of similar administrative problems. Experiences from AP and elsewhere should be drawn upon in carrying forward relatively new reform tools like the bank payment system.

Future Prospects

The system of bank payments for the NREGA in Orissa looks set to be expanded, with a number of other districts preparing to take it on as the model for removing corruption and ensuring correct payments. However, there seems to be little discussion of how a qualitative improvement can be brought about in the system. As we have argued, some thought needs to be put into the strengths and weaknesses of the system before such expansion occurs.

A major concern is the ad hocism that has persisted in the implementation of bank payments. Bank policy vis-à-vis NREGA wages at a variety of levels should be clarified and standardised as much as possible. Methods of transfer of funds vary from place to place. It is advisable that uniform, transparent procedures be introduced everywhere. Equally important is to avoid accentuating delays in wage payments and the flow of funds. We have already discussed how Andhra Pradesh has used advance payments to address this problem. Delays can also be reduced by negotiating with banks so that local branches are allowed to honour letters of credit from the GP, without having to seek the permission of the regional office. Related to this, means need to be devised to ensure that labourers are intimated directly when money has been credited to their accounts. In Andhra Pradesh, as we saw, there is a system of pay slips being distributed to labourers when letters of credit are issued to the post office. Apart from the question of intimation, this kind of collective gathering for the distribution of pay slips would ensure that the workers as a collective body remain a vital cog in the transparency processes of the NREGA. Such collective processes would offset the otherwise individualising tendencies of bank payments as a system of receiving wages. Public distribution of pay slips also facilitates the regular maintenance of job cards – a weak point of the system of bank payments in Orissa.

Enhancing Transparency

Bank policy on the question of the kinds of accounts to be opened also needs to be clarified. So far, bank accounts in Mayurbhanj have been opened in the name of male household members. This has significant drawbacks, in terms of gender equality as well as transparency. The best alternative would be a system of individual accounts, though even jointly operated accounts would be preferable to the current system.

It might be useful, also, to devise new protocols for passbook entry as they relate to NREGA wages. As mentioned earlier, the current practice is to club payments from different weeks and for different members of the family into one entry. This makes it quite difficult for the recipients to verify that they are getting their due. It would enhance the transparency of the system if there were some indication of the period for which payment is being made as well as of the person to whom it is due (as per the muster roll). Alternatively, a new kind of passbook can be designed which could cover these demands specific to the NREGA.

There is also some evidence that middlemen are being able to withdraw money from the bank for groups of people with simply the signature of the labourers on the withdrawal slips.10

Protocols relating to the NREGA wage payments must strictly disallow such withdrawals without the physical presence of the account holder. At the other end, some amount of information must be disseminated about the procedures to be followed at banks – the processes of deposit and withdrawal, and the importance of the various documents related to the bank (passbooks and withdrawal slips in particular).

It is only when people become more comfortable with banks and banking procedures that there can be a reasonable expectation of savings. Evidence that the payment of NREGA wages through banks is leading to savings has been quite thin so far. Either accumulated debts or manipulation by contractor has meant that most of the wages received by labourers are withdrawn immediately. Nevertheless, if the system succeeds in the long term, it would address some of the problems that seem to impede savings – contractors and indebtedness in particular. In that case, the system of bank payments may well come into its own. Banks can also be effective in solving the problems of storage of money that people in rural areas face. NREGA wages are often received in large amounts, and it is likely that banks, as a safe way to store money, might displace such repositories as gold jewellery.

Last but not least, it is important that bank payments should not be seen as superseding the other transparency measures that the NREGA sets in place. In particular, accurate maintenance of job cards and muster rolls must be strictly enforced. From Mayurbhanj itself, it is clear that bank payments, in and of themselves, cannot eliminate corruption. Improving the system of bank payments can only go part of the way towards that end. Building a culture of transparency and accountability in the implementation of NREGA remains extremely important.

4

EMPOWERING PEOPLE-PROJECT INITIATION UNDER NREGA

GANJAM DISTRICT

The NREGA guidelines lay much stress on public awareness (Chapter 2.4, Page 7) and also in maintaining proper transparency in execution, to have quality products. The provisions in Para 10.7 made it clear to form local level committees like Vigilance & Monitoring Committee & Beneficiary Committees.

Multimedia communications were made; even through Kalajatha & out-reach models using local languages. In almost all villages the provision of the Act were discussed in Palli Sabhas/ Gram Sabhas. Still then, it is found that major section of the primary stake holders remain un-aware about the working systems/ the wage rates/ working hours & work site facilities etc.

Hence in order to effectively reach out to the jobseekers and make them aware of provisions of NREGA, a project initiation meeting (PIM) is conducted in the village/ worksite on the first day of starting of a project as envisaged in 11.2.2 of the guidelines chart I point no 7.

CONVENING THE MEETING

(1) The PO of Panchayat Samiti or the Executive Officer of GP who execute the project, initiate action to call for such meetings in the beneficiary village. Most often the meetings are conducted in the worksite itself on the first day of starting of a project.

(2) Wide publicity through beat of drums, announcements through loud speakers are made in the beneficiary villages before holding the meeting. All the primary stake holders are invited to attend such meeting

Action Points

(a) New project is started under NREGS as per guidelines based or demand. However because many of the jobseekers are not aware of the provisions of NREGS, they might not have applied. Hence this meeting is used to explain the provisions of NREGA and this in turn makes them aware of their rights and demand for job. Thus one of the main objectives of PIM is to explain the provision of NREGS and motivate job seekers to demand for job.

(b) Registration of jobseekers, who have not registered are done instantly, obtaining an application from such beneficiary.

(c) Importance of job card is explained and availability of job cards with beneficiary is checked. Handing over of job cards to other persons if any are also caught red handed in such meetings.

(d) The nature of the work to be done in the project & the wage rates, which they may get, are discussed. Time rate for seven hours/piecemeal rates/ expected out-turn in a days work are illustrated to beneficiaries.

(e) Sample pits are excavated at work site to show and explain output based payment in earthworks.

(f) Worksite facilities like providing drinking water/ first aid/ crèche for children & their watch-ward etc. / work sheds/ other social benefits are also discussed.

(g) Payment system through banks is explained. In many places Bankers attend the meeting to open no frill account then & there.

(h) Wage Payment dates are also declared in the meeting. They are motivated to receive their payments, after entering the no. of days worked & the amount paid to them in their respective job cards.

(i) Village Level Vigilance & Monitoring Committees are formed in the said meeting and their role is explained.

(j) The provisions of Social Audit and complaint redressal mechanism explained to the jobseekers

(k) Transparency pillar giving the project details is constructed and leaflets explaining various components of the project are distributed to the jobseekers.

(l) Future project plans/ availability of other works in the private sector particularly in Agriculture sector/ Lean periods of works/ future job requirements are also discussed in the meetings, which provide scope for the job seeker to prepare his plan to avail continuous jobs.

(m) Photographic/ Video documentation of the meeting is done and kept in case records. Further the proceeding of the meeting along with signature of the participants is also kept in case record as an important document.

Advantages

- Job seekers are made aware of their rights under NREGA. This empowers the job seekers effectively and they are able to demand for work and also work site facilities. In villages of Ganjam district demand for work has increased three to four times after this initiative.
- Components of the project are explained to primary stake holders so this helps in achieving maximum transparency in implementation of the project.
- Provides a single window platform for people near their villages in the work sites to learn about NREGA, that particular project, demand for job, apply for job card, open bank accounts, forming of monitoring committees, grievance redressal, plan for future wage employment etc.
- As the PIM is conducted on the first day of work, in the work site, there is enthusiasm amongst job seekers to learn. Actual job seekers only turn up in the work sites and this also helps in giving proper focus to their apprehensions and queries
- When it comes to the National Rural Employment Guarantee Scheme (NREGS), there is little to put the Congress-ruled states apart from the Opposition-governed ones.

- If some non-Congress-ruled states (Gujarat, Kerala, Rajasthan, Tamil Nadu) delayed formulation of rules for the scheme at the time of its launch, Gujarat also stalled constitution or functioning of required State Employment Guarantee Councils (SEGCs). Others like Tripura, West Bengal and Uttar Pradesh failed to appoint State Rural Employment Guarantee Commissioners in time (SREGCs).
- Quite like Congress-ruled states, the SEGCs in Tamil Nadu and Uttar Pradesh only partially monitored implementation of the scheme, while in Gujarat, Karnataka, Rajasthan, Tamil Nadu, Uttar Pradesh and West Bengal, no technical resource support groups, with engineers or other experts, were set up at the district and state levels.
- Revolving funds were not made available at the district, block and gram panchayat levels in Tripura, Kerala, Uttar Pradesh, West Bengal, Rajasthan and Tamil Nadu, while Gujarat, Karnataka, Tripura, and West Bengal delayed the release of state share. In Uttar Pradesh, state share was not paid in full — all "adversely affecting" the implementation of the scheme.

THE CAG AUDITS' OBSERVATIONS:

Madhya Pradesh

- Unemployment allowance of Rs 4.75 lakh paid to 1,574 households for 18 days in Barwani from Central Government funds despite rules putting the burden on states
- Muster rolls in sample districts found to be issued on dates later than the start of work
- In the audited districts the average daily wage was Rs 45, well below the minimum Rs 60 stipulated under the Act
- CEO, zilla panchayat, Sidhi, spent Rs 20.80 lakh on spraying of hormones for jatropha plantation on contract basis, against the rules
- Wages of Rs 10.68 lakh paid even before the issue of muster rolls
- Names of 96 labourers appeared simultaneously in various muster rolls at different worksites for the same period

- Rs 12.05 lakh spent by the PWD, Dhar, on repair of roads and renovation of meeting halls

Rajasthan

- Rs 20 lakh released to six districts as unemployment allowance remained unutilised
- Little evidence found to back the state government's claim of generation of 999 lakh mandays at an average of 91 days per household
- Payment delayed for one to 209 days without compensation
- The proportionate increase in expenditure during the last quarter of 2006-07 indicates that advances given to panchayat were treated as final expenditure
- In sample gram panchayats in Udaipur district, payments were made to labourers without measuring works

Uttar Pradesh

- In four of the six districts covered by the audit, 40,587 households demanding employment were neither provided work nor given unemployment allowance
- In five of the six districts, the funds released were short by Rs 13.26 crore

Tamil Nadu

- Unemployment allowance was not paid in any of the villages on the ground that such contingency did not arise. However, the fact could not be verified; records were improperly maintained
- Measurement books for projects were not maintained in any of the sample villages

Karnataka

- Payments of wages, to the tune of Rs 62.04 lakh, delayed by three-four months. However, no compensation paid
- A road project worth Rs 8.75 lakh taken up in Gulbarga taluk without technical sanction

Kerala

- Cases of muster rolls not carrying job card numbers of households, work number, signature of concerned officers etc

- In three audited projects, excess payment of Rs 2.25 lakh due to application of wrong per unit rates

Gujarat

- About 63 per cent of the works during the year remained incomplete
- None of the 1986 works taken up to provide irrigation facility on land owned by STs was completed
- Fraudulent payment of Rs 5,482

Tripura

- Under reporting of expenditure by Rs 12.14 lakh in one district
- Rs 9 lakh transferred to divisional forest officers, Manu, for construction of houses in violation of rules
- Rs 52.44 lakh spent on construction of motor stands, where wage payment was less than stipulated

West Bengal

- Rs 61.21 lakh from an earlier scheme (NFFWP) was spent for works under the NREGS without observing the norms for the new scheme
- Rs 38.49 lakh spent on 20 projects for execution of non-existent work
- Rs 6.13 lakh spent on social forestry projects with little to show for it
- Concluding its observations, the draft CAG audit has recommended that all funds diverted or misutilised from the scheme should be recovered from state governments, and that the Ministry of Rural Development should take effective steps to ensure "swift and immediate action" by state governments to remedy these deficiencies.

The other recommendations, to the Central Government, are:

- An interest commensurate with the delay in release of state share for the scheme
- Incentives for maintenance of records, like offering a small percentage of the total expenditure — say 0.5 per cent — for data entry in muster rolls, job cards, employment register, project register etc

- 1Appoint Employment Guarantee Assistants in each gram panchayat
- Amend the NREGA for partial reimbursement of payment of unemployment allowance by the Centre
- Explore a nationwide agreement with the Department of Posts for all NREGS payments
- Add additional categories of works and consider empowering state governments/SEGCs to add other region-specific works
- A dedicated administrative and technical set-up for successful implementation of the scheme, especially for 200 districts in Phase 1
- Amend the current pattern of funding administrative expenses as a percentage of total expenditure.

NREGS IEC - Not mere a Buzzword!

- Information – Education – Communication (IEC) means the forms of activities by which you educate & communicate with people about new schemes.

IEC – Why is it Relevant?

- IEC is particularly relevant for National Rural Employment Guarantee Scheme. Through advertisements, the important aspects that need to be communicated are:
  i. Salient features of the Act
  ii. What are the unique qualities/features of NREGS
- Before launching NREGS, it was extremely important for the district administration to spread information about the scheme. The scheme was new and it was important to distinguish it from the other ongoing rural development wage employment schemes.

IEC – Important things to be taken care of:

- IEC of a new scheme is not easy as it seems to be. It is just not that you go & read out the entire provisions of the National Rural Employment Guarantee Act & its guideline to the people. You have to do it very strategically & in a planned manner. There are some important things which we had kept in our mind while doing IEC

IEC – What is to be told?

- It is extremely important to know what is to be conveyed to the people through IEC. The District Administration mainly conveyed:
- Salient features of the scheme – It covers the various processes from the beneficiary point of view like registration, issue of job card within 15 days, demand for work, allocation of work within 15 days, payment in public place that too within 15 days, task based payment, *GroupWise task/napi (measurement) /payment system* (introduced later), social audit, importance & maintenance of Muster Roll, other transparency related issues, worksite facilities – shade in the form of tent, safe drinking water, medical kit with all relevant medicines, crèches, *aaya* (lady caretaker for small children).
- Uniqueness of the Scheme -The features which make this scheme unique from other existing rural development wage employment schemes –
- The people were informed of their entitlements and the consequences of violating the Act for the administration. They were told that it has now become their right to get–
  - o 100 days of employment
  - o Registration within 15 days
  - o Job card within 15 days
  - o Employment within 15 days of application, if not given, entitled to get unemployment allowance
  - o Payment within 15 days, if delayed entitled to get interest
- How big the scheme is? – The District administration explained the scope of the scheme to the Panchayati Raj Institutions & the village people during Gram Sabha/ Ward Sabha/*Ratri Choupal*(Village gathering held in the evening) by giving an example:
- Average no. of rural households in a GP = 1000
- Total no. of man days that can be generated in a year in a GP (Assuming all families work for 100 days) = 1000 * 100 = 1,00,000

- Total funds that can be used in a GP in one year as labor component (the minimum wage per man day being Rs 73) =1,00,000*(Rs) 73 = Rs 73 lakh
- Total funds that can be used in a GP in one year as material component (considering the labour : material = 60:40) = 2/3 * Rs 73 lakh = Rs 48 lakh
- Total funds that can be used in one GP in one year (labour + material) = Rs 73 lakh+ Rs 48 lakh = Rs 1 crore 21 lakh
- The same calculation when done in respect of the district - Total no. of rural families in Jalore district = 3 lakh (in reality it is 2.94 lac, but for the shake of easy calculation, take it to be 3 lacs)
- Total no. of man days that can be generated in a year (assuming all families work for 100 days) = 3 lacs X 100 = 300 lacs
- Total funds that can be used in the district in one year as labor component (the minimum wage per man day being Rs 73) = 300 lacs X Rs 73 = Rs 219 crore
- Total funds that can be used in the district in one year as material component (considering the labor : material = 60:40) = 2/3 X Rs 219 crore = Rs 140 crore
- Total funds that can be used in the district in one year (labor + material) (Maximum potential) = Rs 219 crore+ Rs 140 crore = Rs 359 crore

THREE THINGS

- Three things are extremely important to utilize maximum funds - & this was communicated to the villagers during IEC.
- The maximum funds that can be used under NREGS is a function of A, B & C.
- Mathematically, Maximum funds that can be used under NREGS = A X B X C Where, A = total no. of households opting for work, B = average no. of man days per family, C = average wage rate
- So, maximum funds can be utilized only if A, B & C are maximized, i. e. to say

- Firstly, maximum no. of households should come to work under this scheme.
- Secondly, maximum no. of average man days per family that should be generated
- Thirdly, the average wage per man day should be as high as possible (more closer to Rs 73)
- For implementation & supervision of the groupwise task/*napi*/payment system, 3500 mates were trained. Out of that 1400 were ladies.
- The result of the above groupwise task/*napi*/payment system was very good -
- The average wage of the district which was Rs 45 in May increased ÀÛÆÜ Rs 8 in June - July ÀÛÆÜ Rs 54 in AugustÀÛÆÜRs 65 in Sep-Oct, finally raised to Rs 69 in Nov-Dec (out of Rs 73) – Most of the laborers now getting Rs 73/-

TYPES OF WORK THAT CAN BE TAKEN UNDER NREGS

- The stakeholders were informed of the relevance and context of NREGA and the different works that can be taken up for the rural development of Jalore. The average rainfall of the district being 425 mm & there is a need to undertake more water & soil conservation works. Moreover, Jalore being a desert district, the settlements are scattered settlement in *dhanis3* & there is a need for gravel roads. The marginalized section namely, SC/ST/BPL/IAY beneficiaries got attracted to NREGS when they came to know that individual land development work can also be taken. The beneficiaries believed that the scheme would not only would provide employment but also change the fate of their rural development.

CHOICE IS WITH THE PEOPLE

- The stakeholders were told that in NREGS, the choices & decision making are with the people not with the officials. By this, what we mean is – earlier the administration used to decide when to give work, how many man days a household can generate in a year & how many members of a household can work in a particular fortnight. But, in this scheme the decision making power is with the people. During the IEC campaign the highlighted issues were:

- *15 din mein job card, 15 din mein kaam aur 15 din mein daam* – we highlighted 15 day part
  - o the unemployment allowance provision
  - o the interest provision in case of delayed payment
- Better worksite facilities – We promised & provided tents for shade, safe drinking water, good medical facilities, crèches & aaya for the kids. Especially, the crèche & aaya part became popular in Jalore as we knew that 80% of our workforce was going to be mother/ladies. We were sensitive enough to realize that a mother cannot work efficiently & happily seeing her child suffering & crying on the floor under the hot sun.

IEC FOR WHOM ?

- The various stakeholders for IEC are –
  - i. people at large
  - ii. Ward Panch
  - iii. Sarpanches
  - iv. PS4 member / ZP member
  - v. *Pradhan/Zilla Pramukh7*
  - vi. MP/MLA
  - vii. Press/media
  - viii. Mate
  - ix. *Gram Sevak/Rojgar Gram Sahayak9*
  - xi. *Patwari*
  - xii. Agriculture Supervisor
  - xiii. ANMs/AWWs/other VLWs
  - xiv. PO NREGS/BDO/AEn/JEn
  - xiv. DLOs/BLOs
  - xv. SDMs/TDRs
  - xvi. CEO & other ZP officials
  - xvii. Core group
- EC Strategy for Stakeholders –

- Strong emphasis was given in Jalore to involve each of the stake holders because each has a definite role to play. Hence, each had to be sensitized with the real philosophy of NREGS & with the cause of the rural poor.
- The administration wanted to convey the important role these stakeholders can play in its effective implementation & also that without their active support it was impossible to start the scheme. We wanted each of our stake holders to feel important & proud in being a part of NREGS campaign so that they take part actively in its implementation.

STAKEHOLDERS – THEIR INFLUENCES

- Each of the stakeholders has its own influences, catchment area and hence, her/his fan followings. Now, suppose any of the stake holder's notions are not cleared, then her/his followers would not join NREGS campaign & the result would be that they would start doing anti campaigning of the scheme, which would prove to be fatal in its successful implementation. On the contrary, we wanted each of the stakeholders to be the advocates of our NREGS, specially the elected representatives, the PRIs & the media personnel. We wanted them to communicate the people at large about the beauty of the scheme.
- Training /Workshops – separately / grouping
- The administration organized most of the IEC training/ workshop separately for each of the stakeholders and in few cases in a group of selected stakeholders.
- Why?
- Each of the stakeholders has a different but important role to play. You have to make each of them feel important & indispensable. For this you have to address them separately because it is a human tendency for one stakeholder to feel jealous when the other stakeholders are also given equal importance. The concept of making them feel important & indispensable would have been diluted if they are addressed together.
- Moreover, there were lot of notions among the stakeholders

that some of them would gain & some would loose (not in monetary terms, but in terms of importance & respect). Now these notions had to be cleared & it can be cleared more easily if they are addressed separately.

NOTIONS – TO BE CLEARED

- In order to clear the wrong notions the district administration had planned two kinds of training workshops:
  i. Separate workshop for some stakeholders and
  ii. Workshop for a group of stakeholders
- Workshop of MP/MLA/ZP/PRADHAN – Earlier in SGRY, the financial control was jointly with the Zilla Pramukh and CEO ZP at ZP level and Pradhan & the BDO at the PS level. Now in NREGS, it is jointly with the Collector and CEO ZP at district level and PO NREGS & BDO at the PS level. We knew there would be a notion among Zilla Pramukh/Pradhan that they would loose this control. And as expected it was reflected in our joint workshop of MP/MLA/ZP/Pradhan. This was immediately countered by one of the MLAs that even in MLALAD, the financial control is with the Collector/BDO, so there should not be any problem.
- Workshop of ZP/PS members – Earlier in SGRY, because of the provision of SGRY 20% / SGRY 30% component, ZP/PS members used to recommend works like MPs/ MLAs in their jurisdiction & they used to take pride in it. Now, in NREGS this informal facility has been taken away as all the works would be selected by gram sabha. We knew there would be a notion among the ZP/PS members about loosing this privilege. Earlier in SGRY, the funds used to be limited to few lakhs (say on an average Rs 4 lac per GP). In the gram sabha proposals used to come in bulk (say around of 35-40 lacs). Now at the time of execution, only few works used to be taken up & moreover, the Sarpanches to some extent used to enjoy this discretion informally. This led to a situation where people started thinking, "gram *sabha men jaane ka koi faayda nahee hai1*". And this led to poor attendance of Gram Sabha.

- It is interesting to note that during one of the workshop one of the PS member got stuck to the notion of loosing the power of selection of work. Legacy mindset of existing administrative functionaries oriented to allocation based programme and a hierarical based relationship in PRI act as a deterrent to openly accept the demand and rights based NREGA scheme.

ROLES OF THE STAKEHOLDERS – TO BE UNDERSTOOD

ROLE OF ELECTED REPRESENTATIVES & THE PRIs

- The role of elected representatives & the PRIs is extremely important as far as successful implementation of NREGS and its IEC is concerned. They are more popular among the masses and people listen to them. They can influence them more easily. Moreover, the full potential of NREGA cannot be harnessed if it is implemented in a typical bureaucratic manner.
- Inclusion and active involvement of people and their elective representatives are the agents for ensuring success. The greatest strength which has led to success achieved so far is that the scheme has been under the leadership of elected representatives & the PRIs.

ROLE OF PRESS / MEDIA PERSONNEL

- The media is also an extremely important stake holder. Newspaper coverage has a direct impact on the minds of the people. Through media one can reach directly to the distant rural people. A separate workshop was organised for media & they were also sensitized to the real philosophy & scope of the scheme & how it can change the fate of the people at large & ultimately the fate of rural development. Since, we had very little time, barely a month for our preparation, making all arrangements as per the provision of the guidelines of NREGS & then to implement such a big & voluminous scheme, some managerial problems were bound to take place in the initial days of implementation. The media was informed of the relevance of the Scheme and of the need to report accurately since bad publicity in the initial 1 days of implementation can be damaging. The media cooperated with the district administration completely. They overlooked the minor mistakes in the initial days of NREGS implementation; and highlighted the success stories & the benefits of the scheme on a regular basis. This became one of the most important tools of Jalore's IEC.

ROLE OF GRAM SEVAK

- Many would argue that when there is provision to keep a private person, a *Rojgar Gram Sahayak* in every GP exclusively for NREGS, then why Gram Sevak's role is so important. The role of gram sevak is extremely important because he is the secretary to the GP and is usually well known in the village He is the key functionary for IEC, implementation & supervision. She/He is loaded with so many ongoing schemes so, she/he needs to be pepped up to handle such a big scheme. Moreover, it is he who will have to maintain the accounts & supervise the scheme. The *Rojgar gram sahayak* is there to assist her/him.

ROLE OF PATWARI

- Many would wonder what the role of a *patwari* is here. The two key functionaries which are extremely important in a GP are Gram Sevak & *Patwari*. With the new and significant role of Gram Sewak, the *Patwari* might feel insecure.
- Considering the fact that most of our rural households are farmers & land based & they need the help of patwari on a regular basis, so she/he is in a very crucial position to influence them. Hence, the district administration decided to involve the Patwaris in NREGS from day one & gave then specific, important & much required role. The role involved:–
  - i. IEC
  - ii. Feedback mechanism – with the growing importance of the Gram Sevak, there are chances of misuse of her/his authority. And for this you have to have an independent source of feedback.

iii. Patwari play an important role while sanctioning the works of individual beneficiaries namely that of the SCs, STs, BPLs & the IAY beneficiaries, especially with regards to the land development works, report – *Khasra/ Zamabandi/Khatedari* details.

iv. We have assigned them along with the Agriculture supervisor a role of "*Gram Prabhari*". There is a strong logic to introduce the concept of Gram prabhari. Considering the length & breadth of a GP, it is practically impossible for the *Rojgar Gram sahayak* to go to all the worksites on the very first day of the fortnight (ie on 1st & 16th day of every month) to distribute MR, engage laborers & enroll them on the MR & supervise the work. For engaging & enrolling the laborers, we have trained the mates/worksite supervisors. To ensure that the MR reaches the worksite on the very first day, we call the trained mates and the *gram prabhari* a day before the first day of the fortnight (say 30th April in case of May Ist fortnight) & the RGS gives the MR to them based on the rough estimated labors to be deployed.

- Supervision of the worksite on the very first day of the fortnight by any govt official is crucial from the worksite management point of view. If on the first day, all the arrangements like availability of MR, shade, safe drinking water, crèche, aaya, medical kit etc. are all right then we don't have to worry much for the rest 14 days. Moreover, it is the first day where the labors are enrolled on the MR. For this we have introduced the concept of *gram prabhari* who visits the worksite in her/his village & supervises all the arrangements.

ROLE OF MATE

- The role of a mate is extremely important. She/he is the fulcrum of the scheme. He is the one who is going to supervise the work on a daily basis. We have trained them to form small group of 5, give them separate task, GroupWise *napi,* record them on a *mate map pustika* on a daily basis, so that separate payment can be made to each group based on their task. This has not only proved to be a boon for efficient worksite management but also in enhancing the average wage of the district from Rs 45 in May to almost Rs 70 (out of Rs 73) in Dec-Jan by the introduction of groupwise task /*napi*/payment system.

ROLE OF SDM/TDR

- One would wonder why SDM/TDR need to be trained. There are various reasons for it –
    - i. The administration believed that "Executers should not be the sole supervisor". This has two bases. Firstly, an executer would never share some of her/his mistakes with her/his superiors(the reasons need not to be quoted) and secondly. Thus some outside agency (as a Hawk Eye) in the form of SDM/TDR/DLO/ BLO performing a supervisory role apart from the general supervision being done by the PO/BDO/Other ZP and PS officials to know the ground realities so that corrective steps can be taken on time was required.
    - ii. SDM/TDR has more credibility in the field than any other block level officers. In order to break any kind of deadlock, they are the most appropriate agency. In fact, in the initial 3-4 fortnights, when the average wage was low as a result of strict enforcement of the task based payment with an aim to erode the famine mentality, there were few occasions when laborers tried to create undue pressure on the NREGS administration by coming to the PS HQs in large chunks. That time SDMs/TDRs were actively involved to convince and pacify them.
    - iii. SDM has magisterial power in the form of sections of CrPC namely, section 107, 108, 109, 110, 122, 133, 144, 145 (TDR also has magisterial powers in some of the above sections like section 107 & 109 etc).Moreover, the TDR has power of eviction of encroachments under section 91,LR Act, Rajasthan. We knew these powers would act as a deterrent in breaking deadlocks, countering nuisance makers, during execution of NREGS.In fact we took their help specially in widening

of gravel roads (more than half the roads were encroached)

Role of ZP officials/PO/BDO/AE/JE

- The role of ZP officials/PO/BDO/AE/Jen are of immense importance (needless to say) as they are the main executers and they were trained effectively. Thus, we have just seen how important all the above stakeholders are. Therefore, each of them needs effective training.

Reading the Act

- All the officials including the training of trainers were advised to read the Act/Guideline carefully. This is the first important step of NREGS IEC. Unless one does it she/he can not understand the spirit of NREGS. And unless we understand the spirit, we cannot implement it successfully. The act/guidelines are so beautifully drafted and it has so many enabling provisions that if we ensure their implementation, the scheme is bound to succeed.

Role of Core Group

- Before starting IEC, it is important for the core group to understand that this is one scheme which different from other wage employment rural development schemes. Hence, the role of core group is extremely important. In fact, they are the most responsible working group for carrying out various IEC activities. The success of IEC lies in the commitment of the core group/training of trainers..

FORMS OF IEC/TRAINING

- The various forms that were used for IEC / Training in Jalore –
    - o Training of trainers
    - o Training/Workshops of each stakeholder
    - o Ward Sabha/Gram Sabha
    - o *Ratri Chaupals/Kala Jathha*
    - o Advertisements
    - o Pamphlets/ leaflets/booklets
    - o Hoardings/ Banners/Posters

- o Mouth publicity
- o Quizzing/Slogan writing on walls
- o IEC thru PRIs and Elected Representatives

IEC - AT WORKSITE

- Worksite IEC is extremely important to target the most important stakeholders i.e. the laborers. We had designed a small questionnaire/quiz & the district officials would quiz labourers during their inspection. By this, the real philosophy of NREGS was communicated to the heart of the most important stakeholder i.e., the laborers and their families (more than 1.3 lakh families).

GRAND LAUNCHING OF THE SCHEME

- By organizing a grand launching of the scheme, we mean engaging maximum labor in the first fortnight and opening of works in most of the GP/villages. This is very important part of an IEC strategy because if we do it then we are able to reach to maximum number of people in the first fortnight itself so that they become the advocates of NREGS for others. It is extremely important to note that we should ensure almost everything what we promise them during IEC on the very first day of NREGS implementation.
- It is also important to note that the first day of NREGS work should start with a mega function at the district HQ representing all the stakeholders so that the scheme gets due publicity.
- NREGS is a big, important & unique scheme & it can provide enormous employment opportunities for the rural poor and can change the face of rural development if it is implemented in its spirit. If we treat & try to implement it as yet another scheme, it is bound to be not as effective. So, effective IEC & training of all the stakeholders is of immense importance. It is important that each of the stakeholders should start, own the scheme & finally become the advocate of NREGS. Then the scheme is bound to succeed.

LOCALISED IMPLEMENTATION IN GULBARGA DISTRICT OF KARNATAKA

Following the Enactment of the National Rural Employment Guarantee Act (NREGA) 2005, the ambitious *National Rural Employment Guarantee Scheme (NREGS)* has been implemented in selected 200 districts of the country. This was later extended to 130 more districts during the year 2007-08. The main objective of the scheme is '*to provide for the enhancement of livelihood security of the households in rural areas of the country by providing at least one hundred days of guaranteed wage employment in every financial year to every household whose adult members volunteer to do unskilled manual work*'. Unlike the hitherto prominent poverty alleviation and rural development schemes, this Act ensures the right to work as a statutory right guaranteed and protected by law. The passing of the Act in 2005 signifies a paradigm shift in the strategies of the rural development.

This present paper examines the implementation issues and the immediate impact of the scheme on rural population. Gulbarga district of Karnataka state is taken as a case study. The implementation issues are important because this scheme represents a deviation from all the previous ones in many ways. The present study examines the impact of NREGS on poverty alleviation, creation of durable community assets, agricultural wage level, distress migration and women empowerment.

This scheme is different from all other such schemes that have been implemented in the country so far. A few non-negotiable features of this scheme gives a hope that this could be implemented plugging the loopholes for leakage of government money. This is a demand based programme where there is no limitation of the funds for the implementation. Any individual from the rural household can register under this scheme irrespective of the economic status of the family. Participatory planning and decentralised implementation are the specialities of the scheme. It is mandatory to implement at least 50 per cent of the works by the Grama Panchayat (the units of local self government at the village).

There are certain inbuilt safeguards in the scheme to ensure that the money is spent on labour oriented works and it reaches the targeted beneficiaries. Firstly, the contractors are banned in the implementation of the programme. Secondly, it is mandatory to spend at least 60 per cent of the funds for the payment to the labourers. Thirdly, Priority must be given to labour intensive projects like watershed development, social forestry, wasteland reclamation etc. Finally, payment of wages to the workers is to be made through accounts opened in the name of labourers so as to prevent the exploitation of middlemen and to cultivate saving habit in people.

IMPLEMENTATION OF THE PROGRAMME

Being a demand driven scheme, the basic idea is that the labourers who are willing to do manual work are to be registered with the registration officer. Whenever, they require work, they should approach the authorities and formally place a requisition for work. The registration officer in the state is Secretary of the Grama Panchayat (GP). The GP will issue a job-card to each family which will entitle them to demand work as per their convenience. The job-cards are issued within 5 days of registration. Any labourer with a job card can ask for work and it should be provided to them within 15 days failing in which they are eligible for getting unemployment allowance. The labourers have to be paid as per the prevailing rate of minimum wages in the state. The minimum wages in the state is Rs 74 per day. The families registered under the scheme amount to more than 30 million in all over the country. The corresponding figure for the district is 200688 families out of a total of 388394 families in the rural areas of the district.

Participatory and Decentralised Planning for the Scheme

As a beginning, the task of identification of the potential of the village with the developmental requirement and the resources available were carried out. This was done as collective effort of various stakeholders and the community. A meeting of all the villages were carried out for this purpose. The villagers identified the requirements of the village and prioritised these demands. They were helped by one NGO in these tasks. Their responsibility was to ensure community participation in the planning process. Along side, various line departments also identified the works related to their departments. All these suggestions were combined and the perspective plan for the five years was formed. The works were prioritised and those that are expected to be carried out for an year were taken out separately. Detailed estimates were prepared for these works. This is known as the shelf of projects. These plans were approved by the elected body before implementing.

Administrative Mechanism

For the purpose of implementation of the scheme, the Gram Panchayats2 are designated as the primary implementing agencies. The Executive Officer of the Taluka Panchayat (Intermediary Panchayat) is designated as the Programme Officer (PO) for NREGS. The Chief Executive Officer of the Zilla Panchayat is designated as the District Programme Coordinator. There are five implementing agencies in the district. Department of Watershed Development and Social Forestry are the implementing agencies in the district other than the three tiers of the Panchayat Raj system. Technical support for the implementation is provided by the Panchayat Raj Engineering Division which has one Junior Engineer for a cluster of three to four Grama Panchayats.

Fund-flow

The fund for NREGS is allocated at the ratio of 90:10 by centre and state respectively unlike other programmes where the ratio is 75:25. The Central government releases the money to the districts directly who in turn releases it to the sub-district level to be used for various works. The payment for the labourers under all works is made by the Grama Panchayat irrespective of the implementing agencies.

PAYMENT AND BANK ACCOUNTS

It is mandatory to make payment under NREGS only through accounts. This is followed very strictly in the district. This is very much helpful in ensuring that the payment is reaching the real beneficiaries as no middle men come into the picture. However, such a step does not come without its own share of problems. The major issue was to find out banking institutions at the door steps of the workers. Penetration of banking institutions and the banking habits are not encouraging in the rural areas. Thus, a major share of the accounts was opened by the Post offices. Once the scheme was six months old, post offices turned out to be the biggest bottleneck for the implementation of the programme in many places as they were not able to cope up with the manifold increase in their work. The increased in workload without any capacity addition resulted in delay in making the payments to the labourers. Finally, most of the accounts were shifted to the banks who agreed to cope up with the extra workload by working more every day. The first impressions from the field are that the people have accepted this system of payment as there is no scope for middle men in the scheme of things. This is slowly inculcating a habit of savings in the minds of the rural population which was hitherto unheard of. All the accounts opened were joint accounts in the names of the women of the household also. This is one step towards the gender sensitivity and women empowerment.

NREGA AND GENDER

NREGA is a highly gender sensitive scheme. It is mandatory that at least one third of the workers should be women. The share of women at the national level is 40%. The share of person-days worked by the women in Gulbarga district is 49% which is a little more than their share in the population. It is again necessary to provide various facilities at the worksite like drinking water and baby sitters. The provision of baby sitters will free the women of all the worries of tacking care of their little kids. This provision is women friendly in another way that this will spare the elder siblings from rearing the younger ones. Thus the scheme promotes the education of girl child also. Women are more attracted towards the scheme because the wage level for women labourers are less than that of the male counterparts in the market. While a male labourer gets Rs 100 per day on an average during harvest seasons and Rs 70-80 during the lean season, a women labourer gets about Rs 50 during harvest season and Rs 30-40 during lean season.

It is undisputed that the scheme has the potential to mobilise women in large numbers and groups (which was earlier difficult). This presents an opportunity to the Government to form productive self help groups among them and provide job training. Thus, the ideal progression from the unskilled labour to the skilled labour through the convergence of the entire scheme should materialise as an offshoot of the NREGA. This is true in the case of the men also. Such social change and upward mobility is the final aim of any poverty alleviation schemes.

Experiences from the Field

The programme is being implemented for the last one year and the figures by the end of March show that all the families and individuals who demanded work have been provided with the work. NREGA has so far employed 148,735 people from 77,594 households in the district. This has generated 28,77,000 person-days by taking up 3537 works. The expenditure made for the payment of the labourers is 62.01%.

The scheme has a positive impact on the household income level. This is mainly because of three reasons. Firstly, NREGS provide 100 days of guaranteed job to each household who are in need of manual unskilled work in rural areas. Considering with the daily wage of Rs. 69 paid under the scheme, each family is ensured about additional Rs 6900/ per year. Secondly, women labourers have taken advantage of the scheme thereby increasing the family income as they are paid lesser wages elsewhere. Thirdly, NREGS has ensured continued job to rural household during the lean season. The impact of the scheme on consumption, health expenditure and saving habit is visible. A majority of the beneficiaries reported increase in their consumption, health expenditure and saving. Under the scheme so far more than 0.65 million accounts have been opened in the district. More than one lakh accounts are opened in the name of the beneficiaries in the post offices. This had started to have some impact on inculcating banking and saving habits among the people who were hitherto untouched by such habits. Some of the beneficiaries reported that about 50per cent of the income earned under the scheme is either saved at home or at banks. On the other hand, it has to be noted that most of the households still withdraw the whole amount from the bank accounts immediately after the amount is credited.

Although it is too early to surface the impact of the scheme on agricultural wages, the filed surveys show that on an average wage rates have started increasing in the district. This has resulted in shortages of labourers for other types of works. Simple theory of demand and supply states whenever there is shortage of supply of labourers demand being constant, agricultural wages are bound to increase. This has been very well evidenced through the interviews with beneficiaries, farmers, engineers and contractors. The uptrend in wage level will increase cost of cultivation. The non availability of labourers will negatively affect the agricultural productions. It may ultimately lead to change in the cropping patterns. Preference will be given to those commercial crops which require manual labourers in lesser number.

Another social implication of this trend will be rift and antagonism between labourers and farmers and the possibility of emerging class conflict among the landlords and labourers. Another objective of the scheme is to analyse the impact of NREGS on the migration of rural people. People from the district migrate to other cities like Bombay, Pune, Bangalore and Hyderabad in search of job. The status of migration is not well documented in the district. Most of the jobs created are in the local areas and this has a positive impact on preventing distress migration. Though the survey does not give any conclusive proof, still it is observed that the implementation of the scheme has some positive impact on migration. A word of caution has to be made at this point, that these observations cannot be generalised as it is too early to make conclusions about the scheme without the completion of the lean season.

Like other projects the NREGS has been successful in creating sustainable assets in the district. The major thrust areas of the NREGS are water conservation, social forestry and reclamation of wasteland. These projects not only help in creation of jobs and assets but also increase the efficiency and productivity of the land in the long run. For instance, watershed development projects help in increasing in the water table of the area that ultimately results in increased availability of water for both drinking and irrigation. Consequently, more areas can be brought under cultivation and existing areas can be productively used. Similarly, social forestry programme leads to the afforestation of lands which is the need of the hour in the dry areas like Gulbarga. Two such case studies have been prepared along with this paper. Monitoring and transparency is the major thrust of NREGS. It is necessary that social audit to be conducted where all the documents regarding the scheme especially the muster rolls are made available to the public for inspection. They have the right to question the correctness of the muster rolls. The social audit for the first year in Gulbarga is scheduled to be held during the next month. The details of the muster roll are planning to be put in the public domain. Another significant feature of the scheme is the emphasis on capacity building as this is a paradigm shift in the rural development and poverty reduction activities. Thus training and IEC activities form an important part of the project. We have also attempted convergence with other schemes along with NREGA. The example is combining of the adult literacy programmes at the worksites. Many of the workers are illiterate and hence are the target group for the adult literacy activities. The objective of this initiative is to replace the thumb impressions with signatures in one month. Another inititative being attempted is to carry out primary health check up for the workers in the worksite itself.

CONCLUSIONS

The above discussion in this paper leads to certain conclusions. The study has found positive impact of the scheme on these variables. The study reaches the following conclusions. This scheme is successful in creating an impression in the minds of people that it would help in minimising the pilferages and ensure the benefits of government programmes reach the real beneficiaries. The scheme has an impact in raising the standards of living and the agricultural wage level in the villages. It is leading to the creation of durable community assets. More importantly, the payment to the labourers is done through the accounts in banks and post offices. This had laid the foundation for inculcating the savings habit in the minds of people. If implemented properly with revision of minimum wage from time to time, the distress migration from rural areas especially during the off season can be checked. Finally, the scheme has the potential to change the rural edifice of the district and can act as a model rural development scheme. The authors put a word of caution that all these are first impressions of a scheme that will be there for at least five years.

SUCCESS STORIES

Case 1: - Earthen Drain in Saidapur Village

This is a case where the selection and implementation of the work has been successful in having an impact on the productivity of the village in addition to creation of opportunities for work to the people. The authors visited the site of the work in Saidapur village in Jewargi Taluka in Gulbarga district. There is an irrigation tank in the village to provide irrigation facilities to 500 hectares of land. However, on passage of time, another 200 hectares of land in the downstream of the tank became water logged due to the seepage water from the tank. The small canal leading from the tank also was of no use because of the small size and getting silted. The Grama Panchayat did not have any funds at their disposal for taking up cleaning de-silting and widening of the existing small drain. The NREGS was the opportunity the villagers have been waiting for ages and they did not want it to go unutilised. The work of an earthen drain was taken up leading to reclaiming of 200 hectares of land by two seasons. The 200 hectares of land brought under cultivation will add to the total productivity of the village. The conservative estimate for the agricultural income puts the revenue at Rs. 5000/ a hectare of dry land. This leads to the conclusion that the investment of Rs.4,80,000 (approx) had ensured that the income of the village. This kind of works serves the exact purpose of NREGS.

Case 2: - Renovation of Traditional Water body in Mashal Village

Mashal village is situated on the North western side of the taluka bordering Maharashtra state and is the head quarter of the Gram Pachayat. The area being covered by black cotton soil and is under-laid by boulder trap/weathered trap. Due to over exploitation of the ground water for agriculture and allied purposes and scanty rainfall in the last five years, drastic lowering of water table was noticed in the village. The village faced a very acute water crisis due to these reasons. The bore-wells drilled in the village under the Calamity Relief Fund every year produced very less amount of water. This has been a problematic village always for the administration. Arrangements for the water supply through the tankers had to be made from the month of January to June. The average cost for the tanker water supply for the village per year worked out to be Rs 1,20,000. In addition about Rs. 1,50,000 used to be spent on drilling of bore-wells for fining out a permanent solution to the water scarcity problems. Thus, the village had to spend around Rs 2,70,000 per year for the last three years. (This works out to be Rs. 8,10,000). National Rural Employment Guarantee Scheme was introduced in the district last year. The villagers were very fast to realise the potential the scheme offer to solve their problems related to the water scarcity. The villagers' meeting held for the purpose of planning for the scheme, the suggestion came from the villagers to take up de-silting and renovation of an existing tank in the village. This suggestion came from the realisation by the villagers that the only solution to their water problem is to take measures to improve the ground water situation of the village. The suggestion was accepted in the meeting and the work was taken up.

The work included de-silting and deepening of the existing tank along with the construction of a 3 KM long earthen drain an inlet for collecting the rain water during the rainy season. The work was constructed as per the provisions of the scheme. The estimate cost for the work is Rs 8,75,000. The work is under progress and an amount of Rs. 6,84,000 is already spent. As the luck was on the side of the villagers, there were untimely rains in the month of December and the tank got filled up. This resulted in the recharge of the ground water in the village. The bore-wells catering to the drinking water for the village got filled up and are working properly. There is no demand for the supply of the water through the tankers in the village. Recently a bore-well was drilled in a nearby hamlet near the tank which produced a yield of 8172 Litres per Hour. There were a few wells catering to the irrigation purpose in the village. These were also filled up bringing more land under irrigation thereby increasing the economic production of the village.

This success story has become an eye-opener for the villagers. Now they know the benefits of taking up such schemes in the villages. The people have demanded taking up more such works in the village which are being taken up shortly.

PAPER ON IMPLEMENTATION OF NREGA IN PAKUR :INNOVATIONS & INTERVENTIONS

About Pakur: Pakur, a small tribal district of Jharkhand, with a total population of 7.01 lakhs and a poor literacy rate of only 30.6%, lies on the extreme northeastern corner of Jharkhand and shares its boundary with Birbhum and Murshidabad districts of West Bengal and Dumka and Sahebganj districts of Jharkhand with 6 blocks and 128 Panchayats and 1180 villages, the district was poor, with critical gaps in infrastructure, with sizeable migration of labour to Bengal and Assam and was living in obscurity.

National Rural Employment Guarantee Act (NREGA) was launched in 200 districts of the country on 2nd feb'2006. Pakur was one of these districts and since then NREGA is being implemented as not just an Employment Guarantee Act but as a revolution & a movement to change the face of rural Pakur. The Act provides a guarantee of at least 100 days of wage employment to every rural household on demand. The worker has choice regarding timing to demand employment. If no work is given within 15 days of demand, then unemployment allowance is to be given. The Act aims at eradicating extreme poverty through productive asset creation. Moreover, it creates a paradigm shift in the model of development. Till now limited and decided funds would flow to the district and downwards to blocks and Panchayats with the amount being dovetailed to the Panchayats ultimately was miniscule.

NREGA changes this to a bottom up approach. Now with NREGA, the Panchayats can get asset creation and employment generation done to their heart's content as this is a demand driven program. "Ask and you shall receive" has become the new mantra. People, for the first time, have the power in their hands to change their destiny and the destiny and face of their village. This paper attempts to present to its readers the model of implementation of NREGA in Pakur and how this unknown small tribal district came on the national map of successful implementation of NREGA and has been adopted as a model for implementation of NREGA by Ministry of Rural Development, Govt. of India and by NIRD Hyderabad.

WHY NREGA

Before we move on to how NREGA was implemented in Pakur, it is important that we dwell on why NREGA is being given such a huge importance and how it is different from the other schemes of Rural Development so far.

The potential developmental benefits of Employment Guarantee Act are :

- Employment Guarantee Act helps to protect rural households from poverty and hunger;
- It enables most poor households in rural India to cross the poverty line;
- It leads to a dramatic reduction of rural-urban migration. If work is available in the village, many families will stay in place instead of heading for the cities;
- Guaranteed employment is a major source of empowerment for women and is an opportunity to create useful assets in rural areas;
- Guaranteed employment is likely to change power equations in the rural society, and to foster a more equitable social order;
- The right to work brings economic security in peoples lives especially women;
- With the NREGA, work becomes a right. Such a guarantee of employment acts as a shield for the rural poor and the landless.

Most importantly the Act gives power and responsibility to the panchayat institutions.

The Act authorises the gram sabha to recommend works to be taken up, to monitor and supervise these works, and to conduct social audits of the implementation.

Hence, NREGA is not just about creating employment, but also about developing the social infrastructure. The assets created under the Act will be a step towards growth through higher investment in rural infrastructure. The potential for labour-intensive public works in the field of community asset creation is massive; this includes areas such as watershed development, land regeneration, prevention of soil erosion, restoration of tanks, protection of forests and related activities and this is why NREGA becomes so critical to the development of rural India.

Component Wise Critical Issues For Implementing NREGA and Interventions Done in Pakur

For successful implementation of NREGA it is important that few critical issues are addressed carefully. Component wise the interventions/innovations done in Pakur for NREGA implementation are: -

Registration

- The Act provides that all rural families in NREGA district may apply for registration for unskilled manual work by way of an application for registration by local rural household to Gram Panchayat (written or oral). It must be kept in mind that registration has to be of a household, but the names of all its adult members willing to do unskilled manual work may be registered. Oral application must not be refused.
- At the outset, it was made very clear to the Panchayat Secretary that he should verify eligibility only in terms of local residence and adult status, and NOT on economic status as NREGA is not confined to below poverty line families. It needs to be remembered that verification has to be completed within 15 days of application for registration. For this not just the implementing agencies but the also stakeholders are needed to be made aware about the scheme and its provisions. Hence, taking the message of NREGA to the last village became absolutely crucial.
- Thus it becomes extremely critical that when we start implementing the Act, we have a huge IEC campaign to impress on the people of what NREGA offers, how it can be availed, the difference it can make and its legal accountability design.
- The first and foremost step undertaken by us was spread the information and awareness about the Act to the last person in the last household. For this various IEC initiatives were taken few of which are as follows: -

Panchayat Vikas Utsav

We divided the 128 Panchayats of the district into 26 clusters of about 4-5 Panchayats each and did convergence of various services like, disbursement of loans and assets under various schemes (like PMRY, SGSY etc.); organizing health camp with free medical check up and free distribution of medicines alongwith free blood sample sputum collection etc on the spot, distribution of scholarships and cycles to students; collection of revenue; distribution of grains under Annapurna, Antyodyaya schemes etc; collection of demand for toilets under Total Sanitation Campaign, creating awareness about Nirmal Gram and finally creating awareness about NREGA, collecting applications for Job Cards, collecting applications for demand for work etc. This way the rural population could avail of many facilities at their Panchayat level which acted as a "Rural Single Window System" and we could talk the message of NREGA to them simultaneously. Through the Panchayat Vikash Utsav, the District Administration could reach out to the people and offer them the benefits of various welfare and development schemes of the government under one umbrella thereby creating an aware civil society.

NREGA Pakhwara

- NREGA Pakhwara was observed between 6-20th November, 2006 in which District and Block level workshops were held to reiterate the critical issues of NREGA. Village level monitoring committees were constituted under NREGA for every on-going scheme.
- Application of job card received and job cards issued, demand was received and work was alloted. During the Pakhwara, copies of the Act and operational guidelines in Hindi were also circulated.

Pamphlet, Nukkad Natak, Miking, Hoarding etc.

- Pamphlets were printed and distributed in thousands in all four local languages viz. Santhali, Paharia, Hindi and Bengali. Nukkad Nataks in vernacular languages were intensively organized. Announcements were made through loudspeakers in every haat in every village. Information Boards were put up at Block and District Headquarters.

SHG Mahasammelan

- District Administration Pakur took a conscious decision that under NREGA all works below Rs. 2 lakh would be implemented through SHGs to empower them and to create ownership of the program in the villages. A massive SHG Mahasammelan was held on 29th Nov 2006. About (12000) Twelve thousand members of SHG were present.
- Hon'ble Chief Minister Govt. of Jharkhand, Hon'ble Speaker of the Jharkhand Vidhan Sabha and other eminent people felicitated the Mahasammelan to encourage people to avail this scheme. After this Mahasammelan, about 200 SHG groups were linked in NREGA for implementation.

Issue of Job Cards

- The most important issues here is that one Job Card is to be issued to a registered household with the photograph and name of each registered adult member of that household on it. Also it needs to be clearly explained to the subordinate staff that cost of Job Card including photograph is to be borne on the programme and that the job card must be issued within 15 days of receipt of application.
- It is important that field staff do not create inordinate time gap between registration and issue of Job Card, must not issue a Job Card to each individual, should not include names of minors on Job Cards, should not price the job card and most importantly should not issue Job Cards on work sites.
- Interventions done in this regard are :-

"Har Haath ko Kaam Mile Abhiyan"

- Har Haath ko Kaam Mile Abhiyan was organised between 7-11 May'07 to encourage people who had job cards to demand for work by informing them of their right to work & the provisions of guaranteed employment for 100 days. Before this, many families had job cards but were not asking for work as they were under the impression that work will be opened in the villages and they will report on their own. It was clarified through door to door surveys in NREGA they have to demand for work and only then work will be started in their village. As many as 20,000 new families demanded for work during this 5 day Abhiyan.

Rozgar Guarantee Diwas

- Each Wednesday and Thursday declared as Rozgar Guarantee Diwas and all Panchayat level officials have been directed to sit there and conduct activities. It acts as a single window place to get the labourers demand for job cards, demand for work and give job card.
- Anybody in Pakur can check all the registers kept at Gram Panchayat viz. Muster Rolls, employment provided/ wage paid to workers, work demand, work allocation, work provided and wage paid.

Training Modules

- For adequate, efficient and impairing training / capacity building, different modules of training for different categories of stake holders/ implementing agencies were developed. Brainstorming sessions, lecture modules, fields visits and hands on training, exposure visits, multi media learning modules and Audio-visuals were used to impart training to ensure better clarity and understanding. It is hugely important that implementing agencies and stake holders are all properly explained to how NREGA differ from food for work and other schemes of rural development and what is going to be their roles/responsibility at different levels.
- In the district of Pakur 6 Different Training modules have been developed for different categories of people viz. implementing agencies, stakeholders etc. These six modules are :
  - o For implementing agencies
  - o For Gram Pradhans/ Gram Sabha chairpersons
  - o For engineers at all levels
  - o For MIS data entry under NREGA
  - o For district and block level officers
  - o For SHGs who are implementing NREGA

Allocation of Employment

- In this, the most critical issue to be borne in mind is that work must be allocated within 15 days of demand. There should be no delay in allotting employment as this will create the liability of the unemployment allowance.
- It was observed during the initial months of NREGA implementation that due to the tough terrain and rocky soil in Pakur labour was hardly able to reach the productivity norms of 100 cft. of earth cutting while enables it to get minimum wage for one day i.e. 76.68 Rs. The most of the labour was getting paid Rs. 35-40 on an average and this was acting as a deterrent to more people to join NREGA as labourer. Also, it was noted that after working for 4-6 weeks, labour was "dropping out of the program" due to the low wages they were earning.

Selection of works

- All works sanctioned with physical/technical/financial details should be in public domain (notice boards/website of the district /wall painting in panchayat office).
  - o Works have to be identified and approved by Gram Sabha and the work list approved by intermediated District Panchayat should be displayed in Gram Panchayat.
  - o Asset register at GP with unique number to each work to prevent duplication.

Innovative work selection

- Contour Bunding and Gully Plugging :- It prevents soil erosion, does ground water recharge, has afforestation on a large piece of land and is a 100% labour oriented scheme. It uses the loose rocks strewn around and works like a loose boulder check dam.
- Not only does this scheme act as a three way water conservation model but also because it is 100% labour oriented and uses local material, this scheme covers all the priority area of NREGA works.

Siphon Project: Mayurkola :-

- Pakur, famous for its stone crushers, had a lot of abandoned mines which had now converted into 30-50 ft. deep water reservoirs. One particular group of abandoned mines which was actually a cluster was interconnected of mines, had turned into a 1 Km wide and 600 in broad water reservoir which had an average of 50 ft. deep water. This water was lying waste and even the nearby patches of agricultural land were barren through most parts of the year.
- It was though that if this water can be tapped for irrigational and other purpose, then it would serve as a boon for the nearby farms and lands. For this the option of motor pump was ruled out as it would have created diesel liabilities and factor of safety and protection of the motor. So, as an innovative mechanism, Siphon project was used to pump out the water from the reservoir and take it by way of PVC pipes to the nearby fields. In first phase, an area of 250 acres was given water through this and seeing the success of the project, another 32 lakhs were sanctioned with which more than 1000 acres are being irrigated now with first time vegetable cultivation in these areas.

Execution of works

- It has to be remembered that only job card holders can be and should be employed on works under NREGA.
- It was instructed from the very beginning that numbered Muster rolls should be issued for each work by Programme Officer as this acts as check on false muster rolls.
- We also started a computerised MIS to create a database of preferred works and resource requirement, registered household, job cards, payment of wages, mandays of employment provided to the registered employment seekers, fund received and expanded at different levels. Since the very initial days of NREGA, it was ensured that Muster rolls must mention Job Card numbers of workers as this acts as a check on false names and contractors and that Muster rolls should be read out on the work site during regular measurement to prevent bogus records and payment of wages below prescribed levels.

- In Pakur, the non-negotiables under the Act like adequate work site facilities for labourers like availability of first aid box, shade for workers, drinking water etc. were made available at all work sites and this was closely monitored also.

Time and motion study

- Time and motion study was undertaken to unbundle tasks and reassess rates of water and revise district schedule of rates so that the average labourer can earn minimum wage after a normal day at work.
- For fixing District Schedule of rates Time and Motion Study was conducted by independent agencies at 20 randomly selected villages under schemes sanctioned in NREGS, with labourers working in NREGS
- The objective of the study was to evaluate the efficiency and work performance of working labour in NREGA scheme and to understand about the real reason of poor performance of labour.
- The independent agency deputed at least one technical person i.e. junior engineer/soil expert/social worker at the site to monitor and facilitate the study. A team of two persons (one executive level engineer and one research officer of the program) was frequently moved to the working site for providing supervisory inputs and monitoring the implemented action. The expert team shared its opinion and observation among each other for analysis and incorporated suggestions for better output of the initiative with detailed discussions with Engineers and executing agencies and stakeholders and multiple rounds of presentations with the GIS mapping, soil condition study, labour output to 3 different slab of rates for (a) very hard soil, (b) medium soil and (c) soft soil was proposed to the State Council. We are awaiting the decision of State Council after which this shall again act as pull factor for the labour.

Monitoring

For intensive district level monitoring 26 Clusters have been formed of 128 Panchayats and 26 District level monitors have been put. Each has to monitor NREGA works going on in 4-5 panchayats allotted to him and a monthly review of their reports is done by the by Deputy Commissioner. The DLMs are senior district level Deputy Collectors and HODs. This internal monitoring by DLMs juxtaposed with external agencies during social audit strengthen the delivery systems. At least 20 schemes and 1 panchayat office to be inspected monthly in the formats which are enclosed in Annexure '1' and '2'.

Transparency

- To ensure the corruption does not creep in implementation of NREGA it is important that we establish adequate audit and evaluation mechanisms ensure widespread institution of social audit and use of findings and establish an effective grievance redressal mechanism at the village, block and district level.

Accountability

- 100% payment of wages is being done through accounts.
- 100% payment of wages through bank/ post office accounts.
- With instruction from Deputy Commissioner and facilitation from Panchayat Secretary office a campaign was started in month of February' 07 to open all accounts in bank or post office. This avoids faulty payment/ exploitation/ bogus entry in muster rolls.

Formation of Vigilance and monitoring committees

- 9 member vigilance and monitoring commitees have been formed for each scheme in all villages to supervise quality of work, to be present during attendance taking time, to check muster rolls, estimates etc from time to time.

Social Audit and Muster Roll Verification in Pakur

- Vigilant monitoring, transparency and accountability and ensure active participation of civil society and people is important for successful implementations of the Act. A massive social audit in 18 panchayats with a simultaneous 100% muster roll verification under NREGA was undertaken in Pakur between 16-22 April. Hundreds of volunteers from Pakur and elsewhere from various parts of the state and outside walked from village to village to visit NREGA worksites, verify muster rolls, and hold public meetings. The aim of the social audit was to empower people to fight corruption and defend their rights under the Act.

Why Social Audit

An innovative feature of the National Rural employment Guarantee Act is that it gives a central rule to 'social audits' as a means of continuous public vigilance (NREGA, Section 17). The basic objection of a social audit is to ensure public accountability in the implementation of projects, laws and policies.

In this perspective, a social audit is an ongoing process through which the potential beneficiaries and other stakeholders of an activity or project are involved at every stage: from the planning to the implementation, monitoring and evaluation. This process helps in ensuring that the activity or project is designed and implemented in a manner that is most suited to the prevailing (local) conditions, appropriately reflects the priorities and preferences of those affected by it, and most effectively serves public interest. Thus, social audits can be seen as a means of promoting some basic norms in public matters:

- Transparency: Complete transparency in the process of administration and decision making, with an obligation on the government to *suo moto* give people full access to all relevant information. The information about works should be displayed in the local language proforma given in Annexure B-13 at the worksite and in proforma B-14 at a prominent place in Gram Panchayat.
- Participation: An entitlement for all the affected persons (and not just their representatives) to participate in the process of decision making and validation.
- Consultation and consent: In those rare cases where options are predetermined out of necessity, the right of the affected persons to give informed consent, as a group or as individuals, as appropriate.

- Accountability: The responsibility of elected representatives and government functionaries to answer questions ad provide explanations above relevant action and inaction to concerned and affected people.
- Redressal: A set of norms through which the findings of social audits and other public investigations receive official sanction, have necessary outcomes, and are reported back to the people, along with information on action taken in response to complaints.
- The expectations we had in terms of outputs from the Social Audit exercise were mainly the following:-

AWARENESS AND MOBILISATION

A With respect to Registration and receipt of job cards under NREGA

- The people must be encouraged attend all Gram Sabhas in large numbers and be vigilant.
- The social Audit team must encouraged people to protest if either ineligible people are being registered or given job cards, or eligible ones are being denied.
- Rural labourers must be encouraged must check the authenticity of all the information that is recorded and verify all lists and registers.
- Gram Sabha should be informed that must regularly check whether the lists and registers are being updated as required.

B. Applying for work, getting work in time or receiving unemployment allowance

- The labourers working under NREGA should be clearly told that they must Insist on a written and dated receipt for work application.
- If application is refused, or correctly dated receipt not given, or neither work nor unemployment allowance given in the prescribed period, then the labourers must make complaint to the programme officer for follow up.
- The Gram Sabha should be encouraged that monthly meetings must be attended in large numbers and

grievances addressed and information checked and verified.

C. Participating in the identification of projects and sites, approval of technical estimates and issuing of work order

- The people should ensure that the projects/works/sites selected are as per their wishes and reflect their priority.
- The people must participate and ensure that the estimates are realistic, that the rates being quoted are as per local availability and that no unnecessary items of expenditure are being included.
- The people need to remain vigilant and check the final estimate and work order to ensure that they are in accordance with what was collectively decided.

D. Participation in the supervision and measurement/evaluation of work

- Gram Sabha and members of village monitoring committee specially Must periodically verify the information on the board and in the muster rolls.
- Must also periodically ensure that the work is going as per the sanction/work order; must take random samples of the material.
- Must participate in the verification and assessment exercise, and ensure that the work done conforms with what was commissioned and is of use to the people.
- 2. Generation of Demand for new job cards and demand for work
- Huge awareness, amongst the rural areas will have ripple effect and encourage more people to come.
- Create demand for and motivate people to demand for work.
- Why we did muster roll verification now
- In the last financial year 2006-07, a total of 2178 works were taken up in the district in which 1127 were completed and 1051 were on-going as on 31.3.2007. An expenditure of Rs. 28.73 Cr was done and more than forty thousand households were given employment. A total of more than

15 lakh persondays was generated. In current financial year also, in 2 months alone, more than 6 lakh persondays have been generated and more than 10 cr expenditure has been done 552 works have been completed and 1375 are going on.

- After the initial session of the workshop, Members of Social Audit team were divided into 4 sub groups. Each team was trained in separate subjects during technical session. First sub group was trained on mobilization by NIRD. 2nd group was trained on Physical verification of the work sites by technical persons.
- Senior officers of the 3rd group was trained on document and verification by the members of the NREGA watch and district senior officers and the 4th sub group was trained on the subject of preparation of Report and filing of Muster Roll consolidated sheet by Sri Balram of NREGA watch and others. After sub- group wise training programme all the members were trained once again for two hours by Deputy Commissioner, Pakur & Sri Balram NREGA watch and Members of NIRD Hyderabad.
- Deputy Commissioner, Pakur and Sri Balram and NIRD personnel's at the end of the session elaborately highlighted the provisions of NREGA.
- Following this two days of intensive training teams were dispatched by Bus to their respective Panchayat. A Master Kit was made available to the each team of their Panchayat with all relevant papers for Social Audit. Master Kit contained 300 blank form for demand for work, 100 blank form for registration Job card, a blank register, copy of NREGA operation guidelines , Five copies of book on how to verify muster rolls published by Pakur District administration and few blank papers and stamp pad were given to enable the team to taken labours statements 1000 pamphlets in four different languages spoken in the district (Bengali, Hindi, Paharia, Santhali) , Posters for IEC and banners were also given.
- Team performed social audit work in the respective Panchayat from 18th June to 21st June'07. The sub-group

of the team which worked on mobilisation . Team members asked the villagers about how many formulas have Job cards, how many persons have demand for job, work of how many days has been provided in each job card and how many day's wages have been paid. Wage payments were tallied with Muster Roll sheets and details were collected from the villagers on various aspects.

- The social audit team verified whether the work was done according to measurement book or not verified the physical status of the schemes. The social Team also checked the quality of work and utility and usefulness of the schemes. The DC Pakur monitored the social audit work of 6 panchayat during the period. On 21st June hearing (JAN SUNWWAI) of 18 panchayats was done at the panchayat level in presence of the senior officer deputed from the district head quarter. The DC Pakur herself participated in 3 public hearing. During the course of JAN SUNWWAI team leader spoken about the various features of NREGA & Mobilisation the people.
- Report of Social Audit and Muster Roll Verification in Pakur District revealed that people had huge awareness of the Act and gave demand for 834 new job cards and 1213 demand for work.
- No bogus Muster roll or kachcha muster roll have been reported, no labourer found working at two sites at the same time in two different muster rolls.
- No cash payment has been reported at any site and no machine work has been reported.
- The quality of work and selection of works and worksites has been appreciated.
- Innovative works like contour bunding, loose boulder check dam, siphon project appreciated. Also the result of NREGA pakhwara, Har haath ko kaam mile abhiyan,
- Panchayat Vikas Utsav seen in the field in terms of added awareness. No job cards where labourers have actually worked have been found blank. Job card mention the date of employment and the amount paid and also the account number. No fake signatures have been reported on any muster roll and very few discrepancies have been found.

- Though a few problems have been reported like short payment by post offices, post master fudging withdrawals like when it comes to withdrawal then they pay the labourer amount X and enter in the pass book amount X + 100 etc.
- At times job cards which should be with the labourer have been found with the village head, with the post master, with the labhuk samiti chairperson at times and because of this the tracking and entry could not be done properly and become susceptible to exploitation.

Conclusion

- NREGA in Pakur has been able to provide increased employment to rural households by creating 15 lakh persondays of work in only 3 months of this year, and create durable assets as many as around 1780 this year which are on the verge of completion.
- These durable assets strengthen rural infrastructure and livelihood resource base. NREGA has reduced distress migration in the district and the expenditure pattern is also changing with assets buying/ creation taking priority. The employment generated under the Act has the potential to transform the geography of poverty.

EXPERIENCE OF KERALA

Kerala has one of the highest unemployment rates in the country. But most of the unemployed are educated. Thus NREGA has only limited application in tackling the problem of unemployment among the poor of Kerala. Yet it has a niche ideal for about 4 to 5 lakh people who are willing to do physical labour and for whom an additional annual income of Rs.12,500/- obtained from the Employment Guarantee Scheme would be a substantial boost in income and purchasing power. Therefore right at the beginning a political decision was taken to target the eligible families, visualising NREGS as the nucleus of a concerted and convergent anti-poverty initiative.

Innovative Features

The following are the innovative features in the organization of the Employment Guarantee Programme.

1) The agriculture workers of Kerala are fairly well organized into trade unions. Therefore primacy is given for the organization of meetings of registered workers. This enables proper assessment of demand and in inculcating the workers perspective in the design of the programme - in choice of the works in preference of locations and in deciding the schedule.
2) Kerala uses trained facilitators in the workers meetings as well as in subsequent Grama Sabhas. This ensures that these fora are used effectively to convey the principles and features of NREGA to the lay citizen. These facilitators help in the conduct of these meetings in a semi-structured and orderly manner.
3) Panchayati Raj Institutions are in the central place in the planning and implementation of NREGA. They are the sole agencies responsible for this. Since Kerala has a very strong decentralization experience, Panchayati Raj Institutions have considerable capacity in the planning and implementation of local development works. They have used this capacity to full advantage in the implementation of NREGA. It is significant to note that as of now the entire implementation is in the hands of Village Panchayats.
4) A strong engineering support system has been put in place. In addition to one diploma/degree holder working on contract at the level of the Village Panchayat, there is a system of accredited engineers. Such engineers are drawn from amongst retired engineers, staff working in Engineering Colleges, Polytechnics/ ITIs, engineers working in NGOs etc. These engineers are paid for their work, at rates fixed by Government. Further, if any engineer from a government department or agency is willing to help the Village Panchayat over and above his normal work, he is also allowed to do so and is paid at 50% of the rate applicable to others.
5) Technical Sanction is given not by individual engineers, but by a Technical Committee of engineers. The Committee normally includes a government engineer, a retired

engineer and an engineer working in an academic institution. This has introduced transparency in the issue of Technical Sanction.

6) Since disputes are common regarding measurements, an appellate system has been put in place at the district level. This has facilitated speedy sorting out of disputes.

7) In order to mobilize the workers and the public and to assist the panchayat in carrying out its duties, Village Panchayats have been given the freedom to identify one public servant of their choice having the time and inclination to do social work from any government department and such persons are posted on working arrangement as NREGA co-ordinators.

8) The most radical feature of implementation of NREGA in Kerala is the central place given to Kudumbasree in the implementation of the programme. Under Kudumbasree every family below poverty line is organzied into a Neighbourhood Group (NHG) at the local level consisting of 15 to 40 families with each family being represented only by a woman. The NHGs are federated into an Area Development Society (ADS) at the level of the Ward of the Village Panchayat (a Village Panchayat Ward in Kerala has a population of around 1500 to 2000). The ADSs in a Village Panchayat are federated into a registered body called the Community Development Society (CDS). Each NHG, ADS and CDS has five volunteers carrying out different functional roles.

   The ADS has been entrusted with the task of organizing public works under NREGS. Muster Rolls and other records are maintained by the ADS, implements are provided to labourers by them and the transparency and monitoring requirements are also carried out by them. Welfare amenities to the workers are also provided by the ADS. Since ADS is an organization of the poor and is basically a woman's group, there has been greater sensitivity and community participation in the implementation process.

9) In order to promote transparency, it is mandatory that the estimates are summarized in the local idiom as understood

by ordinary people. At the beginning of every work, the nature of work, expected out turn and the likely wages are explained to the workers' groups.

10) Since Kerala has limited public land, it has been decided to take up eco-restoration works in degraded forest lands. It is significant to note that Village Panchayats would implement the programme in forest areas with the technical supervision being done by field level officials of the Forest Department representing a new kind of relationship between a Panchayat Raj Institution and a government department.

11) A conscious decision has been taken by Government in keeping with the spirit of NREG Act to limit road works to 10% of the total expenditure and to give special priority to integrated watershed development works.

12) Another unique feature of implementation of NREGS in Kerala is that there is total financial inclusion of each and every worker; that is, the wages are paid only into the individual bank accounts of workers, and no exception has been made till date.

ACHIEVEMENTS

Compared to the earlier wage employment programmes there have been significant achievements under NREGS. They are:

1. So far through a combination of transparent processes and procedures, local action and constant vigilance it can be proudly be claimed that implementation of NREGA has been totally corruption free. The factors contributing to this situation include: -
   a) A clear political decision was conveyed to the Panchayats that the scheme has to be implemented strictly according to the letter and spirit of the Act. There were several pragmatists arguing for an asset focused programme ignoring the processes and conforming to the procedures on paper, and it was argued that Kerala would lose out as the demand for unskilled labour is very limited and as the wages are much higher than the statutory minimum wages in

more than 90% of the State, it would be better to go for public works. But this opinion was firmly rejected.

b) The work is organized through the Kudumbashree system and the poor have a stake in the work right at the beginning.

c) The technocratic power to accord Technical Sanction, measure works and recommend payments has been made more spread out and accountable through the Committee system and in case of difference of opinion the appellate system.

d) A lot of social activists have been motivated to keep constant vigil as a kind of continuous concurrent social audit.

e) Special emphasis have been given to the rights of workers and they have been made fully aware of their entitlements. In a state where workers are fairly well organized this has resulted in their jealous guarding of their privileges.

f) All the payments are made only through the individual bank accounts of workers. This is the ultimate preventer of corruption.

Yet there are apprehensions that once material purchase starts, corruption would come in, in some form or the other. The state is earnestly trying to put in a system which deters corruption and the details are being worked out. Till then the focus would be on labour-intensive works.

2. Implementation of NREGA has contributed to very high levels of women empowerment, particularly in the following aspects.

   i) As the work is organized by women's groups, the gender perspective gets built in automatically.

   ii) As women are comfortable working along with their neighbors, nearly 80% of the workers have been women.

   iii) For the first time equal wages are really paid and this has boosted the earnings of women.

   iv) As the wages are paid into Bank accounts the habit of thrift which was already inculcated through the

Kudumbashree experiment has further been strengthened.

v) As the Bank deposits are increasing, the intra-household status of the woman has also been improving commensurately as she controls substantial cash resources and withdrawal can be only on her decision.

3. NREGS has given rise to a new work culture. Hitherto workers were controlled by contractors and their middlemen who knew how to extract work. When NREGS began the out-turn was very poor as the workers could not be supervised properly. But soon the workers themselves realized that they would be losing collectively and a new internal dynamics evolved with peer pressure forcing workers to put in their maximum effort. At the same time a kind of social responsibility also became evident as more capable workers became more than willing to put in extra effort to make up for those who genuinely could not do hard work beyond a point, like the women and the elderly.
4. Public works have gained respectability. Hitherto they were seen as highjacked either by a contractor or a local leader. Now the workers see it as their right. They tend to distinguish between wages provided by a contractor and wages directly given by the Panchayat. The latter is almost equated with a salary. This has motivated a large section of people who were hitherto unwilling to work into join the work force. There was an interesting instance of a penurious descendant of the erstwhile Kollengode royal family in Palakkad taking an active part in NREGS and even motivating her relatives to join on the logic that self-help and access to legally entitled emoluments from a public source is better than charity from relatives.
5. NREGS has suddenly increased purchasing power of the poor and there is visible local economic development. This is particularly true of Wayanad which was ridden with farmer suicides. The peasants have managed to get substantial relief from NREGS by getting over their inhibition in working as labourers in richer farmer's lands by moving on to the now-respectable public works.

New Initiatives

Now that a working model for operationalization of NREGA has stabilized certain new initiatives have been started. They are:

(1) A National Rural Employment Guarantee Mission has been approved and a Mission Director posted.

(2) A convergent Anti-Poverty Sub-Plan is to be prepared using the Kudumbashree network. The components of the Anti-Poverty Sub-Plan would include:

- NREGS - for wage employment
- SGSY and Kudumbashree programmes – for skill development and self employment
- SSA
- NRHMfor Human Development
- ICDS
    - o Including nutrition for children in the age group 0 – 3 and adolescent girls
- Annapoorna and Anthyodaya Anna Yojana for food security
- IGNOAPS } Social Security
- Asraya of Kudumbashree } Social Security
- Health Insurance } Social Security / Minimum needs infrastructure
- IAY } Minimum needs infrastructure
- People's Plan } Minimum needs infrastructure

The detailed methodology has been developed and firmed up in about 100 Village Panchayats whereby at the local level Neighbourhood Groups of the poor prepare micro plans focusing on individual and family needs and at the level of the ADS these are consolidated and components relating to community assets added and thereafter the plans are integrated by the CDS at the level of the Village Panchayat by bringing in elements related to human development and economic development. The plan prepared by the poor is negotiated with the Panchayat and approved.

(3) A strong natural resource management focus has been given to NREGS. One of the topmost environmentalists in the country has been recruited as a consultant and

agricultural graduates are being taken as young professionals. It has also been decided to take up a mega scheme for Bharathapuzha River rejuvenation with action plans emanating from the Village Panchayat as building blocks.

(4) A methodology is being developed to integrate NREGS and People's Plan. Village Panchayats get more than Rs.1 crore on an average under People's Plan. If intelligently dovetailed it is expected that substantial improvement in quality of assets can be attained.

(5) In order to meet the problems due to shortage of technical staff it has been decided to rope in voluntary services of reputed non-government organizations. Already in one district a firm offer has been received and in principle clearance given. The details are being worked out.

(6) Using the excellent network of Kudumbashree it has been decided in the State Employment Guarantee Council to develop a cadre of bare-foot technical volunteers from among the poor women.

(7) In order to develop the skills of the workers it has been decided to set up Labour Banks. A pilot has been launched in one Village Panchayat. The Labour Banks would be supported under People's Plan to take up other public works and even private works.

(8) It is well-nigh impossible to identify works in the plantation areas as well as in the coastal areas. It has been decided to seek the expert support from Government of India to come out with a shelf of projects which can be taken up in such geographical areas.

(9) An innovative form of training has been developed by KILA where there is a shift from the cascading model to a "ripple" model, according to which outstanding Panchayats become the master trainers and the neighbouring Panchayats formally learn from the experience of the best performers.

(10) Monitoring has been strengthened with the decision of the State Employment Guarantee Council to put in a system of State level and District level quality Monitors by

identifying persons with reputation for integrity and competence. The State level Monitors would be of two categories – outstanding individuals whose views are widely respected by society and senior Technical Experts capable of giving authoritative feed back on the quality of implementation. Further the State Employment Guarantee Council has decided to request a team consisting of eminent experts like Smt. Aruna Roy, Prof. Jean Dreze, Shri P. Sainath and Shri Nikil De to conduct an independent assessment of Kerala's performance and offer suggestions for improvement.

Though there were several teething problems it is clear that the policy focus on natural resource management and corruption-free implementation and the administrative measures introduced to operationalise the policy especially the involvement of the Kudumbasree network have resulted in a strong foundation being laid and opened up space for pro-poor innovations.

FINANCIAL INCLUSION UNDER NREGA: PAYMENT THROUGH CHEQUE

For the National Rural Employment Guarantee Act, a Job Card is the basic legal document which enables registered households to demand guaranteed employment.

Though the use of these Job Cards is an important transparency safeguard in the implementation of the Scheme, from the workers point of view, the process of maintenance of these Cards observes certain constraints:

- An illiterate worker who does not understand what is written on the Job Card, may not be able to verify entries on the number of days worked, wages being paid
- The custody of Job Card may not be with the worker
- The Job Card, when taken for updating entries is not returned on time
- The presence of ghost workers or unregistered workers on the worksite
- The Pradhan provides work to only a section of villagers who voted for him (in some cases more than 100 days).

The Cheque-book Pilot

To increase transparency and accountability in the NREGA process, the district administration is trying a simple experiment at villages, Taharpur and Niswapur, of Block Kadora.

Under the scheme, the administration has distributed *shramik* coupons, designed to look like a commercial bank's cheque book. Each cheque, with a counterfoil, has a value of Rs 100 (Minimum wages in Uttar Pradesh).

At the start of the financial year a team of district level officers, distribute the NREGA cheque books under their personal supervision. *This is a very important step to ensure the cheques reach the real beneficiaries.* The use of the cheque books can be viewed under two situations:

Situation No 1: Cash Payments

In case of villages where the NREGA beneficiary does not have a bank account or for some reason the payment is not done through the bank, the NREGA cheque book is being used in the following manner:

At the time of payment a worker submits to the Gram Rozgar Sevak, the number of coupons equal to the number of days he has worked.

Let us take the example of a labourer say Suresh. At the time of weekly payment day/ Buktaan Divas, Suresh who has worked for 5 days would give 5 cheques to the Rozgar Sevak.

The Rozgar Sevak in return would give Rs 500 to him. In case the Rozgar Sevak pays Suresh Rs 300 he would give him 3 cheques only.

This way the Rozgar Sevak would not be able to with draw the extra Rs 200 in the name of Suresh. Further, at the time of inspection the Rozgar Sevak would have to show cheque books equalling the amount of labour wages he has withdrawn from the bank.

Say if the Rozgar Sevak claims that he has paid Rs 50,000 in a village as wages from the start of the financial year he has to show 500. For verification, the coupons can be physically counted quickly within a few minutes.

Situation No 2: Payment through Banks

Though opening of bank accounts is an ideal method for the payment of wages, it does not weed away some of the practical problems in NREGA. For instance, there might be a case where the labourer is not paid for the total number of days he worked or that he is not paid in time.

At the end of each day, a worker asks the Gram Rozgar Sevak to put the NREGA seal on the counter foil. The worker keeps the counter foil and gives the cheque to the Sevak.

Let us take the example of Brijesh, at the end of each working day Brijesh would approach the Rojgar Sevak and ask him to put the NREGA seal on the counter foil. In return he would give a cheque to the Rozgar sevak who would use it to cross check / maintain his daily accounts.

If brijesh has worked 5 days, on the day of the payment Brijesh would visit his bank to check his account should have a deposit of Rs 500. In case he is paid less, say Rs. 300, he can use the counter foils with the NREGA seal as proof to confront the Rozgar Sevak and claim his balance money.

Advantages of Shramik Cheque Book

- Supplements the Job Card: Since no written work is involved, the NREGA cheque book system adds another transparency safeguard without requiring additional time from the staff.
- Personal possession: In addition to Job card which a worker usually hands to the Rozgar Sevak for entering details of work, the labourer can keep the cheque book in his custody. He gets the seal from the Rozgar sevak, on the spot at the end of the day.
- Helps illiterate labourers: Inability to read a Job Card is a major reason for the exploitation of the poor labourers. The use of NREGA cheque book requires basic numeracy skills that almost all workers possess.
- Equal opportunity to all labourers: Since all beneficiaries are a fixed number of cheques (100 in this case), it is difficult for the Rozgar Sevak to be choosy about whom to employ and whom not to employ.

- Makes inspection easy: At the time of the inspection all one has to do is to check a Shramik coupon and ask the Rozgar Sevak how much the labourer has been paid. The amount can be quickly compared with the counter foils to see if the total amount is paid or not.
- Psychological edge: Till now the labourer had been running after the Pradaan or the Rozgar Sevak for work. This has created a sense of dependency for the labourer on the Rozgar Sevak or the Pradaan. With the cheque book system the Rozgar Sevak would be asking the labourer for the cheque as he has to balance his accounts book. This balances the power equation between the two, and this sense of empowerment could easily be categorized as the strongest advantage of the cheque book.

5

THE SEEDS OF REVOLUTION THROUGH NREGA

BACKGROUND

Jalore got included for NREGS1 as a IInd phase district in the end of March, 07 with a direction to launch it on 2nd May. We barely had a month for planning, preparation, effective training & IEC, arrangement of logistics, printing of job cards, MR & other stationeries, holding Gram Sabha, preparation of annual action plan & the work estimates, registration & job card distribution, arranging basic work site facilities, mobilization & engagement of labors. This was like reproducing a baby in 3 months in stead of 9-1/2. We started our preparation with the belief "if the collector has the will, nothing is impossible." & started working almost round the clock. Finally the scheme was launched on 2nd May, 07, with around 30,000 labors on the MR2.

The month of May witnessed the average wage per man day as Rs 45, which was extremely poor considering the minimum wage being Rs 73 (which is also the maximum wage that a laborer can get in a day).This was a matter of great concern, but at the same time it was expected in the backdrop of the prevailing work culture (famine mentality) in the district. It didn't worry me much as a rough sketch was already stored in my heart to improve it.

In Rajasthan, we follow the task schedule i.e., the average wage is calculated based on the task done by the laborers in a given fortnight. There were many reasons for this low average wage. But, the most important of them was the prevailing decades old collective *napi*3/payment system, which had completely spoilt the work culture & in turn, had given birth to an extremely inefficient culture (famine mentality), where the laborers believe in working less & expecting more wages.

One year of NREGA – Are Dalits Faring Any Better Today?

The National Rural Employment Guarantee Act (NREGA, hereafter) that came into effect in February 2006 has been viewed as one of the flagship interventions of Government of India aimed at poverty reduction. During the days following its launch, it was received with an overwhelming sense of optimism, on account of its stated commitment to provide employment on demand and to provide compensation for any lapses in timely delivery of employment. Most significantly, the scheme was launched with a promised outlay of Rs. 16,419 crore for the year 2006-2007 alone and offered a golden opportunity to pro-actively reach out to poor communities affected by burgeoning agrarian crises, devastating disasters and an acute dearth of gainful livelihoods.

Given the strikingly high incidence of poverty in most habitations of the dalits, the touchstone of NREGA's success definitely lies in its ability to make a meaningful difference to the lives of millions of dalits living in difficult circumstances.

This article seeks to examine key issues relating to NREGA's reach and performance in relation to the dalits and early trends of its impact.

What Does the NREGA Promise?

- 100 days of adult employment for every rural households; 1/3rd of workers to be women
- Registration of work through the Gram Panchayat / Block Program Officer & Provision of 'Job Card'
- Allocation of work within 15 days from the date of application by the Gram Panchayat / Block Program Officer
- Payment of the statutory minimum wage applicable to agricultural workers in the State
- Payment of unemployment allowance if work is not provided within 15 days of application
- Creation of durable assets & livelihood resource base of the poor through works

Work done by Contractors is not Permissible

The Paradox of Excellence

According to a report of the Ministry of Rural Development (ref. Table 1), nearly one-fourth of the 701 million employment days generated by the National Rural Employment Guarantee Scheme in India up to March 16, 2007 were availed by scheduled castes.

Punjab, Haryana, Uttar Pradesh and Tamil Nadu accounted for the highest coverage of scheduled castes under NREGA, delivering between 55-70% of all jobs to them. On the other hand, the coverage of scheduled castes in states like Gujarat, Rajasthan and Tripura did not even match up to the existing proportion of scheduled castes in the population of the state.

Similarly, the inclusion of scheduled castes in states like Madhya Pradesh and Chhattisgarh, which ranked higher than most states in terms of the number of employment-days generated, did not significantly exceed the actual SC composition in the state's population (with provision of only 16.76% and 12.85% employment days to dalits respectively).

- Associated with Praxis – Institute for Participatory Practices and Wada Na Todo Abhiyan
- Ashok Bharati is the Founder Convenor of World Dignity Forum, Co-ordinator of NACDOR & associated with Wada na Todo Abhiyan
- National Conference of Dalit Organizations

In view of the fact the scheme doesn't differentiate between the poor and the non-poor, or between dalits and non-dalits in terms of eligibility for employment, the relative inclusion of dalits in delivery of employment can be taken as a good indicator of a state's commitment to equitable development. Given that the scheme needs to be extended with greater urgency to communities known to suffer from greater degrees of poverty, treatment of dalits at par with other population sub-groups points at the lack of a good understanding of poverty and the lack of commitment to use the scheme as an opportunity to reach out pro-actively to the poorest population sub-groups. This also points at the need for extending reservations to dalits in identification of beneficiaries, which is a constitutional right of Scheduled Castes and Scheduled Tribes. The NREGA in its current form has no such provision.

Entitlements Under NREGA – Myriad Ways Of Denial

During the National Tribunal on NREGA organized at the India Social Forum by Wada N Todo Abhiyan and PACS in November 2006, hundreds of dalit labourers recounted numerous instances of denial of their entitlements under NREGA.

For instance, Anita Devi, a landless Musahar woman from East Champaran district of Bihar mentioned how job cards were issued in her village only after people organized a dharna in September 2006. However, even after officially applying for work in September, she had not been given any work till the second week of November, making a mockery of significant provisions like 'unemployment allowance', which makes any labourer eligible for receiving unemployment allowance on a daily basis, if not provided employment within 15 days of demand. As a matter of fact, not a single labourer present at the NREGA Tribunal could recall any payment of unemployment allowance, to anyone for even a day. Various instances of irregularities in provision of employment opportunities were brought to the fore by dalit labourers at the Tribunal held at the India Social Forum.

Common grievances included (i) issue of extremely limited number of job cards, (ii) unreasonable delays in issue of cards, (iii) job cards lacking necessary records, e.g. dates of employment provision, wages paid etc., (iv) demand of bribe for issuing cards/ photographs, (v) excessive delays in employment provision despite demands being made long before, (vi) underpayment of wages, (vii) underreporting of number of days of employment provided and payment of less wages accordingly and (viii) non-payment of unemployment allowance. Significantly, none of the panchayats represented at the tribunal could recall distribution of more than fifty job cards. In many panchayats of the country, it is common practice for supervisors and engineers to deny minimum wages payable to labourers by quoting deficiencies in the quantum of work performed by the latter, which affects labourers from the dalit communities the most on account of their relatively limited ownership of land and other productive assets.

Limited Reach Vis-à-Vis Hot Spots of Hunger and Disasters

Since the launch of NREGA, several appalling cases of starvation deaths have occurred in the country, mostly involving dalits as victims. In some cases, as in the case of Sarupiya Devi of Darbhanga district, Bihar, who worked for 40 days under the scheme before dying of hunger, the fatal delay in payment of wages points at the typical apathy of administrators of the scheme towards marginalized people. Unfortunately, Sarupiya Devi's death, publicly discussed and condemned during a jan sunvai organized by the All India Agricultural Labour Association in August 2006 at New Delhi while the Monsoon session of parliament was underway, did not create any sense of urgency towards expediting the delivery of the scheme, and till date, NREGA remains a virtual non-starter across a large number of panchayats in Bihar. Similar instances of hunger deaths of people who could never avail of employment under NREGA despite possessing valid job cards were also reported from some other places, e.g. Rohtas. The exclusion of a large number of dalit communities in disaster-prone regions of several states, e.g. Jharkhand, Orissa and Bihar, where the scheme hasn't progressed beyond tokenistic issue of job cards to a handful of rural households, is appalling.

Misappropriations by Non-Dalits In Heterogeneous Communities

A critical area of concern relating to NREGA' reach vis-à-vis communities of the dalits is the high likelihood of misappropriation of employment opportunities by non-dalits in communities where dalits co-exist along with socially dominant castes. For instance, in villages like Badanpura in Karauli district of Rajasthan, people hailing from dominant castes are known to forcefully claim a share in the wages of dalit labourers earned from supply of labour under NREGA, by pressurizing the sarpanch. As a result, not a single labourer from the dalit community has ever been able to claim their daily entitlement of Rs. 73/- payable as minimum wages in lieu of unskilled labour.

Instances of Assertion and Actualization of Entitlements

In several places, dalit communities and their organizations had to forcefully assert themselves against instances of denial of their entitlements under NREGA. One of the significant acts of assertion of dalit labourers was seen in Nagphana (Bolangir district, Orissa) where hundreds of labourers went on a mass-strike in protest against non-payment of wages as per the standard piece-rate amounts specified under the provisions of the Act. The labourers insisted on payments on a pro-rata basis for every additional quantum of work performed in excess of the standard specifications and did not turn up for work till the contractors agreed to pay them their due wages. Subsequently, the labourers also set up a committee of their own in the village, which keeps copies of all relevant documents and muster rolls relating to employment activities and other schemes in the village, including works implemented directly by the panchayat. Similar acts of protest were organized at Villupuram (Tamil Nadu) where dalit labourers refused to accept wages falling short of the minimum wages prescribed by the state government.

During 2006, significant campaigns were undertaken under the banner of NACDOR – a national level confederation of dalit organizations – in several states of India, with the objectives of bringing about mass awareness about NREGA and exposing glaring irregularities. NACDOR's initiatives to this effect included Rozgar Adhikar Yatras, Public Tribunals and direct dialogues with government functionaries.

Rozgar Adhikar Yatra, Madhya Pradesh

A Rozgar Adhikar Yatra to promote awareness of and participation of in the National Rural Employment Guarantee Act in Madhya Pradesh was organized across 18 districts of MP. The Yatra brought to light the key difficulties being faced by people, particularly Dalits, in accessing the NREGA.

The administrative process for obtaining Job Cards has been very slow and payments of wages have been delayed. The creation of ecologically sustainable infrastructure and the improvement of the land of marginalized and Dalit farmers have not been prioritized as per the provisions of the Act. Workers have been deprived of relevant equipments and crèche facilities for the children, and contractors are being permitted to work in a clear-cut violation of the provisions of NREGA.

The Rozgar Adhikar Yatra concluded with a public awareness meeting and a massive rally to the Madhya Pradesh Legislative Assembly. A delegation met with Chief Minister and delivered a memorandum of suggestions for effective implementation of NREGA. This included recommendations for the training of Panchayat representatives in implementing the NREGA, training of the elected Dalit & Adivasi representatives, and the provision of compensation allowance in absence of work allotments.

Source: National Conference of Dalit Organizations (NACDOR)

Salient Programme Implications

Dalits, bearing a greater susceptibility to exclusion due to social reasons, need to be purposively targeted and reporting of their coverage under the scheme must be made mandatory for all panchayats known to be inhabited by dalit communities. Similarly, known hot spots of hunger, natural disasters and epidemics, mostly coincident with habitations of dalit communities, must be purposively targeted under the scheme.

Only a clearly articulated policy of affirmative action favouring pro-active inclusion of dalits can make a scheme like NREGA effectively contribute to poverty reduction. The scheme needs to be envisaged as an opportunity to address the disparities between dalits and non-dalits, by according preference to dalit labourers, locating work-sites closer to dalit habitations and deputing a greater number of administrators/monitors hailing from dalit communities.

Outcomes of the National Tribunal on NREGA

On 10 November 2006, more than 1000 people representing experiences of NREGA across 14 states gathered at the capital, Delhi to contribute to an evaluation of the program from the perspective of the most marginalized communities. Depositions extended across six hours, and culminated with the presentation of key findings before a Jury comprising of K. R. Venugopal - Former IAS officer, Former Secretary to the Prime Minister and Special Rapporteur, National Human Rights Commission, and Annie Raja – General Secretary, National Federation of Indian

Women (NFIW). The Jury recognized that the implementation of the NREGA is among the most significant steps taken by the United Progressive Alliance towards the fulfillment of the promises made to the people through the National Common Minimum Program. There is also a notable level of expectation, energy and efforts among civil society groups across states to ensure that the NREGA is successfully implemented across the country..

The Jury noted that there were reports of exclusion from almost every section of the marginalized and across states, pointing to the urgent need for concerted action between government agencies and civil society organizations to ensure that the program reaches those who need it the most – the poorest of the poor. The government must purposively seek to include scheduled castes, women and other marginalized sections of society in the NREGA.

The inherent exclusion of women from the equal opportunity for employment – by virtue of the provision for only one member of the household to gain work – was also adjudged as one of the weakest links of the program.

The stipulated wage provided through the program – an average of Rs. 60 per day – is judged to be grossly inadequate, and a wage revision to the amount of Rs. 120 – 130 is recommended to ensure that a family is able to meet its basic entitlements of food, clothing, housing, education and health.

The Jury concluded that the NREGA can only succeed with a combination of strong political will and able administration. The role of civil society organizations towards opinion building and advocacy needs to be sustained and strengthened towards this objective.

NREGA: FROM ACCOUNTS TO ACCOUNTABILITY

The ghost of corruption has haunted many public interventions in India, and the National Rural Employment Guarantee Act (NREGA) is no exception. Bank payments of NREGA wages were recently introduced on a mass scale, and projected as a foolproof remedy against corruption. Recent evidence, however, suggests that the banking system itself is not above corruption — corrective steps are urgently needed.

Rush to Bank Payments

The main technique of embezzlement in public employment programmes, including NREGA, is to fudge the "muster rolls" (attendance sheets): fake names or inflated attendance figures are entered in the muster rolls, and middlemen pocket the difference. This used to be possible, indeed very simple, because of the cloud of secrecy that surrounded the muster rolls. The NREGA sought to change that based on a range of safeguards, starting with the transparency of muster rolls. For instance, NREGA muster rolls are supposed to be available at the worksite and filled there every day in the presence of the workers, giving them an opportunity to check the details at any time. Similarly, payment details from the muster rolls are supposed to be entered in the workers' "job cards", enabling them to monitor these payments.

Another factor that facilitated corrupt practices in the past was that the same person or agency was in charge of maintaining muster rolls and paying the wages. Since both functions were in the same hands, fudging muster rolls was both easy and profitable. The separation of these two functions is a powerful safeguard against embezzlement. Even before NREGA, this was the norm on drought relief programmes in Rajasthan. There, muster rolls were prepared by Gram Panchayat functionaries with the help of the "mate" (worksite supervisor), whereas wages were paid by the patwari (a Panchayat level employee of the revenue department). This makes it harder to siphon off funds by fudging muster rolls, unless the different actors collude with each other.

The need to separate payment agencies from implementation agencies was an important argument for the recent introduction of bank (or post office) payments of NREGA wages. There are other good reasons for introducing bank payments. For instance, paying wages directly into the workers' accounts reduces the risk of harassment by payments officials. Further, it encourages saving habits and the use of bank facilities.

However, there are also significant drawbacks with bank payments. The coverage of banks and post offices in rural India is still patchy, which means that labourers have to travel some distance to collect their wages (as opposed to getting cash in hand in their own village). In some states at least, bank payments have been associated with delays in the disbursement of wages, as the relevant transactions work their way through the system. There is also a danger of women being excluded, if bank accounts are opened in the names of men only, as has happened in some districts.

From a long-term perspective, the payment of wages through banks is probably a move in the right direction. However, the transition to bank payments has been made in a very rushed and haphazard manner. And the results have often been sobering. The Deoghar social audit

A social audit of 17 NREGA works in five Gram Panchayats of Karon Block in Deoghar District (Jhardhan), conducted on 12-16 October 2008, unearthed some alarming facts related to bank payments. Briefly, the loot is far from over: funds are siphoned off through manipulated bank accounts of NREGA workers, in collusion with bank staff. In Deogarh, banks are rapidly being integrated in the system of corruption.

Consider the case of the construction of two NREGA wells in Ranidih Panchayat: one on Koka Baori's land and the other on Paane Hembrahm's. Both were approached by the Panchayat Sevak, who offered to get a well constructed on their land. Once the well was sanctioned, a contractor took charge (an infraction under the Act). When cheques arrived in the name of the beneficiaries, they were asked to collect it from the bank and hand it over to the contractor to pay for material costs.

As far as wage payments were concerned, it was a simple matter for the contractor. Two years earlier, he had kindly opened bank accounts for many NREGA labourers (often without their knowledge), with a little help from the rather cooperative staff of the Deoghar-Jamtara Central Cooperative Bank. The contractor and Panchayat Sevak manufactured muster rolls with wages adding up to the labour component sanctioned for the wells. Whenever money is transferred to the labourers' accounts, the trio of bank officials, contractor and Panchayat Sevak step in: they coolly pocket the excess money after giving their due to the labourers who actually worked. Most of the labourers we spoke to said that they had never been to the bank, and that they were paid in cash at the worksite by the contractor.

While other banks in the area did not have the audacity to indulge in such open loot, their practices were not entirely above board either. In some cases, we heard that labourers had been made to sign withdrawal slips in bulk at the time of opening their bank accounts, to facilitate proxy withdrawals later on. In the case of Allahabad Bank and Vananchal Bank, bank officials said that labourers came in person to withdraw their wages, but usually accompanied by men who "do not look like labourers". These men, believed to be the contractors' cronies, stand outside the bank and force the labourers to hand over the excess money that has been claimed in their name. For us, this story was a nightmare come true: one year earlier, a master (or rather mistress) contractor in Orissa had told us that if bank payments of NREGA wage were introduced, "the contractors will become dacoits."

Magic Bullet or Shot in the Foot?

How typical Deogarh's experience is we do not know. But this experience certainly shows that bank payments alone are not an adequate protection against corruption. In fact, in Jharkhand's anarchic environment (not unique to Deogarh), they have even facilitated embezzlement in several ways. First, while all NREGA-related documents (e.g. muster rolls, job cards, measurement books) are supposed to be in the public domain, it is not clear whether banks are going to accept this principle for their own records, including the details of NREGA accounts. Meanwhile, the rush to bank payments has led to reduced transparency by withdrawing key documents from public scrutiny.

Second, payments through banks and post offices introduce new players into the corruption game — the staff of these institutions. It is not clear how these officials (who are often employees of the Central government, rather than of the State governments or Panchayati Raj Institutions) are to be held accountable for NREGA-related matters. They tend to be more difficult to "catch" than other functionaries such as the Panchayat Sevak or Gram Rozgar Sevak.

Third, embezzlement of wages paid though bank accounts typically requires the involvement or cooperation of the labourers themselves, in one way or another. Labourers generally have a stake in blowing the whistle against corruption, but when they become part of the nexus of corruption, this voice is effectively silenced.

Last but not least, bank payments have led to an alarming neglect of other transparency safeguards. For instance, muster rolls are no longer signed by workers at the time of wage payment, since wages are paid directly through banks. In fact, in Deogarh we found that muster rolls had been reduced to a naked attendance sheet, without any payment details. The only person who signs is the person who fills the muster roll in the first place, and his or her "supervisor", often acting in collusion. Apparently, a similar setback is happening in Rajasthan. This is unfortunate since Rajasthan had largely stamped out the embezzlement of NREGA wages based on more "conventional" safeguards such as the transparency of muster rolls.

This is not to say that the transition to bank payments should be reversed. But this transition certainly requires great caution (including strict monitoring of banks and post offices), and must be combined with strict enforcement of all the transparency norms. The Central government seems to regard bank payments as a "magic bullet" against corruption, but the bullet is in danger of ending up in its own foot.

NREGA NOT JUST ABOUT DROUGHT RELIEF, BUT RELIEF AGAINST DROUGHT

On the eve of NREGA becoming a pan-Indian programme from April 1 2008, the Centre for Science and Environment (CSE) releases its assessment of two years of the National

Rural Employment Guarantee Act (NREGA); study looks at the Act's implementation across 9 states and 12 districts.

NREGA is not just about drought relief but relief against drought, says CSE. Wants programme strengthened but revamped so that it provides not just wages for work done but 'work' that will make ecological regeneration possible.

NREGA has huge potential for regenerating village economy in India, but only if its focus remains on the creation of productive assets, the study argues.

The Act brings with it huge possibilities of making a difference to the lives of 45 million rural households of our country. Over the two years that it has been in existence, NREGA has already created half-a-million assets and provided jobs to around three per cent of India's population.

CSE study shows that people essentially want two things – productive assets and regular wages. Wherever the Act has failed to meet these needs, its implementation has collapsed.

Key Findings

Creating productive assets, ecological regeneration for economic change The CSE study finds that despite NREGA's official focus on jobs, the programme is witnessing a dipping demand for employment under it. This is not because rural India does not need jobs any more, but because of the Act's lopsided focus and its imperfect wage-for-jobs scheme. To begin with, governments have failed to articulate the Act's development potential. Instead of implementing and evaluating the Act purely in terms of employment creation, the focus should have been on the real impacts on local development through productive assets creation. In terms of assets creation, finds the study, most of the NREGA money has gone to road construction projects, instead of works related to water conservation and harvesting. Of the 27 states where the NREGA was implemented, only five have made substantial allocation to water conservation. During 2006-07, Andhra Pradesh alone accounted for about 67 per cent of the total water conservation works under NREGA in the country.

This has happened as irrational wage calculations have made projects like water conservation less lucrative. Panchayats are increasingly demanding more roads and other construction works because road construction gets them the minimum wage and sometimes even more than that. The nexus of local government officials and contractors is also a reason behind building works getting priority.

Bad Planning, no Maintenance

The programme is also plagued by another set of problems, finds the CSE analysis – that of incomplete and abandoned works, and lack of maintenance of completed works. Out of a total of 769,582 works under progress, only 158,277 (20.56 per cent) have been completed. Till August 2007, only about 14 per cent of water conservation works under NREGA had been completed. In fact, road construction projects were getting done at a faster rate.

The study has found that bad planning for water conservation structures is putting a large number of the assets created into disuse.

For instance, water harvesting structures have been created without any provision for catchment's protection. On top of this, 'maintenance work' does not come under the ambit of NREGA as a permissible activity. As a result, districts, which already have large numbers of water harvesting structures and want to use NREGA money for their maintenance, can't do so.

The way Ahead

The CSE study lists a set of steps that will ensure that impact. These include:

- o Measure not just the wage provided but also the asset created and its effectiveness. This will make village development, through productive assets creation, the primary objective.
- o Make wage payment people and development friendly, provide a premium wage for development pro grammes, which will ensure that work done is completed and is useful.
- o Continue to emphasise water conservation works under NREGA by providing additional incentives
- o Make the completion and maintenance of works under NREGA mandatory.
- o Give importance to afforestation under NREGA by linking it to other forestry programmes – Joint Forest Management or watersheds.
- o Do more to strengthen village-level planning and decision making by revamping the current operational structures.
- o Equip panchayats with the necessary personnel and funds for effective implementation of the programme.

NREGA IN PRATAPGARH

The National Rural Employment Act-2005 (NREGA) is a People's Act towards the realization of the right to work. Its main motive is to provide a legal guarantee at least 100 day's of employment to every rural household whose adult members are willing to do unskilled manual labour through which it is expected to enhance people's livelihood on a sustained basis by developing the economic and social infrastructure in rural areas.

National Rural Employment Guarantee Scheme has been launched in the first phase on 2 February 2006 in the district Pratapgarh (UP) along with 22 other districts of the State.

DISTRICT – PRATAPGARH

District Pratapgarh comes under Allahabad Division and it is located 60 Km. from Allahabad and surrounded by district Sultanpur in North, Allahabad & Kaushambi in South, Jaunpur in East and Raibareily & Fatehpur in West. It was established in 1858 and with its head quarter "Belha". The name is synonymous with Belha Devi Mandir, which is situated on the bank of river Sai. Later it was named after King Pratap Singh who built a fort in the city, thus it derived its name PRATAPGARH.

FLAWS IN THE SYSTEM

The NREGA is a piece of new-age legislation which invokes the framework of legal rights to provide employment in rural areas. The rights framework should, ideally, provide an antidote to government irresponsibility in the form of accountability under the law. In practice, however, this transition towards an accountable system has not occurred – far from it. In our survey, we found that NREGA workers had to put up with numerous infringements of their rights without being able to do much about it: lack of work, delays in wage payment, non-payment of minimum wages, absence of worksite facilities, to cite a few. Most of these irregularities remain unaddressed, often even unnoticed. The persistence of corruption is another aspect of this lack of accountability.

Three related problems have contributed to this state of affairs: confusion about the operational requirements of the Act; absence of any grievance redress system; and lack of independent monitoring.

To start with, there is a troubling lack of clarity about the various actors' basic responsibilities under the NREGA. The Act directs each State government to notify an "employment guarantee scheme" to give effect to the work guarantee. The combination of a Central Act with State-specific schemes (and generally, the complex Centre-State relations behind the NREGA) calls for rigorous coordination between Central and State governments. This is not happening; to illustrate, the Union Ministry of Rural Development does not even have a copy of each of the State schemes. The result is a confusing duality in the source of norms.

Schedules I and II of the NREGA spell out mandatory features of the schemes, for example, the minimum entitlements to be guaranteed. However, most of the State schemes fall short of these norms and fail to define an adequate operational framework to fulfil the work guarantee. In many States, schemes have been notified as a mere formality, and the programme is actually run through oral or written instructions issued from time to time.

The Central government, for its part, has issued operational guidelines on various functional matters such as selection of works, worksite management, payment procedures and record keeping.

Unfortunately, the status of these guidelines is ambiguous. In response to the Comptroller and Auditor General's (CAG) widely publicised report of widespread non-compliance with the operational guidelines, the Ministry of Rural Development clarified that these guidelines were not binding. With operational guidelines reduced to a "best practice" template, the NREGA is being implemented in a dangerous vacuum.

Beating Around the Bush

One aspect of this vacuum is the absence of clear remedies against infringements of the Act. Curiously, the NREGA talks the language of rights but there is virtual silence on available remedies when rights are violated. So far, the Central and State governments have failed to put in place any system to respond to people's complaints. Interesting ideas have been floated, such as the appointment of ombudsmen or the activation of lok adalats, but they are yet to see the light of day. Transparency and accountability rules have been drafted and discussed for months, without getting anywhere. According to the Ministry of Rural Development, the Law Ministry now takes the view that the Central government has no mandate to make such rules under the NREGA – an illiterate reading of the Act. Meanwhile, transparency safeguards (including job card maintenance, muster roll norms and social audits) are languishing in the operational guidelines. Since the guidelines are now treated as "advisory", these safeguards have no teeth.

A third issue is the lack of independent monitoring of the NREGA, whether in the States or at the Centre. The Central Employment Guarantee Council (CEGC) was intended as an active, powerful, independent monitoring body for the NREGA at the national level. However, the council is virtually non-functional. The performance of the State Employment Guarantee Councils is no better – in fact, it is worse in most cases. These watchdogs, too, have no teeth – they are not even barking.

Similarly, no independent survey has been conducted so far on a national scale to evaluate the implementation of the Act. It is a mystery why a government that spends about Rs.25,000 crore a year on the NREGA is unable to spare a few crores for an independent evaluation, to find out where the money is going and what the programme is achieving. The Central government bears a heavy responsibility for this state of affairs. The NREGA is a national Act and about 90 per cent of the funds for works come from the Centre. The Central government is duty-bound under the Act to put in place mandatory operational norms to protect labourers' entitlements. Failing that, the new hopes that have been kindled by the NREGA in rural India are likely to be dashed.

Alternative to Migration

> "For us, getting work in our village is a big thing. Since I don't have any land, I am completely dependent on casual labour." – Gondi, a 45-year-old woman (Surguja district, Chhattisgarh)
>
> "Because works have started opening, the idea of leaving the village doesn't enter our mind." – Dilsay (Surguja district)

"Migrating for work is very expensive. Half of our earnings are spent in commuting alone. When he used to go to the bazaar to work, he had to face exploitation from his employer." – Sita Bai (Sirohi district, Rajasthan)

"Before the NREGA, we had to go far for work. There was no place to stay, so we slept with our children on the footpath where dogs also slept with us." – Dinesh, 20 years (Badwani district, Madhya Pradesh)

These testimonies sum up the importance of the NREGA in the lives of many migrant labourers. It is a valued source of local employment, if not – at times – the only source. In their minds, migration is associated with hardship and they resort to it only when there is no alternative.

Such is the outlook, for instance, of Baleshwar Mahto, a resident of Uttari Dehati in Bihar's Araria district. Baleshwar goes to Punjab every year in search of work to sustain his family. He had planned to go there last June as well. However, he got NREGA employment in his own village and so he decided to stay back. Baleshwar will definitely go to Punjab next time – the trip has only been postponed.

Meanwhile, he enjoys this respite. The NREGA is a triple bonus for him: apart from providing local employment, it enabled him to combine this work with tending his own fields and spending more time with his family.

Baleshwar's story illustrates the situation faced by many in Araria. Large numbers of people there are forced to look for work in Punjab, Delhi and Gujarat as employment is hard to find locally. What is available is very poorly paid, with wages varying from Rs.40 to Rs.60 a day during the harvest season, even less (Rs.25 to Rs.50 a day) otherwise. Baleshwar takes up such employment only when he is forced to stay back in his village, for instance, owing to illness in the family.

In their survey responses, migrant workers often spoke about the hardships associated with migration. In the cities, they live in deplorable conditions, with no access to basic facilities such as shelter, sanitation or even safe drinking water. In the case of men-only migration, women and children face material and psychological insecurity, and family relations often suffer.

The NREGA is a potential liberation from these hardships. Naresh Hirshi Dev from Palamau (Jharkhand) put it succinctly: "To be with your family and get work in the village is a real relief."

Says Noor Zaheer, survey coordinator, about the condition of migrant workers in Himachal Pradesh: "Migrant workers who came to Himachal for fruit picking were paid a pittance [just a little more than what they would have got at home], made to sleep in torn tents and given poor meals." This year, however, they had a choice. Says Noor Zaheer: "They refused to work for less than Rs.200 a day. They also demanded waterproof tents and decent meals. They said if they had to work for Rs.100 a day, they need not have come all the way to Himachal Pradesh. They could have earned it at their doorstep at the NREGA worksites. The orchard owners had no option but to comply."

More than half (57 per cent) of the sample workers stated that the NREGA "helped them avoid migration", and a similar proportion (also 57 per cent) felt that migration had decreased in their villages after the NREGA was launched. As expected, these figures were even larger in areas with high levels of NREGA employment or high rates of migration before the inception of the programme. For instance, in Pati block (Madhya Pradesh), a hub of out-migration where the NREGA has been deployed in a big way, 92 per cent of the sample workers felt that migration had gone down and 88 per cent said the NREGA had helped them avoid migration.

The responses were similar in Dungarpur (Rajasthan), where some people had even returned from Mumbai and places in Gujarat on hearing that NREGA work was available in their villages.

Even in areas where the scale of NREGA work is much smaller, for instance, Sitapur in Uttar Pradesh and Araria, there is some evidence of an impact on migration. One possible explanation is that a few days of assured employment in the lean season is enough to persuade some workers to "stay back" for the entire period.

However, it is also possible that the promise of local employment is luring workers to stay back and that if these hopes are dashed migration will resume. Delays in wage payments could intensify this potential "discouragement effect" and push people back into the web of migration. If this setback is to be averted, NREGA employment must be expanded and made more predictable.

What Works Against Women

Women at work in Badwani, Madhya Pradesh.

KAMLA DAS, 25, belongs to a landless family in Salba gram panchayat in Chhattisgarh's Surguja district. Her husband does not earn anything, so she is especially appreciative of the opportunity the NREGA has given her to earn in her own village: "Now women can also earn, so the family's earnings increase. The NREGA is very important because women get the same wage as men."

The NREGA has enabled her to stop working for a local landlord, who pays women less than men. She has used her earnings to buy rice to feed her family, books and clothes for her children, and fertilizer (they are sharecroppers), and also to celebrate Holi. However, she has faced some harassment from the mate, who pressures the women to work harder. She is also worried about her four-year-old child, who is alone at home when she goes to work. She would like to bring her child to the worksite but this depends on a child-care facility being made available there.

The participation of women in the NREGA was below the stipulated minimum of 33 per cent in the survey sample, and in many of the survey areas, it was abysmally low. Uttar Pradesh and Bihar were at the bottom, with women accounting for only 5 and 13 per cent of the NREGA workforce respectively; the situation was only marginally better in Jharkhand (18 per cent) and Chhatttisgarh (25 per cent). The only States where women were well represented were Madhya Pradesh (44 per cent) and Rajasthan (71 per cent).

What prevents women from joining the NREGA in larger numbers in the other States? We were often told by gram panchayat functionaries that women were not interested in NREGA work. But when the field investigators spoke to women directly, most of them expressed a keen desire to work. The interviews revealed five important barriers to their participation in the NREGA. First, in many areas there are tenacious social norms against women working outside the home. In Uttar Pradesh and Bihar, field investigators met women who said they had not been able to register and were told that this programme was "not for them".

Women in Sitapur, Uttar Pradesh, reported that when there were more applicants than could be accommodated at a worksite, they were turned away to make way for men. Some of them also faced verbal sexual harassment – they were teased, ridiculed or verbally abused by male labourers and other villagers.

The second big hurdle is the lack of child-care facilities. The Act requires that when there are more than five children under the age of six at a worksite, a female worker should be spared to take care of them. But field investigators did not find child-care facilities anywhere (except at two or three worksites, that too possibly as "window dressing"). The lack of these facilities can be crippling for women, especially those with breastfeeding babies.

Third, the continued illegal presence of contractors at many worksites affects the availability of work and its benefits for women. In some places, the presence of contractors actively impacted women's participation in NREGA work. At some sites in Madhya Pradesh, contractors offered work only to young, able-bodied men. At worksites where contractors were involved, 35 per cent of women workers said they had faced some harassment, as against only 8 per cent at contractor-free worksites.

Fourth, in some States productivity norms are too exacting because the "schedule of rates" is yet to be revised in line with NREGA norms. For instance, in Jharkhand the standard task for a day's work at the time of the survey was digging 110 cubic feet (in soft soil), which is far too much. Certain types of NREGA work limit the participation of women. This applies, for instance, to the construction of wells on private land; women are not employed after digging reaches a certain depth.

Fifth, delayed payments also come in the way of participation of poor women. Delays in wage payments make things particularly difficult for single women, who cannot afford to wait as they are the sole earners in the family. When the wages do not come on time, they are often forced to return to previous, less-preferred forms of employment. Women's battle to be full participants in the NREGA goes beyond being able to get their names on job cards and getting work. An important part of the NREGA is participatory planning, where the list of NREGA works is decided. Only a small proportion of women workers in the survey sample had attended a gram sabha, and even fewer had spoken at a gram sabha. Many do not go to gram sabhas because they do not feel welcome or because they believe these meetings are not for women.

Much of this is changing, and participation of women in the NREGA is certainly improving. But there are also new challenges.

One of them is the introduction of wage payments through banks. In most places, only one bank account is opened per job card, and generally the account is opened in the name of a male member of the family. This means women will have to rely on men to withdraw their wages. Ideally, there should be one account per registered NREGA worker or at least joint bank accounts instead of men-only accounts. Even better would be for every individual worker (man or woman) to have his or her own job card, bank account, and entitlement to 100 days of work.

Banned but Still There

CONTRACTORS are banned for work under the NREGA, but the survey found that they were in fact involved at 27 per cent of the sample worksites. The worst State in this respect was Jharkhand, where contractors were found at more than half (57 per cent) the sample worksites. A common excuse for this is the shortage of staff: gram panchayats, the main implementing agencies for NREGA work, do not exist in Jharkhand. In fact, it is the only State that has not held elections to panchayati raj institutions since the 73rd and 74th amendments to the Constitution.The survey teams encountered contractors to varying extents in all the States except Rajasthan. Often, they get a foot in the door on account of delays in the flow of funds. When funds are delayed, contractors step in to ensure timely payment to labourers and suppliers. In return, they are given a free hand in forging muster rolls, job cards and other NREGA documents.

Why is the involvement of contractors such a big issue? This question has to be seen in the light of the unscrupulous character of most contractors in rural India. They are there to make money, in a highly competitive environment where cheating and exploitation is the way to get ahead.

The semi-criminal, petty contractor, roaming around on a motorcycle, wearing dark glasses and a scarf and chewing paan, is not a fictitious Bollywood character – he is a familiar figure in most Indian villages.

On a more serious note, the survey findings amply confirm that private contractors are best kept at bay. This is so for at least three reasons:

Corruption: Corruption levels tend to be higher where contractors are involved. For instance, in a survey in Orissa in October 2007, we found higher rates of embezzlement of wages at worksites managed by contractors. Worksites with contractors were more likely to have muster rolls with fake names. More than half (55 per cent) of the wages did not reach the labourers concerned, whereas the figure was low (25 per cent) for contractor-free worksites.

Exploitation: Contractors typically thrive by exploiting labourers – making them work hard and paying them as little as possible. This often goes hand in hand with harassment. For instance, 35 per cent of the women working at contractor-managed worksites reported being harassed. This figure is much lower (8 per cent) for contractor-free worksites.

At one worksite in Surguja district (Chhattisgarh), women were verbally abused for working too slowly; the contractor made them work for 10 hours a day and turned away those who came late.

At another worksite, also in Surguja, the survey team noted: "The women who complained about these work conditions were verbally abused by the contractor, who also threatened to replace them with workers from other gram panchayats. Our team learned from a worker that these workers from other gram panchayats were paid at the rate of Rs.50 a day."

Accountability: It is easier to keep gram panchayats or Line Departments' employees on their toes than to hold private contractors accountable. In fact, in our experience, contractors are very difficult to "catch" even when there is proof of their mischief. For instance, at Masmohna in Jharkhand's Koderma district, the survey team found conclusive evidence that a private contractor had cheated NREGA workers and embezzled their wages. This evidence was presented at a massive public hearing attended by three members of the Central Employment Guarantee Council (on June 18, 2008) and confirmed again in a detailed follow-up by the Koderma Sub-Divisional Officer (SDO).

Yet, in the first information report (FIR) lodged against the culprits, which is supposed to be based on this very inquiry, the contractor's name is missing. He apparently has the "protection" of the local Member of the Legislative Assembly.

Patronage

Many contractors enjoy the patronage of political leaders (and return this favour by funding election campaigns). This nexus of corruption and crime, which also involves corrupt bureaucrats, has been the bane of public works programmes for many years.

The NREGA seeks to break this nexus and replace it with a transparent and accountable system where panchayati raj institutions are in charge. If this new system is to see the light of day, contractors have to be kept at bay.

All is Not Well with the Wells

The fields of Mahua Tand in Jharkhand's Deogarh district are full of wheat. Farmers and field hands are busy irrigating their lands. The rains have not been very helpful this year, and pumpsets and wells are the saviours of crops. Our social audit team is inspecting two NREGA projects in Mahua Tand, both involving the construction of a well on private land – a common type of NREGA work in Jharkhand.

The well constructed by Taufique Zarra reminds the team of the tragic Tapas Soren episode. In the short video recording of his last words, Tapas Soren testifies that a corrupt government machinery had driven him to take his own life. He had tried to construct a well on his own land under the NREGA but was unable to cope with the frequent demands for bribes. A helpless and distraught Tapas set himself ablaze at the Collector's office in Hazaribagh to highlight his plight and warn others about this trap. But Taufique, unaware of Tapas' fate, fell into the same trap.

Taufique hails from a below-poverty-line (BPL) family and his sole source of income is the little agricultural land he owns. In the absence of a reliable source of irrigation, he is often at the mercy of unpredictable rain. Having heard that wells can be constructed on the land of BPL families under the NREGA, Taufique applied. Soon enough, he was informed that if he could pay Rs.2,500, a well would be allotted to him, he said. The NREGA mandates that a shelf of works be prepared in the gram sabha, but no such attempt was made in Mahaua Tand.

He said he paid the bribe and the well was sanctioned, and he became both the beneficiary and *abhikarta* (manager) of the project. As an *abhikarta* Taufique signed an agreement with the government and was in charge of executing the work. He was to fill the muster rolls, purchase materials and oversee the worksite. He also had to pay workers' wages and for materials as the work progressed, but funds were often delayed and depended on his ability to pay the "PC" (percentage, a term for illegal commissions) to government functionaries. The PC had to be given in cash before the bill for his payment was passed, he alleged. Taufique took a loan of Rs.20,000, sold a buffalo and mortgaged his land to arrange for the PC and the construction costs.

For Taufique, this well was a chance to escape poverty but today, he says, he is struggling to make ends meet. Luckily, Taufique was not driven to suicide. But the whole PC system did push him into a web of indebtedness. Maybe for every Taufique who survives this gamble, there is a Tapas Soren who may not.

ACCOUNTS OF CORRUPTION

SINCE April-May 2008, the Central government has insisted that NREGA wages be paid exclusively through savings accounts opened for workers in nearby banks and post offices. A major public relations campaign has tried to present this as a solution to corruption. So much so, the progress of the NREGA is being measured in terms of the number of accounts opened – an impressive 4.22 crore, according to a recent statement by the Rural Development Minister's office. This extraordinary investment of energies must, however, be viewed with caution. A recent social audit of the NREGA at Karon block in Jharkhand's Deogarh district showed that corruption persisted, at times with the collusion of banks themselves.

Deogarh Scam

Manchan Rajwar of Ranidih panchayat had no reason to suspect that his NREGA account at the Deoghar-Jamtara Cooperative Bank had been activated. Severely crippled, he had not worked at the site where his name figured, nor signed any withdrawal slips. His passbook was blank. However, an inspection of bank records (during a social audit in October 2008) revealed that many transactions had been made over a whole year. It turned out that middlemen were siphoning off NREGA funds through his account in collusion with bank officials.

Similar tricks were played on many other workers in Ranidih, and also in Ganjebari panchayat where they were paid through the post office at Madankatta. The amounts moving through these accounts could add up to as much as Rs.9,000 within 14 months for a single account.

Even where collusion is not as blatant as in Ranidih, making payments through banks is fraught with vulnerabilities. First, little effort has been made to integrate bank payments with other transparency safeguards, such as payment of wages in public and regular updating of job cards. In fact, there is a dangerous tendency to assume that these safeguards are redundant when wages are paid through banks or post offices.

In Dungarpur district in Rajasthan, the traditional safeguards worked, and bank payments were – at least initially – a step back. Where bank payments were in place, we found (in our May-June 2008 survey) that job cards were not updated and that muster rolls were no longer read out in public at the time of wage payments.

Second, bank payments have often increased delays in wage payments. In Rajasthan, for instance, where wages used to be paid regularly, teething problems with bank payments last summer caused delays of up to 50 days. Such delays cannot be tided over by NREGA workers and must be treated as a serious violation of the Act.

The combination of opaque procedures and delayed payments has created new opportunities for middlemen. Many middlemen have privileged access to panchayat- and block-level officials and are often the first to know when wages have been credited. They then collect workers (both real and fake) and escort them to the bank. There, a combination of loans, coercion and (sometimes) monetary enticements is used to induce workers to hand over the money they have withdrawn. At Karon block, workers from Mahua Tand, Tekra and Ganjebari panchayats stated publicly that this had happened. They had been paid in cash at the rate of Rs.60-70 a day, while the stipulated minimum wage was Rs.86.40. In some cases, middlemen collude with the panchayat sevak to inflate muster rolls, steer the inflated payments through people's bank accounts and pocket the difference.

New Complications

Bank payments have also resulted in new complications. For instance, banking procedures have not been publicised at all. Most workers do not know how to operate bank accounts. This, in turn, increases their dependence on intermediaries. Another serious irregularity in many places is the opening of accounts solely in the name of the male head of the family. This makes it hard for women to keep their own wages. Other problems include extractions from workers to open accounts; people without accounts being turned away from worksites; workers having to spend time and money to withdraw their wages when banks are far away; and staff shortages in banks and post offices.

So far, the introduction of payments through banks has been little more than a stampede for opening accounts. Crucial guidelines and safeguards have been ignored. Consequently, the aim of ending corruption in wage payments has not been achieved. This can only happen when bank payments are combined with other transparency safeguards, as has happened to some extent (with post office payments) in Andhra Pradesh. Otherwise, as is already happening, new vulnerabilities will get entrenched. On the bright side, this experience has demonstrated the Centre's ability to enforce critical guidelines. This power could be used to put in place a more comprehensive structure of vigilance and transparency.

Pati Experience

Once covered with lush teak forests, Pati block in Badwani district of Madhya Pradesh now has a depressing lunar landscape of denuded hills, where only subsistence agriculture is possible. Most rural households there survive on wage labour and seasonal migration. The Jagrut Adivasi Dalit Sangathan (JADS), an unregistered organisation with a membership of 3,500 families, has worked there for many years on issues concerning tribal land rights. Since the NREGA was launched in 2006, the JADS has struggled for workers' entitlements under the Act: employment on demand, minimum wages, timely wage payments, and disbursal of unemployment allowance, among others. This organisational work has achieved important results.

As far as the NREGA is concerned, Pati block is an oasis compared with the other survey areas. Most sample workers were aware of their entitlements under the Act and also how to claim them. For example, more than 90 per cent of the sample workers in Pati had got employment in response to written applications for work. In most of the other sample districts, the work application process was not in place (fewer than one-fifth of the sample workers had made written applications), defeating the whole principle of demand-driven employment.

Similarly, rural workers in Pati are aware of – and strive for – their entitlement to 100 days of employment over the year. Nearly half of the sample workers there had worked for a full 100 days in the preceding 12 months. Average NREGA employment per sample household over the year was as high 85 days, much higher than in other survey areas.

The most heartening aspect of the JADS' work in Pati is the sense of empowerment that is evident among its members. Malubhai is apprehensive of the move to route NREGA wages through banks but defends the JADS when he was asked why it allowed this to happen. "We thought we'd try it out; if it doesn't work, we'll just protest and make them revert to cash payments," he said. This sort of confidence is rare among NREGA labourers elsewhere.

An important episode in this empowerment process was the five-month struggle by the JADS, from June to October 2006, for unemployment allowance. The fruits of that struggle were easy to see during the current survey.

In 2006, when the residents of Pati block were offered work without applying, they insisted on applying. They made collective applications for work and demanded receipts while submitting them. Many JADS members went through the entire process of applying for job cards, then for work, and finally for unemployment allowance (in cases where work was not provided). On June 7, 2006, the unemployment allowance became due to more than 2,000 labourers of Pati.

If work is not provided within 15 days of an application being made, applicants are entitled to an unemployment allowance. The cost is borne by the State government, in contrast with employment costs, which are borne mainly by the Central government. Thus, one role of the unemployment allowance is to act as a "fine" on the State government for failing to implement the guarantee. In this respect, payment of the unemployment allowance plays a key role in the realisation of the work guarantee.

Faced with this demand, the Madhya Pradesh government tried various tactics to avoid paying the unemployment allowance. But the JADS did not give up even in the face of threats of violence and false cases against its members. Finally, in October 2006, unemployment allowance was paid to 1,574 labourers of eight gram panchayats of Pati block. This was the first instance of payment of such unemployment allowance in the country.

This victory seems to have turned the channel of accountability on its head. Often one finds that the panchayat secretary (also known as the sevak) feels accountable only to block-level officials. In Pati, for the first time it seemed that the panchayat sevak was actually a "sevak" of the people.

On April 8, 2008, more than 1,000 workers in Ubdagarh village put in a group application for work under the NREGA. They were demanding 30 days of work on cattle prevention trenches (CPT) in their village, which the authorities concerned were able to initiate within 15 days. When Virendra Patel, the panchayat sevak, spoke about this episode, he seemed to feel that he did not have any alternative – if he had not provided work, he would have had to arrange for unemployment allowance.

The successful implementation of the NREGA in Pati block goes beyond the ability of its residents to claim their rights. It is also evident in their active engagement with the programme in terms of planning, implementation and monitoring.

Madhuri Krishnaswamy (who has been associated with the JADS from the beginning) says: "The struggle for the enactment of the NREGA was associated with a larger vision."

Apart from offering a form of social security for the rural poor, the NREGA was seen as a tool for the activation of gram sabhas, the empowerment of women and the development of rural areas. In this sense, the JADS has fully imbibed the spirit of the NREGA.

Rajasthan way Ahead

"Rozgar Guarantee, Zordar Guarantee" (employment guarantee, powerful guarantee). For Lalubhai of Obri panchayat in Dungarpur district of Rajasthan, this slogan sums up what the NREGA means to him and others in his village. Our field survey, too, puts Rajasthan in a fairly good light. Most sample workers there had spent at least 60 days on NREGA worksites in the preceding 12 months, the main transparency safeguards were in place, and the administration was working overtime to implement the Act. The seeds of these achievements go back a long way: public employment programmes have a long history in Rajasthan. Basic systems are in place and there is a wealth of administrative experience to draw upon. A good illustration of this preparedness was the launch of the Act on February 2, 2006.

In Dungarpur district, unprecedented enthusiasm among the people marked the occasion. Loudspeakers blared out the main provisions of the Act from cassettes provided by the government. Armed with their ration cards (as an identity document), men and women queued up from early morning to apply for job cards. Arrangements to issue job cards on the spot were in place. Many already had a fair idea what the NREGA was about. In Thana panchayat, when a group of villagers was asked what was happening, they said they had been given the right to work.

Perhaps the most impressive aspect of the NREGA in Rajasthan is the staggering scale of works. During the survey, it was not uncommon to find entire hamlets empty until 2.30 p.m., when NREGA work ends (during summer). In many gram panchayats, muster rolls for over 2,000 workers were issued every fortnight. In our sample, 36 per cent of households had worked for a full 100 days in the preceding 12 months. The scale and predictability of NREGA employment have brought Rajasthan much closer to the goal of a "work guarantee" than any other State.

Participation of Women

In a State where the social norms militate against women having independent incomes, it is heartening that the NREGA workforce consists overwhelmingly of women: 71 per cent of the workers in our Rajasthan sample were women. Only one-fifth of these women had earned any cash income other than NREGA wages in the preceding 12 months. For them, the NREGA is a new-found source of economic independence and freedom. "I am the head of the household," said Haski, a married Adivasi woman from Sirohi. Few States, if any, have taken transparency norms as seriously as Rajasthan (see Table 13). Muster rolls are usually available at the worksite and daily attendance is taken on them in front of the workers. Further, wages are paid in a public space (as per guidelines), and job cards are updated at the time of payment. These and other safeguards have considerably narrowed the scope for embezzlement, at least in the wage component of NREGA works (though there have been reports of continued cheating in the material component, such as inflated technical estimates).

Worksite Management

Worksite management has been an important area of innovation in Rajasthan. "Mates" (worksite supervisors), both men and women, have been trained to maintain muster rolls, assign tasks to workers, record their output, and ensure that worksite facilities are available. This experiment is still at an early stage, but there are good prospects of it leading to better worksite supervision, higher productivity, an improved work environment, and an improvement of the transparency norms.

Challenges do remain: for instance, Rajasthan has a very poor record of payment of minimum wages on the NREGA.

Nevertheless, this experience is an impressive demonstration of the possibility of implementing the Act. It also shows how skilful public mobilisation can be brought to bear on State politics. Indeed, these achievements also owe much to citizens' organisations such as the Mazdoor Kisan Shakti Sangathan. Aside from acting as watchdogs (for example, by conducting social audits), these organisations have also been involved in work such as training of mates. They are also charting out a programme of unionising NREGA workers.

A scene from the South

A social audit of the NREGA in Villupuram district in Tamil Nadu in July 2007 and a field survey in Surguja district in Chhattisgarh in June 2008, conducted as part of the six-States survey, brought out to this writer the contrasts between Chhattisgarh and Tamil Nadu.

In Chhattisgarh there were many lapses in implementation, including the involvement of contractors, the fudging of muster rolls, corruption in material usage, low scale of work, and delays in wage payment.

Tamil Nadu, on the other hand, has taken measures to address these problems. It has successfully kept out machines and contractors through close monitoring and strict action against any breach of the ban on both under the NREGA.

Another reason for Tamil Nadu's success is the stipulation (under Tamil Nadu's "employment guarantee scheme") that only works devoid of any material component be taken up. (The Act allows up to 40 per cent expenditure on material costs.) The material component tends to give private contractors a foothold as they provide engineering expertise the gram panchayats may not have. The possibility of doing away with the material component arises partly from the fact that Tamil Nadu has a vast network of canals and other traditional water-harvesting structures. The repair and maintenance of these structures is a vast source of useful, labour-intensive work.

If the Act requires that at least 50 per cent of the works be taken up by gram panchayats, the Tamil Nadu scheme stresses that all NREGA works be managed by gram panchayats. In

Chhattisgarh, there is more reliance on the line departments (for example, the Irrigation Department or the Forest Department), which tend to be less accountable than gram panchayats. Tamil Nadu also avoids delays in wage payment by a well-rehearsed routine of payment on a fixed day every week. In Chhattisgarh, by contrast, delays in wage payments cause great hardship to workers, to the extent that some of them have given up NREGA work. In one work implemented by the Forest Department in Udaipur block, people had not been paid for almost a year.

Tamil Nadu has put in place a good monitoring system. For instance, every worker is required to put his signature or thumb impression on the muster roll every day (by way of marking attendance), making it difficult to fudge muster rolls. The employment guarantee assistant ("Makkal Nalla Panniyalar") in each gram panchayat is expected to phone the block office every day before 10 a.m. to report worksite attendance figures. This information is immediately collated at the district level and officials from different departments do random checks the same day to verify these reports.

In Chhattisgarh, there was no regular monitoring of muster rolls or worksite attendance. At many worksites, the official muster rolls were not available. In Kedma panchayat of Udaipur block, our survey found that more than half of all entries in one set of muster rolls of a completed worksite were fake.

Most importantly, in Tamil Nadu a strong message has been sent from the top that NREGA works are unlike other schemes and that corruption will not be tolerated. This has been done by taking strict action against panchayat presidents, employment guarantee assistants and block development officers who have been found guilty of major fraud. The seeds of such a change could be seen in Chhattisgarh: on the basis of a social audit in Mareya panchayat (Udaipur block) in June 2008, a complaint was lodged with the district authorities and strict action was taken.

To be sure, Tamil Nadu has its own set of problems, including politicisation and some corruption in NREGA works, conflicts over non-payment of minimum wages, low worker productivity, lack of worksite facilities, unmet demand for work and lack of community monitoring. Nevertheless, Tamil Nadu has achieved some success in providing employment on a large scale, paying wages on time and avoiding mass corruption.

Another special feature of the NREGA in Tamil Nadu is that an overwhelming majority (about 80 per cent) of NREGA workers are women. Most of them have no comparable work opportunities in the private sector.

Indeed, Tamil Nadu's strong tradition of active involvement in the social sector is finding a new expression through the NREGA. There is much to learn from this experience, just as Tamil Nadu itself has much to learn from pioneering experiences elsewhere.

GIVING RELIEF TO POOR PEOPLE

The National Rural Employment Guarantee Act (NREGA) offers relief to the emaciated underemployed manual labor and vital to those struggling for a living in drought prone dry land rain-fed farming dependent areas.

The first set of two hundred NREGA districts holds the largest concentrations of the poor who face shrinking livelihoods and a rapidly degrading of its fragile endowments and productive resources. Eking a livelihood meant able-bodied persons seasonally migrating for employment to irrigated areas but scope for work and wage rates in such areas are declining due mechanization abetted by subsidized agricultural equipment and labor saving farming practices.

While NREGA emerged to address declining employment avenues, the way it is now furthered offers no hope and future, leading to anxieties among people. This is because the areas and purpose of investments are not discussed nor is there criteria in the selection of "works".

To address the employment objective, the strategies to adopt must be clear and form the basis of selecting "works" rather than be taken as accepted or assumed that existing ones are right. This leads to NREGA resources being recklessly dumped with fanciful proposals, often in the name of gram sabha. Among strategies, the choice is between growth, income and new employment as outcomes, along with a clear understanding and measuring of the "rate of return". As declining employment led to NREGA, its reversal is the obvious task, as otherwise labor will have to solely depend on employment under government aegis. A hundred days per family limit with a much lower actual provisioning of employment in NREGA in a scenario of declining wage opportunities does not address the fears of labor.

A predominant thinking is that the task of works in NREGA is to offer manual labor and no more. This is the cause for disinterest among the people in suggesting "works" leading to such decisions vested with officials, experts and interest groups. In such a scenario the issue of triggering the employment dynamic through NREGA is overlooked. Policy makers should give priority on how NREGA investments can tackle rising employment deficit by expanding employment opportunities and equipping labor to acquire skills and capabilities to meet emerging labor market offers.

Growth as driver of development is empirically well established and vital to agriculturally backward areas. The issue is whether it should it be central in NREGA as huge investments are available in myriad other development schemes. Experience shows that triggering growth through infrastructure development such as roads, address issues of input access, output markets and value addition.

It utilizes existing productive capacities and natural resources with benefits accruing to existing producers and asset owners while offering little to wage and employment dependent people. A key reason to promote such works is the scope for profits to middlemen and cost manipulation by officials leading often to wasteful investments. Hence roads and physical infrastructure activities must be kept out of or given low preference in NREGA. Where it is taken up the aim must be for a high employment trajectory and a simple way to do so is that such activities be allowed a ratio of 90:10 for labor and materials component. Such reverse engineering in design and materials will lead to enhanced labor value in construction activities, leading to employment. This will address current malaise of the money provided under the ratio being aggregated and activities such as roads and housing receiving 10:90.

Another set of activities in NREGA is of tackling poverty or increasing incomes. Ideas are profligate with little accountability to outcomes. Ad hoc single intervention through bio-fuel plantations, adding of tank top soils on degraded lands and farm ponds etc are undertaken without much thought on how it is being integrated to serve the intended purpose. Such measures have yielded little as it fails to understand and address and harness the underlying resource endowment inadequacies and imbalances. So even if such investments are intrinsically worthwhile, it serves little purpose leading to wasted public investments. NREGA can serve as the key investment to address inadequacies and bottlenecks, not currently available in our land and water development plans and proposals.

The income deriving activities should then follow with the decision on the type of activity left to farmer. Only then will incomes bear fruit and motivate farmers rather than be a bureaucratic whim. NREGA investments must be seen as measures that take the resource to a potential seen as worthy of investment by involved private parties. Direct poverty alleviation plans must be left to others while NREGA helps create the conditions for such investments to flow.

What is urgently needed is to develop the land and natural resources and environmental services with a longer time horizon plan along with steps/measures that reverses degradation and motivates villagers to engage with and work on them.

This will be immensely valuable, as most workers also own small pieces of farmland and not possible to be done with their own resources. Developing this potential is possible only through public investments leading to generating additional incomes and employment.

For instance over a third of our arable land is fallow with most of them being single crop rain-fed farmlands and repeated drought has further worsened the situation. At our Centre we were successful in bringing such lands to productive use and withstand moisture stress by adopting a three-year phased approach to land development.

This involves soil improvement through aeration and humus addition in the first year, water conservation and soil working in the second year, followed by measures for environmental services in terms of pest control and soil microbial activity. This helped extremely degraded lands become productive along with capabilities to withstand drought stress. In addition one acre of land brought to productive use, provides employment of one hundred person days and twenty-eight bullock pair days along with a crop. NREGA must focus on works that lead to generating additional employment.

To widen and trigger the employment dynamic in NREGA, one needs to tackle workload and drudgery issues. Wage seekers now bring whatever tools they have at their homes to undertake the task. The crowbars are blunt and women use heavy metal baskets. This leads to tasks being hard and productivity and wages being low and driving many needy wage earners to shy away from NREGA. Some policy makers believe of hard manual work as the "test" to deserve the wage. Having simple and efficient tools will reduce drudgery, improve productivity and will help bring in a wider segment of employment deserving people to join NREGA. An efficient workforce would be better capable to meet the demands of emerging labor markets.

6

RELIABILITY OF NREGA

The National Rural Employment Guarantee Act, (NREGA) was enacted with the objective of enhancing livelihood security in rural areas by providing at least 100 days of guaranteed wage employment in a financial year, to every household whose adult members volunteer to do unskilled manual work. The Act initially came into force in 200 districts with effect from 2 February 2006. According to the Act, rural households have a right to register themselves with the local Gram Panchayats (GPs), and seek employment. Work is to be provided within 15 days from the date of demand, failing which the State Government will have to pay unemployment allowance at the stipulated rates. It is noted that the Act is a unique laudable Act of Parliament which confers a right on the rural households to demand up to 100 days of employment as a matter of their statutory right. Of the total available funds of Rs. 12074 crore (including the States' share of Rs 813 crore) upto March 2007, the State Governments could utilize Rs. 8823 crore (73 per cent).

A Performance Audit of the implementation of NREGA in the initially notified 200 districts was taken up during May–September 2007, in response to a request from the Ministry of Rural Development, so as to provide assurance that the processes under the Act were put in place and were being adopted effectively by the State Governments. The performance audit report was issued to the Ministry, which sent its response, and also forwarded the comments of 21 State Governments on relevant sections of the report. While doing so, the Ministry categorized the audit findings into (a) specific instances of irregularities and deviations committed by the implementing agencies of the State Governments, and (b) issues relating to the general principles in the Act, guidelines and instructions. As regards specific instances of irregularities/ deviations, the Ministry stated that it could not be expected to comment on such findings, as the relevant evidence was not available with it, nor was it practicable to comment on such findings, as the relevant evidence was not available with it, nor was it practicable for the Ministry to examine such evidence. Further, the Ministry stated that the State Governments were not subordinate organs of the Government of India, but were co-ordinate authorities within the framework of NREGA and the Constitution. However, audit holds that NREGA is a Central legislation, and the Ministry bears overall responsibility for co-ordinating and monitoring its administration and ensuring economical, efficient and effective utilization of funds provided by the GoI.

According to the Ministry's figures, 3.81 crore households had registered under the Act, Out of these, while, 2.12 crore households had demanded employment, 2.10 crore households were provided employment during 2006-07. The applications for work are to be submitted primarily at the Gram Panchayat, and it was crucial to maintain proper records of employment demanded, employment provided, number of days of employment generated, entitlement for employment allowance etc. However, the examination of field-level records by Audit reveled that record maintenance, particularly at GP level was, was poor, demonstrating the lack reliability and authenticity of the reported figures. Also, as the applications for demand for work were not documented or dated, and dated receipts for such applications were not issued in most cases, the eligibility of rural households for unemployment allowance, in these cases, was unverifiable. This would indicate that there is a high probability of only partial capturing of the demand for work.

There were several cases of delayed payment of wages, for which no compensation was paid. While there was a high probability that all demands for work were not being captured, there were also instances of non-payment of unemployment allowance which became due to employment seekers even where the records indicated that demand was not provided within 15 days from date of demand. Yet no one was fined for the violation of the Act. This indicates lack of an effective grievance redressal mechanism which defeated the very purpose of the Act of conferring a statutory right on the rural households for demanding upto 100 days of employment. The poor record maintenance further diluted the purpose of the Act as in the absence of dated acknowledgement of the application for work, there was no way the employment seekers could prove denial of demanded work and could claim entitlement for unemployment allowance.

Systems for financial management and tracking were deficient, as monthly squaring and reconciliation of accounts at different levels to maintain financial accountability and transparency was not being done. The status of inspection of works, and holding of Gram Sabhas to conduct Social Audit Forum was also not up to the mark. Subsequent to the original audit, some of the sampled districts were revisited to check the improvement in maintenance of records in February-March 2008, covering 24 GPs in 12 blocks in 12 districts in 6 States from within the original audit sample. The scrutiny revealed that while there was a definite improvement in record maintenance especially in Uttar Pradesh after the conduct of initial audit, the maintenance of basic records at the GP level, in particular the employment register was still deficient and there was considerable scope for improvement. The Ministry needs to ensure that State Governments take swift action to remedy these deficiencies and strengthen the processes and procedures for implementation of NREGA. The record maintenance at GP level needs to be streamlined. It should be ensured that all applications are dated, and dated receipts of applications are given to the job applicants. Up-to-date data entry of the important documents such as Job Card Register, Muster Rolls (with Job Card number and other details), Employment Register (to indicate employment demanded) and Asset Register is essential to achieve transparency and accountability and minimize fictitious/ duplicate entries, besides providing a basis for verification. All states should also be persuaded to put in place effective grievance redressal mechanisms so as to ensure that the purpose of NREG Act to provide 100 days employment as a matter of right is not diluted. Further, Government of India may consider amending NREGA for partial reimbursement (out of GoI funds) of payment of unemployment allowance, while instituting controls to minimize occasions to pay unemployment allowance. In the present scenario, since State Governments have to shell out funds for payment of unemployment allowance, there is an incentive for non-transparent recording of employment demand.

THE ACT: AN INTRODUCTION

Salient features of NREGA

The National Rural Employment Guarantee Act currently provides right of employment to about 5.4 crore rural poor in 200 most backward districts of the country. The Act provides employment guarantee to every rural household for 100 days in a year. In September 2005, UPA Government passed the National Rural Employment Guarantee Act 2005. This is perhaps the first time that the Panchayats have been provided with the freedom to plan and execute works and is backed by substantial resources, which are at their own disposal. Ideally, the Act and the programme design reflects to bring about a radical change in the rural areas as far as employment generation and creation of sustainable assets for the villages is concerned.

The NREGA programme's efficacy is based on the logic of using the productive capacity of ordinary rural folk to build and nurture productive and infrastructural assets, while simultaneously alleviating the problem of chronic unemployment and poverty. The Act provides an opportunity to build rural infrastructure through watershed development, restoration of water bodies such as tanks and canals, activities aimed at forestry, land development, and soil erosion and flood control, and construction of roads and institutional facilities. Anyone willing and able to perform unskilled manual labour at the statutory minimum wage can apply for work, which must be met within 15 days, failing which an unemployment allowance must be provided by the state.

In the year 2006-2007, a total budget of Rs 11300 crore was set aside to implement the programme in 200 districts of 27 States. In April 2007, 130 new districts have been added in the programme and the NREGA allocation has been increased to Rs 12000 crore for the year 2007-2008. At the state level, State Employment Guarantee Council and State Employment Guarantee Authorities have been formed. Separate fund for the programme called the State Employment Guarantee Fund needs to be created at the state level. The states are supposed to make a contribution of ten percent to the fund for effective implementation of the programme.

Key Findings of the First Monitoring Report

The poorest Areas Civil Society (PACS) Programme supported over 600 CSOs, working in the 108 poorest and most backward districts across six states of India, to enable the poor to realize their rights and entitlements more effectively. This NREGA implementation monitoring report is an outcome of the second round of monitoring of NREGA indicated by the PACS. In the first monitoring report 107 villages of 87 Gram Panchayats have been covered from 20 districts in six PACS intervened states. Moreover a substantial amount of information was collected from the experiences of the Rojgaar Yatras held by PACS in six states reaching out to 2170 villages. In the first monitoring report, it was observed that the status of registration for the job cards was poor in the states of Maharashtra and Bihar. It was also observed that the job cards were not being used properly in any of the states. There was a lack of demand for jobs under NREGA as people were not aware of the fact that they can demand employment under the Act. As far as resources available and the resources utilised were concerned, Madhya Pradesh was the best performing state among the six states and Maharashtra was the poorest performer. The lack of worksite facilities, medical care for injured workers was also conspicuous in all the states.

At the institutional level, it was observed that the districts with high utilisation had started facing shortage of funds because of non-compliance of certain aspects like release of state share, formation of State Employment Guarantee Fund, formation of the State Employment Guarantee Council etc. The lack of funds at the district level also had adverse effect on the Panchayats as they were not able to pay the wages of the workers on time. The top-down approach of planning was also adversely affecting the functioning of Panchayats. It was also observed that there was inadequate flexibility with the

Panchayats to use the NREGA funds for addressing local issues. In this round of NREGA status monitoring, structured research was conducted to generate longitudinal data on selective variables as well as cover new issues and dimensions, which have become more visible and prominent with the maturity of the scheme.

Objectives of the second monitoring report

- To review performance of NREGA with an inter-state and interdistrict comparison
- To understand effectiveness of implementation of NREGA from the poor villagers' perspective in the six intervention states of PACS programme
- To identify institutional and other bottlenecks at different levels affecting implementation of NREGA and pave the way forward

Methodology

The first monitoring report was prepared using the macro level secondary national data as well as primary data from six PACS-intervened states. The same format has been used to prepare the second monitoring report, taking the period from April 2006 to March 2007. This period overlaps with the first monitoring report. However, it was felt that it would be relevant to cover the complete financial year for building a more comprehensive understanding of the programme.

Collection of Data from Secondary Sources

In order to develop a nationwide scenario of the NREGA performance as well as to consider inter-state and inter-district comparison, data from the website of NREGA as well as from the state offices of NREGA were collected. The available macro data is helpful in building a national picture of the programme as field visits or primary data collection from each of the state was not possible in this study.

Sampling Design for Primary Survey

The sampling design was based on the rationale that the voluntary organisations working in collaboration with PACS programme can provide deeper understanding on the issues from the Panchayats of their work. In this report therefore, the status of NREGA, which illustrates ground realities from six states viz. Bihar, Chhattisgarh, Jharkhand, Madhya Pradesh, Maharashtra and Uttar Pradesh, has been covered by collecting primary data.

Since Panchayat is the principal authority in implementation of NREGA, the unit of sampling is considered to be Panchayat. Considering the strength of large-scale presence of PACS initiatives in NREGA districts with partners, it was decided that CSOs working under the PACS programme would collect data at the community, village and Panchayat level. The selection of the CSOs was carried out in such a way that the data represents the diverse socioeconomic and geographic conditions. Overall 283 Panchayats and 600 villages from different socio-cultural backgrounds were taken in 39 districts of the six PACS intervened states.

Study Period

The study period was considered from 1st April 2006 to 31st March 2007 in order to cover a complete financial year. The secondary data was collected during April 2007 so that latest updated of works completed and expenditure etc. could be collected.

Study Process

Preparation of structured schedules: Samarthan, in consultation with PACS, prepared a set of questionnaires that covered the different aspects of NREGA implementation. Questionnaires were developed to capture the progress of NREGA at the state, district, Panchayat and village levels. Apart from structured schedules, some semi structured questionnaires were also developed to capture the views and opinions of different stakeholders.

Identification of districts: The study was designed in such a way that maximum possible diversity within the states could be captured. Therefore, the choice of the PACS partners was carefully done to maximise the geographical diversity.

Orientation of volunteers: The CSOs identified the volunteers who would collect information from the field, using structured and unstructured questionnaires. Around 200 volunteers were oriented in five batches in six states.

Data collection from the field: The concerned State PSTs coordinated with the CSOs to ensure timely and accurate collection of data. The ROs supported the CSO volunteers to collect quality data systematically. Team members from Samarthan also surveyed five Gram Panchayats from the data collection sites in each of the states to have the first hand understanding of the issues and bottlenecks of NREGA.

Data analysis and report writing: The collected data was analysed and the report was prepared using the available primary and secondary data. Draft findings were shared with PACS team for comments and suggestions for the finalisation of the study. Study tools The study was conducted using structured interview schedules. A set of five questionnaires, focusing on different types of respondents, was administered. These questionnaires were framed to collect both qualitative as well as quantitative data with respect to the implementation of the scheme. Questionnaires were administered to collect information at the state, district, Panchayat and village levels. Case studies were also collected from the field to substantiate the findings from the research. Extensive analysis of print media and website was done in order to see the different perspectives on the issues of implementation of NREGA in different states. Different perspectives of the CSOs working in the state could be gathered during the workshops. Interactions were held with the district level as well as state level officials. The details of the questionnaire are as mentioned below:

State level data format: The state level formats were administered with the state level officials implementing the scheme. The format gathered information on the methods of popularising the scheme, the arrangements for people's participation, the state level strategy for implementation of the scheme, and on how the MIS and online monitoring systems are maintained.

District level formats: The district level formats were designed to collect information on the aspects of implementation in the districts. The questionnaire focused on the manpower available at the district, the flow of funds from the Central government, the difficulties that the district administration is facing in implementing the scheme and the suggestions from the district administration for improvement in the scheme. Gram Panchayat level formats: The format captures information on the number of families in the village, the BPL families, and the number of families with and without job cards. The format also captures information on the perspective plan prepared in the village, the budget for the year, the targeted beneficiaries, and the man days of work that would be generated. The format collects information on the details of implementation of the scheme in the village and people's perspective on each aspect. Village level formats: The village level schedule was primarily focused on collecting data from the villagers. The questions included seeking information from labourers on the wage payment, the measurement aspects, the muster roll preparation etc. it also looked into the aspects of worksite facilities available. A section on identifying issues related to women and children was also included in the questionnaire. Data from the community was also collected using focused group discussions. Limitation of the Study

Limited / inadequate information on the website: While data form the six PACS intervened states could be gathered by visiting the state offices, the only source of secondary information from the other 21 states was the national website on NREGA. www.nrega.nic.in. While this data has been quite useful, there were some states and districts which had not put up data on some aspects on the Net. These have been recorded as 'zero' value on the Internet. Therefore, adequate data availability on the Internet is one of the limitations. Moreover, reliability of the data is The Act: An Introduction 11 also questionable in certain cases. However, there is no alternative source for state level data.

Primary data from only selective field sites of the CSOs: Though efforts were made to gather data from different sites that are diverse in nature, the primary data was collected only from the field sites in which the PACS partners were working. Hence, the sample is not truly random meeting the statistical rigour of the sampling techniques.

Inadequate NREGA worksites covered in the state of Maharashtra: Owing to an overlap of the state-run EGS and the NREGA in Maharashtra, the implementation of NREGA works has not been started in most part of the state till the time data was being collected for this study. Out of a sample of 36 Gram Panchayats from where data was collected, NREGA works had started in only three Panchayats.

Since this sample was too small to be considered for a meaningful analysis, the data from Maharashtra has not been included in the sections related to ongoing or completed works under NREGA.

Worksite / Work related primary data based on the records of Panchayats: Since Panchayat records were the only source of data on some of the variables related to work and worksite related aspects, most of the primary data depicts the information collected from the Panchayat records. The data has limitation as it was impossible to generate alternative primary data on budgets, expenditure etc.

GOVERNMENT PERSPECTIVE ON IMPLEMENTATION OF NREGA IN PACS INTERVENED STATES

The NREGS has several key dimensions / processes which are interdependent and have implications on the overall performance. Presentation here has been arranged in the sequence which normally takes place in the implementation of the programme. We have considered all the NREGA states for the analysis.

Issuance of Job Cards

As far as the registration of the families is concerned, different states followed different strategies. The basis of identifying families for registration was the lists of households that were prepared during 2003 BPL survey. At the national level, MIS data on the Government website reported that during 2006- 07, more than 2.09 crore families were registered under the NREGA. The secondary sources also indicate that 3.78 crore job cards have been issued till March, 2007 in all the 27 NREGA states.

Some of the key observations on job cards issued are:

- The villagers of poorer States like Bihar (45.94%), and Uttar Pradesh (55.91%) have lowest access to jobs as relatively low percentage of families have job cards.

- Madhya Pradesh has been distinctively ahead in providing job cards to the families. It has actually distributed job cards to more number of households than the number of households mentioned in the 2001 census.
- Chhattisgarh and Maharashtra have exceeded the national average of job cards issued.

Overall, more than 70% rural households in the 200 districts of Phase I of NREGA have been issued Job Cards. The status of PACS intervened states in issuance of Job Cards is as reflected in the Table 2.1.

Access to Job Cards to the Scheduled Caste and Scheduled Tribe Families

Having a Job Card is the first step to demand employment and claim wages or unemployment allowance if job is not provided within the stipulated time frame. The situation of the registration of the disadvantaged sections as job card holders shows the following trends: It has been observed that among the job card holders, the number of tribals is less in the states of Chhattisgarh (48.13%), Jharkhand (38.35%), and Madhya Pradesh (41.20%). While these figures look impressive as compared to the other states as well as the national average, it has to be noted that these states are highly tribal dominated and most of these tribal families belong to the poorest section of the society. It appears that in these states, inadequate attention has been given to target tribal families.

Similarly, the scheduled caste dominated states have relatively low job cards for the SC families – Bihar (43.13%), MP (14.16%) and UP (54.67%) – as compared to the proportion of scheduled caste presence in these states, especially in the NREGA districts.

Employment Demanded Vs Employment Provided

One of the most important aspects of NREGA is that the villagers can rightfully demand employment. The Government is bound to provide employment in response to the demand or provide unemployment allowance in case it is unable to do so. In order to understand the effectiveness of the Act, it is essential to look at the response of the Government in providing employment against the demand raised by the workers. The major observations from the secondary data available on the NREGA is as follows:

- From the secondary data available on the Internet, the national scenario reveals that, 99% people who have applied for jobs have got employment under NREGA. However, it has been observed that the demand is not natural, rather manipulated, as in the case of states like Jharkhand where the figure is 100%, which possibly reflects that those who could be given jobs were reported as those who demanded jobs.
- Of the total person days generated, women constitute more than 40%. The scheduled caste families have been provided with 25.36% and the scheduled tribe families with 36.45% person days of work.
- Poorer states have not been able to create more employment opportunities for women, as in Bihar only 17.38% and in UP 16.55% women person days could be generated.

Employment to SC and ST Persons

Concentration of SC and ST population vary in different states, therefore figures of SC/ST workdays generated can be meaningfully interpreted with the availability of percentage of SC/ST population in the NREGA districts. However, the following trend emerged from the person days generated:

- The lower proportion of SC having job cards in these states is in itself a constraint for sufficient job creation in the states of Uttar Pradesh, Bihar and Madhya Pradesh. It can be seen from the secondary data available on the Internet that only 56.85% in Uttar Pradesh, 47.08% in Bihar and 15.87% in Madhya Pradesh have been reported as the person days of work generated for scheduled caste.
- Similarly, in ST dominated states like Chhattisgarh (45.45%), Jharkhand (40.29%), Madhya Pradesh (48.6%), and Maharashtra (40.88%), relatively lower person days have been generated among the ST households.
- In many developed states, proportion of person days generated for the SC/ST is relatively high as in Punjab (69.36% SC), Tamil Nadu (56.06% SC), and Karnataka

(53.50% SC and ST). This reflects a positive case of addressing poverty, which is concentrated in selective social groups, even in the developed states.

Number of Households Provided 100 days of Employment

The Act guarantees provision of at least 100 days of employment to each household that demands work and is willing to do manual labour. The percentage of households that have been provided with 100 days of employment is an important indicator for assessing the performance of the states in implementing NREGA. The percentage of job card holder households that have been provided 100 days employment under NREGA, in the six PACS-intervened states, is as mentioned in Table 2.3 (given on the next page). Nationally, only 5.71% households have been provided 100 days of employment in the last financial year. The data clearly shows that even in the state of Madhya Pradesh, which is one of the better performing states in the country, the figure is still below 12%. Maharashtra has been the poorest performer in this regard.

Expenditure on NREGA

The utilisation of resources available with the state government is also an important indicator to measure the success of the state in implementing the Act. The states that are able to utilise more resources reflect that on an average, they have been able to produce more person days of work and create more infrastructures in the villages. The availability of resources and the utilisation pattern for six states considered under the study is mentioned in Table 2.4. Nationally, 66.20% resources have been spent on wages and 31.28% on material or skilled labour. Among the PACS states, Maharashtra is utilising maximum proportion of resources on wages. However, a clearer picture regarding Maharashtra would emerge in the next few months when more works will be initiated in the state.

The secondary data clearly suggests that there is still scope for increasing the utilisation of NREGA resources. The national average for utilisation of NREGA resources is merely 73%. Considering that there is a general perception that the utilisation rate at the Panchayat level will go down as very few works will remain to be taken up as the scheme progresses. The average expenditure per district (in Rs Crore) and the national average is shown in the chart below. Among the PACS intervened states, only Madhya Pradesh and Chhattisgarh exceed the national average. The progress in Maharashtra is the poorest with an average expenditure of only Rs 14.55 crores per district [BA1].

The Government data does give us an idea of the status of implementation of NREGA in the PACS-intervened states. The block and district level functionaries lack capacities in filing up formats or uploading data online on the performance of NREGA. Therefore, the available statewise picture of performance is also not adequately representative of the ground realities. There is a need for a rigorous scrutiny of the data being fed right from the Panchayat level upto the district and the state level. The resource utilisation is a key parameter for the release of the next instalment.

7

FIELD EXPERIENCES: CASE STUDY OF SIX NREGA STATES

REGISTRATION, JOB CARD PREPARATION AND DISTRIBUTION

The mandate of the NREG Act has been the guaranteed employment generation, and is dependent on several administrative factors viz. registration, job card preparation and distribution, application for work, initiation of the work, appropriate and timely measurement/valuation of the work and subsequent release of wage payment to the labourers. Any discrepancy in the chain would consequently effect the employment generation. Table 3.1 shows the status of registration and job card distribution in the sample villages of the selected states. The lack of initiative by the Government is popularising the scheme for all the wrong reasons and has made ways for rumours to creep in. In some Panchayats in Jharkhand, rumours were spread that the programme is meant only for SCs and STs, hence people from other communities did not register under the scheme. Similarly in Tikamgarh district of Madhya Pradesh, there were rumours that those registering for job cards would be sent to Iraq for work.

Job Card is the most important instrument that can ensure that the workers are not being cheated on their entitlements. However, it has been observed in most of the states that the job cards are often kept with the *Sarpanches* (Village Head) or *Sachiv* (Panchayat Secretary). Pramod Kumar Deghariya in Pokata Panchayat of Basia Block in Jharkhand informed that 72 families had registered for job cards in March 2006. However till date, only 48 job cards have been distributed. In Romjaaal village of Banki Panchayat (Bano block – District Gumla), Gram Sabha members informed that their job cards are kept with the Gram Sevak and he refused to give cards back to the workers. In Jhulna Panchayat of Shivpuri District, though all member of the Gram Sabha have been registered and their job cards have been prepared, it has not been distributed to the workers yet.

In Uttar Pradesh, it was observed that only around 45% job cards have been distributed so far. The remaining job cards were kept with the Pradhan or the Secretary. Shivpyari from Kondar village of Asothar block of Fatehpur district of Uttar Pradesh, reported that the job cards of the workers were under the custody of the Pradhan and often the entries in it were found to be false. Similar observations were made by other civil society groups too. According to the reports of the social audit conducted by NREGA WATCH, at Anedi village of Murhi Panchayat in Ranchi District, no job cards were issued to villagers. Many villagers have also not applied for job cards as they are not aware of the NREGA. Two days prior to the commencement of the social audit campaign, the block officials took some sample job cards to the village and showed it to the villagers. Similarly in Siladon Panchyat, Block Khunti, the job cards of the workers were in the custody of the Panchayat Sewak for the past ten months.

There are also incidents where workers were provided work without providing them job cards. The workers in Ladabill village of Meromagutu Panchayat in P. Sighbhum district of Jharkhand, reported that none of the villagers have been issued with a job card as yet, though they were provided work under NREGA.

It has also been observed that Sarpanchs and (Secretaries) kept the job cards with them so that they could misuse them while implementing the works. In Urugutu Panchayat of Ranchi district, separate job cards were issued for each member of the family of the Sarpanch, whereas the Act states that there should be only one job card for one family. In Pada Gram Panchayat of Kedapur Tehsil of Yeotmal district in Maharashtra, the workers said that the Gram Sevaks and Sarpanchs kept blank job cards in their custody and used them it to serve their personal interests. The workers also reported that there is a lot of delay in issuing job cards and it has taken almost eight months for the workers to get their job cards even after registration.

KEY OBSERVATIONS

The primary data collected from six sample states reveals that out of the total families in the sample, villages, 47.69% families have been registered under the scheme. Whereas, the national average obtained from the secondary data suggests that more than 70% rural households have been registered under NREGA. Out of the total registered families, approximately 90% families have received the job cards. However, it has been observed that while job cards have been prepared and distributed, these have been taken back by the Sarpanch or the Sachiv. In several cases, the entries in the job cards are not known to the card holder.

The NREGS does not limit its benefits to BPL families; however, the primary data has been collected from BPL families having NREGA Job Cards. In Maharashtra and Uttar Pradesh, about 96% BPL families have job cards. Chhattisgarh and Jharkhand have the lowest figures at 32.33% and 39.82% respectively. There are several cases where the figures for the number of days of employment provided were inflated in the job cards. This has been done to accommodate the commissions for the block level functionaries like the Junior Engineers and the Block Programme Officers. In Jharkhand and Maharashtra, it was observed that the workers were being asked either to pay an amount of Rs 20-40 for photographs or submit their photographs for the job cards. In many Panchayats in Chhattisgarh, job cards were found in the custody of the Sarpanch on the pretext that the photograph is not attached. Also, the village community is not aware of how to procure it from the Panchayat. It was also observed that job cards have been made even for those who are in service or who do not have to do manual labour.

PERSPECTIVE PLAN PREPARATION AND WORK EXECUTION

The NREGS has made provisions for enabling bottom-up planning for all the works undertaken in the villages. All

Panchayats are supposed to prepare the five year perspective plans for implementation of NREGA. Based on the perspective plans, the annual plans have to be prepared as per the requirement of the Gram Sabha.

In the surveyed Panchayats, it was found that apart from Bihar, Maharashtra and Jharkhand, five year perspective plans were prepared in more than 90% surveyed Panchayats in the other three states. In Madhya Pradesh, perspective plans were prepared in 98% Panchayats surveyed. In Maharashtra, only 41% and in Bihar only 48% of the survey Panchayats had their perspective plans prepared.

While the Panchayats reported that five year perspective plans as well as annual plans were prepared, the villagers' perspective and priorities were missing in these plans. In Jharkhand, in most of the Panchayats that were surveyed, it was observed that the plans were prepared at the district level and implemented at the village level. The involvement of Gram Sabha and the Labhuk Samiti was negligible in preparation of the plan.

The Uttar Pradesh Government has appointed 'Panchayat Mitras' (or Panchayat Friends) for assisting the Panchayats in implementing NREGA, however these newly appointed personnel have yet to be trained. Since the Panchayat Mitras do not have much understanding of the perspective plans, they become dependent on Panchayat Secretaries for understanding the technicalities and the priorities of work to be undertaken. Even the elected representatives need to be trained for effective implementation of the plans.

The Pradhans in Uttar Pradesh were aware of the perspective plans. However, they believed that the amount received by the Panchayat depended on the quota fixed for the block which is received from the district officials. Unless the elected representatives and the NREGA-specific staff is properly oriented, they will continue to work under the influence of the Panchayat Secretaries, and block and district level officials.

INFLUENCE MATTERS MORE THAN PERSPECTIVE PLAN

The individual connections of the Sarpanch of the Panchayat also play a crucial role in deciding the works to be implemented at the Panchayat level. On an average, only around two to three works were initiated in the sample village. However, it was observed through the qualitative data obtained from the Panchayats in Uttar Pradesh and Madhya Pradesh, that the Panchayats which had influential Sarpanchs were able to start several works at the same time. The others had to wait for directions from the block or district level officials.

Efficiency in Technical and Administrative Sanctions

Technical and administrative sanctions are required for all planned activities. In the surveyed Panchayats, it was observed that in only 50% cases, the procedure took around 7 to 15 days for technical clearance. Once the technical clearance is obtained, it takes another 7 to 15 days (in 50% cases) for the funds to be allocated to the accounts of the Panchayat. Thus effectively, if any work has to be undertaken in a Panchayat, it would require around 15 to 30 days before it can actually commence. Since the NREGA works have to be planned for a lean period of work (usually lasting for only four months), such delays would affect the overall implementation of the programme if proper attention is not given on planning the activities.

The status of technical sanction and allocation in sample Gram Panchayats is given in Table 3.2. Besides the delay in technical and administrative sanctions, it has also been observed that the works were included in the shelf of projects without proper planning. Jauhar Singh of Bhanwahi Panchayat from Beejadandi block of Mandla district in Madhya Pradesh reported that the construction of a pond was included in the project without paying any attention over the status of land.

Later on, it turned out that the land was disputed and a local resident, Shiv Lal, claimed its ownership. Hence, the work could not be taken up in the current year.

It has also been observed in the surveyed Panchayats that there are instances where the amount mentioned in the technical proposal sent by the Panchayat are deducted by the block level officials without giving any reason. Thus, the Panchayats have to work on the same activity with a reduced budget. This has also been a reason for reduced wage payment at some worksites.

Works Udertaken

While the basic principle of NREGA is provision of guaranteed employment to people willing to do manual labour, it also envisages creation of sustainable village assets which would, in the long term, improve the overall economy of the village.

If we look at the proportion of works sanctioned, it is evident that most of the works are on water conservation and water harvesting structures, followed by rural connectivity. In the surveyed villages, it was observed that most of the works undertaken were that of rural connectivity followed by water conservation structures. There is an overemphasis on creation of bigger structures that are resource intensive as compared to the smaller works like land development and irrigation works on the lands of SC/ST, despite the fact that there is demand for it. On an average, only 9.7% of the total works undertaken has been on provision of irrigation facilities to the land owned by SC/ST. Some key observations from the field are as mentioned below:

- In Jharkhand and Madhya Pradesh, it was observed that works were undertaken as per the priorities stated by the block officials. Works on SC/ST farms do not figure as a priority of the Panchayats in any of the six states.
- In Madhya Pradesh, more than 90% works have been undertaken by Panchayat in the state.
- In Madhya Pradesh and Uttar Pradesh, some Panchayats reported that the amount proposed under the technical proposal is deducted (even up to 50%) by the block office without giving any reason for such deductions.

Relatively, a high reporting of cases in 'others' category clearly reflects tha either the agencies are unable to appropriately fix the works in the prescribed category or many works other than the prescribed have actually been taken up. Any other work not specified in the eight categories of NREGA requires permission from the MORD.

COMPLETION OF THE SANCTIONED WORKS UNDER NREGA

In the surveyed villages from all the six states, it was observed that out of the 814 works being carried out in the Panchayats only

46% works have been completed as per the annual plan. In Maharashtra, work did not even commence in most of the surveyed villages. Only three villages could be identified where work was being implemented during the survey. The status of completion of the work taken under NREGS in the sample village and as per the secondary data is as shown in the chart below.

Provision for Works and Wages

The Act is based on the fact that the workers would demand work as a right and the Panchayat or the Government would ensure that the person is provided with work within 15 days of receipt of such an application. The workers engaged in NREGA works should also be paid wages within 7 to 15 days. NREGA provides clear cut instructions on the manner and the time frame in which the workers can get their entitlements. This section deals with the ground realities as far as the provision for work and wages is concerned.

Artificial Vs Real Demand for Work

In the surveyed Panchayats, it was observed that people have not really understood the meaning of 'demand' intended as a right to employment under the Act. The implementing agencies have initiated works under the scheme and people are asked to come for the work. Those who are interested come forward and join the work. Often, the Secretary of the Panchayat gets the applications filed at the site of work. The government figures are mostly based on the local records manipulated by the implementing agencies. Therefore, the national figure of employment provided against the demand raised shows a rosy picture. There is lack of awareness regarding demanding work as a right. In Jharkhand and Madhya Pradesh, people reported that they were not aware that they had to apply for jobs. From the qualitative information collected from Jharkhand, it was observed that people thought that having a job card automatically makes the workers entitled for 100 days of employment. It has also been observed that the whole concept of demand for job is fictitious as people are turning up for work as in any other Government scheme and while they are working, the secretaries fill up their applications to demand jobs as a mere formality.

The secondary data on the demand is based on the figures provided by the Panchayat Secretaries to the block officials. However, it is observed from the field that this data is not reliable. In several cases, it has been observed from the field that the number of work days entered in the job cards is inflated. Beena Raikwar, a 58 years old worker from Khirvahpurwa village of Rajnagar block of Chattarpur district (Madhya Pradesh), informed that while she has worked only for 12 days, the entry in the job card shows 18 days. Similarly, Champa Lal of Badokhra Panchayat from Shivpuri block of Shivpuri District (Madhya Pradesh) said that he got nine days of work in a road construction site in Khiriya village while 28 days were entered in his job card.

In the case of Maharashtra, there is an apparent apathy among citizens for demanding work as a right because they feel this will also go the way EGS has gone, in which it was very difficult to get unemployment allowance if work is not provided. Besides, demand for work is also weak because workers feel that they can earn better wages by migrating to nearby towns to earn higher wages. The response of the Panchayats and the implementing agencies to the demands raised by the workers is also quite poor. Often the Panchayats do not provide receipts to the demand raised by the workers. Anandi Saharia, an illiterate worker form Puradhankuan Panchayat of Bar Block in Lalitpur district, informed that he had orally demanded work several times since May 2007, but till date he did not get any work. The Pradhan mentioned that the Panchayat does not have enough money in its account to initiate any work. There is also a fear among the workers that if they demand job as a right, they might end up getting no work at all in the village as Sarpanchs are influential and seeking justice at higher level is more expensive for them. In Patgarh village of Garbandh Panchayat in Garhwa district (UP), 127 villagers had applied for work but they never received any receipt for the applications and neither were they provided employment. Similarly in Mandar Block of Ranchi, there were 175 job card holders in five villages who had submitted applications long back, but 166 of them never got any work.

There is a general feedback on non-issuance of receipt to the workers demanding work. This weakens their case to demand employment. There is also apathy on account of the Government to provide unemployment allowance. Sakina Khatoon of Raghopur Panchayat in Meenapur block of Muzaffarpur district in Bihar, claims that the Secretary discourages women from demanding work under NREGA, stating that women cannot do hard manual labour. When she applied for work in January 2007, she was neither given work nor the receipt of the application. The case of Madhya Pradesh is also no different. In Gumanganj Panchayat of Ajaygarh block in Panna district, the Secretary said that the block programme officer has asked all secretaries not to accept applications for work. Similar experiences were observed in other states as well. Kaushyalya Devi (Kamarthu Panchayat, Gaighat block, Muzaffarpur district, Bihar), along with 15 other women, demanded work under NREGA from the Panchayat in October 2006, but they have neither been provided with jobs nor job cards till date.

Response Time to Call for Employment

From the analysis of primary data, it has emerged that where people are applying for work, in most of the states, people are getting jobs between 15 to 30 days. Only in Chhattisgarh and Madhya Pradesh, more than 50% respondents have received jobs in less than 15 days. In the case of Maharashtra, it was found that none of the respondents had got jobs within 15 days. However, the data from Maharashtra reflects the situation of only three Panchayats where work had started in the surveyed Panchayats, hence it has not been included in the chart provided on the next page.

Measurement based Payment

In most of the cases, wage payment is based on work measurement. Though measurement specifications have been defined in the State Schedule of Rates (SOR), however, the measurement is not done in front of the workers. Many of the workers are unable to calculate the amount of work done and the multiplication factor applied to calculate the wage rate. Pradhan/ Sarpanch/ Labhuk samiti members submit the details of work done at the residence of the civil engineer. In a case observed by the NREGA WATCH, villagers from Chilgu village of Ranchi district in Jharkhand, informed that although the work has been on-going in the village for the last four months, the Junior Engineer (JE) has not measured the work done over this period; as a result, the workers have not received any payments for the work done. The beneficiary (Labhuk Samiti Member) Narian Singh Munda informed that he had to bribe the Panchayat Sewak with three hundred rupees to ensure that the measurements are taken on time.

Labourers find it difficult to measure the payments with 100 days' guarantee on the minimum wage rate. In most of the cases, the Mate or the field site supervisor conducts measurement at the end of the day's work. Due to paucity of civil engineers available with the NREGA as well as the practice of avoiding transparency, work measurement by the concerned civil engineer is mostly not done on the site of the work.

In Jharkhand, in many cases, labourers work in the early morning and finish digging by lunch time. They have to come around 5 pm again to show the work to the mate/supervisor so that his/her attendance and measurement of work is recorded. This wastes the time of the labourer to do any other work, though the payment is on a measurement basis. However, mates want labourers to be involved for the whole day.

Average Wages Realised by Workers

The field realities are much different from what is apparent from the secondary sources of information. In almost all the states, the workers mentioned that they receive much lesser amount as wages than what is prescribed by the state norms. Besides, the workers have said that they could get better wages elsewhere. This has also led to a reduced demand for work. Banwari of Urauli Panchayat from Asothar block of Fatehpur district in Uttar Pradesh has reported that under NREGA, workers are getting only Rs 50 per day as wages and that too after more than two months. He prefers to work in the sand mine where he regularly gets around Rs 100 to Rs 150 per day as wages. This has made him lose interest in the works under NREGA. Raju Ansari from Darhai Padri village in Muzaffarpur district of Bihar also reported that people are getting only Rs 50 per day for the work being done under NREGA.

Since people can find better wages elsewhere, they are slowly losing interest in the NREGA work.

The workers are complaining of low wage rate in Gram Panchayat Adawaal, which is about 20 km away from the block headquarter of Bastar in Chhattisgarh. Many families applied for work and the de-silting of a pond was started within few days, but only 25 labourers came for work and others did not turn up. About 65 workers were going outside the village to work, for which they were getting Rs.30-40 per day. They were not interested in working under NREGA because they had the apprehension that the payments would be delayed and that they will not receive the wage rate of Rs. 62.63 per day.

Delayed Payment to Workers

In the surveyed states, it was observed that on an average, 33% people in the states were receiving wages within seven days of completion of work. In 55% cases, people were getting their wages in more than 7 days but lesser than 30 days. In 13% cases, there was a delay of more than 30 days in wage payment.

In a recent survey conducted by UPVAN in Uttar Pradesh, it was observed that of the 952 respondents, 53% respondents said that they did not get wages within 7 days as mandated in the Act. More than 32% respondents also informed that the wages paid were much less than the prescribed wage rate.

Mode of Wage Payment

NREGA has made provisions for making payments in cash as well as in kind, with a precondition that at least 25% of the total payment shall be in cash. It has been observed in the surveyed Panchayats that in 92% cases, workers were being paid in cash. In around 8 percent cases, workers were being paid in kind as well. The statewise status on the mode of payment is as mentioned in the adjoining chart. Maximum Payment in a mix of cash and kind is being done in Maharashtra, followed by Bihar and U.P.

ADDITIONAL AMOUNT FOR WORKING AT A DISTANCE

If people get work at a place which is more than 5 kms from their village, they are entitled to have additional ten percent of their wages as per NREGA. In the surveyed Panchayats, it was found that in most places people were getting work within the Panchayat. However, there were cases where people were provided work at a distance that was more than five kilometres from their native village. It has emerged from the primary data that on worksites away from the village, additional wages were provided to the workers in only 1.9% cases.

The workers from Badachapudiya Panchayat of Dumka District were given work in Tasria village which is eight kilometres away; however, no additional wages were paid to the workers. Similar cases were observed in Pulwas Panchayat of Lalitpur district in Uttar Pradesh and Khaiva Panchayat of Chattarpur district in Madhya Pradesh. The status of additional wages at distant worksites is given in Table 3.3.

Average Family Income Realised during the Year

The NREGA guarantees 100 days of employment per year to each rural household willing to do manual labour at a minimum wage rate of Rs 60 per person per day. Thus, the minimum guarantee that the Act provides is Rs 6000 per household per year. The average wages realised per family per year in the surveyed Panchayats is given in Table 3.4.

The data collected from the sampled villages, reflects that on an average the families which have demanded work have received only 18.45 days of work under NREGA. The average family income per year in the five states, estimated from 814 works of the 283 Panchayats, is coming out to be Rs 1990.

This is much lesser than the average of Rs 6000 per family per year as of approximate wage payment for 100 days' employment as promised under the Act. 45 From the data obtained from the sample villages, it has emerged that in most of the states, the average income earned by the families is much lower than what is prescribed by the Act. The data from the field study reveals that in Madhya Pradesh on an average, a family is able to earn Rs 4854 per year. Bihar has been able to provide average wages worth only Rs 705 per family in the year 2006-07. From the study, some of the key issues identified with reference to the issue of wage payment are as follows:

- Largely, there is ambiguity in the understanding of the people on the mode of payment (based on the measurement or on a daily basis) and this has resulted in resentment regarding the scheme.
- Unavailability of staff for implementing NREGS is the most important reason for delays in measurement. There are insufficient overseers for measuring the work. On an average, each civil engineer has to look after more than ten Panchayats.
- There is a practice of making payments in instalments, which makes it difficult for the workers to keep track of. Even the records (especially muster roll and job cards) are not maintained regularly. Thus, it is very difficult for the labourer or anybody else to conclude regarding the exact wage that has been paid for a particular work.
- The state of Bihar (along with Andhra Pradesh, Gujarat and West Bengal) has come under the scanner of the Ministry of Rural Development for indirectly increasing the wage rate under NREGA. The indirect increase is caused by reducing the quantum of work that has to be done in a day. According to reports published in the Times of India, the output for women has been considerably decreased in these states, which effectively means that the workers have to do lesser amount of work to earn the minimum wages. The Rural Development Ministry has expressed concern that such a move would ultimately affect the agriculture sector in the state as higher wages under NREGS would lead to an exodus of workers from the agriculture sector to the works initiated under NREGS.

Employment Opportunities for Women

The employment opportunities provided to women in the six states is shown in the chart on the next page. Both the primary data as well as the secondary data indicate that Bihar and Uttar Pradesh have performed poorly as far as providing employment opportunities to women is concerned. In the surveyed Panchayats in both states, it was observed that the employment opportunities for women were lesser than 25 percent of the total workdays generated. The case of Maharashtra has not been included here because out of all the surveyed villages, NREGA works were initiated in only three Panchayats in Maharashtra and the data does not appear to be representative of the entire state.

Gender discrimination is apparent in the refusal by the Panchayats to provide work opportunities to women as well as discrimination of payment to women. Lambardi Bai of Ladhari Panchayat from Bhainsdehi block of Betul district of Madhya Pradesh reported that in her village, preference is given to men for working under NREGA. The Sarpanch and Secretary discourage women to work at these sites, hence they are forced to look for work elsewhere. The workers from Nouawkhar Panchayat of Madhubani District of Bihar also reported that women are considered incapable of doing hard manual labour, hence they are paid lesser wages than men working at the same site. Similarly, the workers in Kundera Panchayat from Banka district and Majhika Harikase Panchayat from West Champaran district have revealed that women are not given any work under NREGA. Sumitra Devi of Meenapur Panchayat of Muzaffarpur district of Bihar also informed that the Panchayats did not prefer giving work to the women because women cannot do hard manual labour. She also complained that there is unequal wage payment to the women.

In Uttar Pradesh, it appears that the cultural and traditional factors are influencing the demand of employment. In many districts of Uttar Pradesh that have traditionally harboured feudal gender practices and have not allowed women to work in the public domain, especially with men from different families, restricted their women folk to seek employment under NREGS. The traditions are reflected in the macro data of the state with very small percentage of the women covered under the scheme at 16.6 percent only as against the required 33 percent.In districts like Sitapur and Jalaun, the percentage of women coming out to work is extremely low, while in hilly districts such as Chandoli, the participation of women has been higher.

In Panchayat Poorunpur in Kasmanda block of the Sitapur district, men clearly stated they would rather go hungry than to send their womenfolk to work with other men folk. However, women were very keen to work and earn some wages. They had even worked for the plantation work under NREGA, as it could be done individually, without the help of other men. Women suggested that if such a work is initiated where they could work with other women, they would be very happy and there would not be opposition from the family as well. However, neither the Panchayat nor the administration had been sensitive to this situation, resulting in the loss of employment opportunity to women. Similarly, the Sahariya tribe in the Lalitpur district has comparatively benefited due to its traditional openness to the manual labour as against the agriculture. While at the same time, the Thakur community in the same district takes it as a stigma to do manual labour as its members would rather migrate to nearby towns and do somewhat similar jobs at higher wages.

TRANSPARENCY AND ACCOUNTABILITY IN NREGA WORKS

NREGA has made provisions to ensure that the works undertaken by the Panchayats and the other implementing agencies can be scrutinised by the public. There are several types of records that have to be maintained at the Panchayat level and these records have to be made accessible to the Gram Sabha whenever required. There are also provisions of conducting social audit for each work that has been undertaken under NREGA. This section of the report deals with the practice as far as transparency and accountability in NREGA works is concerned.

Availability and Maintenance of Records

The Panchayats have been provided with several types of registers to maintain the details of each work initiated under NREGA. Most issues related to transparency and accountability can be addressed if these records are maintained regularly. The availability of various registers in the sample Panchayats is depicted in the chart above. While it has been observed that these records are available, they are not being maintained on a regular basis.

In Madhya Pradesh, Jharkhand and Chhattisgarh, there is a practice of preparing 'kuttcha' muster rolls at the worksite and the final data is entered later on. At the time of payment of wages, the 'Sachiv' (or Panchayat Secretary) collects the job cards of all the workers and returns them only after a few days. This gives the Sachiv enough time to make all 'corrections' in the records so that the records appear in good shape. In Jharkhand, the job card formats do not have a column on wage payment. Thus, the worker does not have any official record stating the wages that (s)he has earned. Such discrepancies are paving the way for corrupt practices in the implementation of NREGS works. In Chota Baru village of Murhi Panchayat in Ranchi district, the NREGA WATCH volunteers reported that no muster rolls were available at the worksite and that the job cards and the muster roll were found in the mate's house.The muster rolls are maintained on the basis of daily attendance of the worker at the work site. However, the payment is made on 'piecerate' basis. Since the payment is not based on the number of days that the worker has worked at the site, one cannot conclude whether the worker has been paid full wages or not.It has also been observed that the responsibility of maintenance of records mostly lies with the Sachiv, whereas the 'rozgaar sahayak' (or Employment Assistant) and the members of vigilance committee are also responsible for maintaining some of these records.

Monitoring and Vigilance Committees

There is a provision of constitution of Monitoring and Vigilance Committee at the village level so as to keep a check on the implementation of the NREGA works. Though these committees were formed in some Panchayats, they were hardly found functional. There are issues pertaining to their training, roles and responsibilities and even the constitution of the committees. In Madhya Pradesh for instance, there are no clear cut guidelines for formation of these committees. As a result of this, the committees formed for earlier developmental programmes have been considered for NREGS also. Though in 48% sample Panchayats, Monitoring and Vigilance committees have been formed, it was observed that in only 38% cases, these committees were provided training on their roles and responsibilities.

Only in 38% cases, the vigilance and monitoring committees were issuing work completion certificates. However, it was observed that since the committee members were not clear about their roles and responsibilities, often these work completion certificates were prepared by the Panchayat Secretary and signed by the committee. There have been several instructions from the

Central Government on building capacities of the vigilance and monitoring committees. However, the states are yet to respond to these orders.

Social Audits and Self Disclosure

Social Audit on the works undertaken under NREGS is another mechanism that can ensure transparency and accountability in the implemented works. It was observed that social audits of works were conducted only in 27% sample villages. There is also very little focus on self disclosure by Panchayats on the details of the works being undertaken. It was observed from the field data that in only 22% cases, information regarding works was put up on display boards. In Madhya Pradesh, social audits under NREGA are being carried out by the Civil Society Organisations. In Sidhi district, the cost of the social audit per Panchayat has worked out to be as low as forty rupees. It is clear that such organisations who have been awarded the task of conducting social audit at Panchayat level will not do justice to the cause. In Tikamgarh district, in the name of social audit, the NGOs were given Rs 200 per Panchayat to fill up formats which had questions related to the plantation works undertaken by the SHGs as implementing agencies under NREGA.

In Uttar Pradesh, the entire monitoring aspect is State led. The office orders of the UP Government suggest that most of the monitoring will be done by the officials at the state, district and the block level. In order to get another perspective, a few organisations have been awarded the work of conducting social audit of works under NREGS. No efforts are being make to develop the capacities of the community (who are the real stakeholders) to conduct social audits. As observed in most states, in Jharkhand too the Government is not very clear about the manner in which social audits should be conducted under NREGA. Mass social audits were conducted in some parts of Jharkhand by NREGA WATCH – an informal coalition of organisations working on effective implementation of NREGA in the state. While such efforts are laudable, social audits will not become effective unless the capacity of the Gram Sabha is enhanced to conduct social audits on a regular basis at the Panchayat level.

8

TRENDS AND SIGNS OF IMPACT

Trends and Signs of Impact

The impact of NREGA will be visible in more concrete terms only after completion of at least three years of the scheme. However, certain trends as well as output and outcome oriented impacts have been captured at this stage of the programme. NREGA's impacts are visible at two levels: (a) Employment guarantee or assured wage income for the poor families; and (b) Creation of assets providing short term or long term benefits. We have made an attempt to capture the gains of the NREGA in the following section.

Reduced Distressed Migration Pattern

The NREGA income in wages has two dimensions. The families owning small agricultural land, which is insufficient to generate food security for the whole of the year or create additional surplus of cash to meet other basic needs, are supplementing the agricultural income with the wage income of NREGA. There are large numbers of small land holding families having low agricultural produce. NREGA income provides a significant value addition to meet their higher order needs, which is critical for their survival or growth and development of their families.

There are families who are completely landless and depend on wage labour, look for work in the agriculture sector or civil works. In the off season of agriculture, such families migrate to towns. Civil works opened up in village have given them options to earn in their village itself, even if the wage rates are lower in the NREGA civil works. Even if the younger family members migrate as skilled labourers, middle aged unskilled family members prefer to stay in the village and work under NREGA. Among the sample villages, overall half of the villages reported that migration has been considerably decreased due to the availability of jobs at the local level. The graph shows the responses of sample villages about the decrease in migration. Now, migration has reduced in the NREGA villages and labourers are able to spend more time with their families as they do not have to migrate in search of work. The guaranteed employment increased the income of labourers which could be used for fulfilling their daily needs like food, cloth, etc. and ensure the dignity of labour.

Food Security and Improved Nutrition for Children

It was a general response that due to the employment generation under the scheme, some changes occurred in terms of their food security, which resulted in improvement in their diet. An analysis on better food for children reveals that villagers are able to include vegetables in their diet and can ensure food security for the family. In some cases, the diet pattern of labourers has also changed considerably since some people have reported that they have also been able to include meat occasionally in their diet.

The prime object of NREGA is to provide guaranteed wage employment to rural poor through creating community assets. At the grassroots, these community assets fulfil the basic amenities of the local populace and bridge the gap of general amenities.

Additional Income Provided Better Opportunities for Health Care

As far as the impact of NREGA on health is concerned, in some of the sample villages, people stated that they are using NREGA payment for treatment of their family members. The employment generation increased their income and now villagers have more money in hand. Hence, they are able to spend it on the health of their family members to go to the town for better treatment. The additional income, especially payments in cash for the daily wages, immensely help poor families to spend it on health issues. The health treatment in town requires a lot of cash to seek advise of the professional private doctors.

NREGA WAGES IMPROVED ACCESS TO EDUCATION FOR CHILDREN

It was found that some of the villagers spent their NREGA income to improve the quality of education of their wards by paying the admission fee, purchasing books, providing tuitions, buying of school uniform, bicycle etc. Due to the construction of a connecting road, children got better connectivity to go to school by bicycle or on foot and now, children are more regular in terms of attending the school.

IMPACT OF THE SUSTAINABLE PRODUCTIVE ASSETS CREATED UNDER NREGA

The NREGA has a strong focus on creation of such structures which may enhance livelihood opportunities for the poor families. Works related to improve the water structures or bunding/wells on the lands of the SC/ST families will definitely enhance the agricultural productivity for the small and marginal farmers. We feel that impact on such aspects will take some time. Some of the outcomes of the works as mentioned on the NREGA work sites have been presented here as illustrations: (see the table below)

Some of the key impacts of NREGA are

- The infrastructure created under NREGA as illustrated above has significantly benefited agricultural productivity, especially for the small and medium size cultivators. Moreover, fishing and other water related production has enhanced opportunities for the poor, especially SC/ST families, who depend on the water structures for their livelihoods.
- Families working under NREGA for wages have got an additional wage income over and above the agricultural work/wages. The additional monetised wage income has been useful in meeting the contingency needs viz attention for health of the family.
- The additional income has transformed the composition of the food consumption pattern. Very poor families are also able to supplement nutritional items like vegetables and pulses and are having a more balanced diet. The evidences are illustrative and over a period of time, if

there is a reduction in the malnourishment of children (Grade- IV and Grade-III malnutrition) in NREGA Panchayats, the impact of additional income will be sufficiently substantiated.

- There is a clear tendency of using the additional wage income for the education of children. It builds a case of inherent demand for children's better education. Most of the NREGA benefited families utilised their income for accessing children's education or supplementing with additional facilities to improve the quality of education. This long term investment of NREGA wage income will build for capacity of the families for their upward mobility. Conclusion and the Way Forward

CONCLUSION AND THE WAY FORWARD

The present study has thrown light on various aspects of the implementation of the Act in the different PACS – intervened states. Apart form analysing the Government perspective, based on the secondary data available on the websites and state level records, the study has also focused on grassroots realities by collecting first hand information at the district, Panchayat and village level in these states. The study brings out both positive aspects as well as the shortcomings in implementation of the Act. The major conclusions drawn from the study are as mentioned below.

A comparison with the experiences of the monitoring report released last year, revealed that in all the six states, awareness has risen regardy registration, job cards distribution, wage payment, etc. However, new challenges like delayed wage distribution, measurement based payments, quality of work under NREGS, work site job facilities, fake muster roll entries, job card possession and job cards on rent, etc., have come to the fore.

Since April 2007, additional 130 districts have been included under the purview of the Act. There is a need to be more careful in identification of families under the scheme so that the job cards are not misused. There is also a need to include the message of measurement-based payment in the IEC materials in all the states so that the confusion prevalent in the first phase districts is removed. While the status of registration of rural households is reasonably good at a national average of 70%, it has been observed that there are several issues as far as distribution of job cards is concerned. The analysis of the data on job cards distribution reveals that the under developed states, which have a larger concentration of SCs, have not provided the job cards to the SC households in adequate numbers (Bihar - 43.13%, MP-14.16% and UP-54.67%). The primary data reveals that among the six PACS-intervened states, 67.67% BPL households in Chhattisgarh and 60.18% BPL families in Jharkhand have not been provided job cards.

Whereas most of the families registered under NREGA have been issued job cards, it has been observed in most of the Panchayats surveyed that the job cards have not been distributed to the workers. From the primary data, it is evident that job cards have been distributed to only 42.86% households. The situation is the poorest in Bihar (21.31%), followed by Jharkhand (37.54%). In several places, the job cards are with the Sarpanch or Secretary or even with the mate. Besides, it has also been observed that there are numerous cases of false entries being made on the job cards. In order to ensure that the NREGA funds are not siphoned off like in other schemes, there is a need to ensure that the worker keeps the job cards in his/ her custody and also ensures that the Panchayat fills it regularly and properly.

It has been observed that in 72.5% Panchayats, five year perspective plans as well as annual plans have been prepared. However, these plans are not actually prepared in consultation with the Gram Sabha. Instead, these are prepared either by some external agencies or by the block level officials. It has also been observed that the priorities of works mentioned in the annual plan is often influenced by the block and district officials, instead of the Gram Sabha. There is also lack of awareness on how the plans and priorities in the plans can be modified by the Gram Sabha.

Sometimes, the implementation of the planned works gets stuck because of the delays caused in getting technical sanctions. In 50% cases pertaining to the field study, it has been observed that on an average it takes nearly 30 days for getting the required sanctions for initiating the work. Inadequate planning of works thus leads to loss of person days for the workers. The demand of jobs, as reported in the secondary sources, is manipulated. An analysis of the secondary data, as well as the findings from the field, indicates that people are not aware that they have to demand for work. As of now, people are getting work because a good number of works has been started in different places.

There is also apathy on the part of Panchayats in providing receipts against the applications given by the workers demanding jobs. It has also been observed from the field study that the response time in providing employment under the Act is not very encouraging. With an exception of Madhya Pradesh (58.6% cases) and Chhattisgarh (54.4% cases), in all the other states the average response time for providing employment against demand is between 15 and 30 days. It was also observed in all the states that there were some cases where people got jobs after more than 30 days. Jharkhand had the maximum number or respondents (14%) who started that the response time for providing employment was more than 30 days.

Payment of wages is the most talked about aspect under NREGA. The Act has made provisions to ensure that the workers get a minimum wage that is not less than Rs 60 per person per day. At the time of the launch of the NREGA, only 11 out of the 27 states had a minimum wage rate of Rs 60 per person per day. Thus, the Act had raised a lot of expectation, particularly among the workers, in terms of getting much higher wages than earlier. However, the aspect of measurement based wage payment was not popularised and this led to dissent among the workers on receiving wages lesser than Rs 60. The delay in measurements and the lack of transparency in measurements only added on to the prevailing confusion on wage rate.

The average annual wage being realised by the families in the six sample states is Rs 1990, as compared to Rs 6000 envisaged in the Act. The poorest performer has been Bihar, with an average annual wages per family of only Rs 705. As against the guarantee of 100 person days of work per year, the average number of days of work provided is only 18.45 days in a year. Among the six states considered for the study, Chhattisgarh has provided the maximum work per family (41.74 person days of work per family per year) and Bihar has been the poorest performer with an average of 6.84 person days of work per family per year. The primary data reveals that as far as providing employment opportunities to women is concerned, apart from the States of Bihar (24.2%) and Uttar Pradesh (24.5%), all the other states have provided more than 33% work opportunities to women. The state average, based on the secondary data, shows a grimmer picture of Bihar and Uttar Pradesh who have provided only 17.4% and 16.6% work opportunities, respectively, for women. There are also issues regarding the wage rate being paid to women in these states. It has been observed in that there is a difference in the wage rate paid to the men and women. The basis of discrimination in all the states under the study, is the perception that women are not able to do hard physical labour as men. Alòng with providing employment opportunities for people, the NREGS also aims at creating sustainable assets which would, in the long term, have an impact on the economy of the village. Considerable attention has been given to taking up environmental conservation works. These include creation of soil and water conservation works. There is a great possiblity of these works showing possitive results in the coming year. The infrastructure development works, (particularly the rural connectivity works), have also been commendable.

Perhaps the most neglected area in the implementation of the programme is ensuring accountability and transparency. Be it regular filling of job cards, maintenance of records, formation of active vigilance and monitoring committees or conducting proper social audits is concerned, none of these aspects are being looked into seriously. Due to lack of awareness on the provisions for ensuring accountability and transparency, the Gram Sabha is also not much bothered about these aspects. The workers are taking the NREGA work as any other Government initiated poverty alleviation programme.

Among the positive indicators of the programme, it has been observed in all the states that there has been a decrease in migration because of the works initiated under NREGA. There are issues pertaining to wage rate and timeliness of wage payment. However, it was observed that the marginal increase in the wage rate has enabled the workers to use the additional money for ensuring food security for their families. Workers have also reported that they could afford medical expenses of family members and provide better education facilities for the children with the increased income from NREGS works. The productive assets, created under NREGS for improving irrigation facilities. have also demonstrated positive results.

THE WAY FORWARD

Developing NREGA as an Employment Right

The National Employment Guarantee Act clearly articulates 100 days' job guarantee for every rural household. However, the intent of the Act is not reflected in the programme. A close look at the state-wise data on 'job demanded' and 'job provided' clearly indicates that those who are provided jobs are reported as those demanding jobs. There is a huge unmet demand which is not getting adequately articulated in the official performance monitoring system. There is a need to systematically analyse the available resources for awareness generation and its application at the state level. In most of the states, the resources are wasted in publication of posters, pamphlets, hoardings and publicity advertisements. A systematically and professionally planned communication campaign with the available resources will make a significant difference in generating the demand for employment. The civil society organisations should be involved by the Government to widespread the intent of the Act at the grassroots so that the really needy families should feel confident enough to demand jobs. If jobs are not provided, they should ask for unemployment allowance as their right.

Greater Autonomy to Panchayats to Plan and Execute need Based Works

The scheme still has quite a top-down orientation. The perspective plans have been prepared by hiring agencies to complete plans of every Panchayat of a district within three months. Therefore, real needs of the Gram Sabha have not been considered in their perspective plans. There are many state-led campaigns determined by the political leadership which are pushed down by the district level officials overruling the priorities of the

Panchayats. Similarly, technical sanctions by the engineers and evaluation of works are also designed in such a manner that twists the arm of Panchayats for bribing or accepting the commands of the Government officials. Appropriate mechanisms are required, which allow Panchayats to enjoy the flexibility of the programme and encourage them take up works that are extremely important to build long term sustainable productive structures that may enhance the livelihood promotion capacity within the village. Panchayats should be allowed to involve external resource persons/agencies, duly recognised by the Government, for technical sanction of the project as well as evaluation of the work done so that the monopoly of the Government civil engineers may be diluted. There is a need to build greater accountability norms for the Panchayats where Gram Sabha and Government officials can 3 play a critical role as enablers to promote greater transparency and accountability towards Gram Sabha. Panchayats need greater capacity building support to improve their knowledge and skills to keep their accounts, muster rolls, measurements of works, as well as maintenance their records and conduct social audits. The current level of capacity building support is far inadequate in terms of the expected roles, complexity of works and volume of resources available with the Panchayats.

Introducing Flexibility and Poverty Focus within the Programme

It is difficult to understand the criteria of allotment of resources to the states/districts by the centre. The most obvious criteria used is the number of job card holders in the district as well as the number of job card holders demanding jobs. Both of these parameters are not relevant for the allocation of funds as a high number of job cards in a district does not reflect the potential demand of genuinely deserving households requiring employment guarantee. Similarly, the fear of payment of unemployment allowance from the state exchequer suppresses the real demand for employment guarantee. There is a need to review the poverty indices of the poor districts, including agricultural production, rainfall, suicide deaths in rural areas, etc., to allocate higher volume of funds. Districts of Vidharbha of Maharashtra and Bundelkhand of M.P and U.P, etc., are strong contenders for greater allocations and attention. Such a disaggregated analysis and attention will improve the overall performance of the scheme for targeting the poorest of the poor to ensure 100 days of employment.

Improving MIS and Performance Indicators

There are serious gaps in the capacities of the block and district level functionaries filing up formats or uploading online data on the performance of NREGA. Therefore, the available statewise picture of performance is also not adequately representative of the ground realities. There is a need for a rigorous scrutiny of the data being fed at the Panchayat level going right upto the district and the state leave. The resource utilisation is a key parameter for the release of the next instalment. There is a need to improve the quality of internal and external agencies reviewing the content and emerging issues of the monitoring and evaluation agencies. There is a need for more systematic attention for in-depth analysis of the poorest of the poor or poorly forming districts. There should be a formal mechanism to share the evaluation/monitoring reports as well as the action taken report at the national as well as state level. It would be worthwhile to put such reports in public domain.

Broad Base the Parameters of Performance Monitoring

The current parameters, which are prescribed in the Monthly Progress Reports (MPRs) by the Government of India to the states and the district, miss out on many important parameters. It is pertinent to incorporate parameters like the proportion of works done by the departments and Panchayats to know whether at least 50% works are being done by Panchayats or not. Similarly, there is a need to monitor the number of Panchayats/villages where no works have been started or where one lakh rupees have been transferred in any quarter.

There are many Panchayats which are unable to receive adequate funds under NREGA to initiate works under NREGA. The monitoring system also does not capture the data on the available human resources placed at different levels. Moreover, details of expenditure of the contingency fund are also not published/monitored. Similarly, there is no data available on the trainings conducted to strengthen the capacities of staff/Panchayat at different levels.

Promoting Large Scale Support in Social Audits

With greater resources being spent in every Panchayat, it is high time to establish a norm for effective social audit by Gram Sabhas. Most of the states have been busy establishing implementation mechanism by recruiting the staff and developing the norms for expenditure. The attention now should be to mainstream the social audit process. It is fortunate that many kinds of methodologies of social audit by various social activists, action groups and field level functionaries of the Government have been attempted. There is a need to systematically review and decide on the 'common minimum' steps and processes that must take place in every social audit. Organisations may add on new dimensions, based on their capability and commitment to the social audit process.

Strategy for PACS in the Intervened States

PACS and partners should, in the near term, focus on the following activities to improve the situation at least in the PACS intervened districts. Organise campaigns with a focus on increasing the demand for work. As of now, people are not demanding work as a right and this has been the reason for poor performance of some of the states. In the intensive Panchayats where PACS partners are working, efforts should be made to identify deserving families and individuals which have been left out of the registration process. These families should be registered and efforts should be made to ensure that they receive the job cards. The perspective plans of the Panchayats should be discussed at ward level meetings in the Panchayat. If additional work needs to be added in the perspective plan, then it should be added in the perspective plan (duly approved by the Gram Sabha). If the activities need to be reprioritised as per the needs of the village, then efforts should be made in that direction.

The PACS partners should facilitate the Panchayat to prepare labour budget for the activities prioritised in the perspective plans. This would enable the Panchayats to effectively plan the implementation of the works so that maximum people can be benefited from the scheme.

BIBLIOGRAPHY

Alderman, H.: Food subsidies and the poor, Oxford: Pergamon Pressm 1991.

Bandyopadhyay, N.: An evaluation of policies and programmes for the alleviation of rural poverty in India, Bangkok, ILO, 1985.

Berg, A.: Malnutrition: What can be done?: Lessons from World Bank experience, Baltimore, Johns Hopkins, 1987.

Chadha, G.K.: Employment, earnings and poverty: A study of rural India and Indonesia, London, Sagem 1994.

Copestake, J.: The integrated rural development programme, Bombay, Oxford University Press, 1992.

Drèze, J. and A.K. Sen.: Hunger and public action, Oxford, Clarendon, 1989.

Gaiha, R.: Does agricultural growth matter in poverty alleviation?, Delhi, Faculty of Management Studies, University of Delhi. Mimeo, 1994.

Harvey, C. and S.P. Lewis: Policy choice and development performance in Botswana, Basingstoke, Macmillan, 1990.

Jamison, D. and L. Lau: Farmer education and farm efficiency, Baltimore, Johns Hopkins, 1982.

Lipton, M. with R. Longhurst: New seeds and poor people, London, Unwin, 1989.

Ostrom, E.: Governing the commons, Cambridge, Cambridge University Press, 1990.

Sen, A.K.: Poverty and famines: An essay on entitlement and deprivation, Oxford, Clarendon, 1981.

Walker, T. and J. Ryan: Village and household economies in India's semi-arid tropics, Baltimore, Johns Hopkins, 1990.

INDEX